Children's Childhoods:
Observed and Experienced

Children's Childhoods:
Observed and Experienced

Edited with an Introduction
by

Berry Mayall

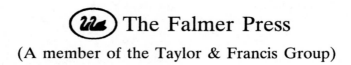 The Falmer Press

(A member of the Taylor & Francis Group)

UK	The Falmer Press, 11 New Fetter Lane, London EC4P 4EE
USA	The Falmer Press, Taylor & Francis Inc., 29 West 35th Street, New York NY10001

First published in 1994

Transferred to digital printing 2002

The Falmer Press is an imprint of the Taylor & Francis Group

A catalogue record for this book is available from the British Library

Library of Congress Cataloging-in-Publication Data are available on request

ISBN 0 7507 0369 5 cased
ISBN 0 7507 0370 9 paper

Jacket design by Caroline Archer

Typeset in 10/12pt Times by
Graphicraft Typesetters Ltd., Hong Kong.

Contents

Contents

Introduction

Children's Childhoods: Observed and Experienced — the title of this book — draws attention to a range of possibilities for exploring childhood and to the wide-ranging focus of the chapters collected here. Between them, the authors are concerned to study such topics as: to what extent childhood belongs to children — or to adults; whether children's understanding of childhood can serve as a basis for reconstructing childhood; whether the development of a sociology of childhood is, can be and should be for children or for adults; what contributions can be made by adult observation and study of children to understanding childhood; what are the methodological and ethical issues intrinsic to collecting data from and with children and to providing accounts based on the data.

That such topics are under consideration is part of the history of developing interest in the sociology of childhood; and the papers themselves have constituted part of an enterprise arising from the editor's own wish to learn more about childhood, viewed through sociological eyes. Early in 1991, together with colleagues (Margaret O'Brien and Kathryn Dodd), I called a meeting to consider whether there was a perceived and expressed wish to provide a forum for discussing research on children and childhood, with the broad aim of working towards the structuring of a discourse on childhood, which would be distinctive, as compared to traditional psychological discourses and paradigms. The Childhood Study Group flourished as a London-based group and more recently a seminar group — Childhood and Society — has been established with a wider geographical membership, based in Keele and London, and convened by Alan Prout and me (funded by the ESRC). The chapters included in this book were presented under the auspices of the Childhood Study Group. My thanks are due to Margaret and Kathryn for their collaborative efforts to arrange and run the early meetings; later on motherhood and teaching commitments required their full attention!

The book includes ten chapters, which address a range of theoretical concerns, through debate, through consideration of interrelationships between theory and data collected from and with children, and through consideration of policies, laws and practices impinging on children's lives. Between them, the papers consider children's experiences and activities in a range of settings: the home (Halldén, Buckingham, Mayall), the neighbourhood (Ward, Morrow), the hospital (Alderson), the school (Bird, Mayall, Oldman). The

1

papers deal with interrelations between children as well as between children and the range of adults they encounter (parents, teachers, health professionals). They deal with everyday life and also with extreme situations and experiences. They consider prospects for advancing sociologies of childhood, through consideration of similarities and differences between women's studies and children's studies (Oakley) and through consideration of the implications of conceptualizing children as a social class, in tension with other social classes (Oldman). Two of the papers focus directly on children's rights; Gerison Lansdown provides an analysis of current UK legal provisions and of recent cases in the areas of health, welfare and education; Priscilla Alderson takes up her themes and reconsiders them in the light of issues raised by a study of children's participation in consent to surgery.

The purposes of the chapters are essentially political. The authors' investigations are concerned to consider the status of children, to show how children do not fit adults' images, and thereby to describe how 'modern childhood constructs children out of society, mutes their voices, denies their personhood, limits their potential' and to consider how they do or do not 'surmount the obstacle of childhood' (Ennew, 1994), how far we adults fall short of implementing children's rights, what children's own experiences and discourses tell us about their understandings of the rights and wrongs of their daily lives, and what resistances children make to the childhoods proposed for them. These studies are distinctively conceptualized as compared to studies carried out within the traditions of developmental psychology, which typically have focussed on the individual and have aimed for description of the decontextualized universal child (Zuckerman, 1993). The basic vision behind child psychology research and practice has been that of a sequence of ordered developmental stages through which children progress at certain ages. Yet, as John Morss (1990) has pointed out, the bases of child development theory are best regarded not as scientific, in the sense of being tested and proven, but as assumptions based in biological and philosophical theories current in the early nineteenth century. But these traditional understandings of childhood have lent force to the other major and basic concept within child psychology, that of socialization. Adults have the task of teaching children what they need to know in order to take their place as adults in the social and psychological worlds inhabited by adults. As developing people and as objects of socialization, children have thus been conceptualized as lesser than adults, in that they are progressing towards the goal of mature adulthood; they are also the legitimate objects of adult attention, rather than persons in their own right. Whilst these ideas about childhood have some obvious common sense value (and indeed it is difficult not to think of children and childhood using these concepts) clearly they do not offer an adequate explanation of children's activities and of how people become adults. The linking of stage to age, (for which Piaget takes some responsibility) has been challenged through a range of studies (for example, Boden, 1979; Light, 1986); attention has shifted to children's creative participation in learning, for, as has been noted, if children only learned what they were taught, human beings would have become extinct in a generation (Wartofski, quoted in Qvortrup, 1993). Furthermore, the goal of describing the universal child has faltered and been modified in the face of disciplinary challenges, which strongly indicate the need to contextualize study of children's activities (for example, Ingleby, 1986).

As Alan Prout and Allison James (1990) explain in their comprehensive and path-breaking chapter, critiques from many sides have combined to pave the way for more appropriate and certainly newer understandings of childhood. Thus, from within psychology itself, the study of children has moved away from the search for the universal child, and has contextualized children and findings about them within social contexts. The traditions of interactionism and social constructionism have served to shift arguments forward. Interactionist perspectives have alerted us to children's own activity and creativity in promoting their own knowledge and development and their own social positioning, and we have learned to think of children and of childhood as social constructs rather than as natural phenomena (see Prout, 1992).

Nevertheless, whilst thinking about children has moved on, the notion that children are best understood as incomplete vulnerable beings progressing with adult help through stages needed to turn them into mature adults, has socially recognized status, both theoretically and as enlisted in policies and practices affecting children's lives. Developmental psychology underpins the training of teachers and the organization and ethos of schools (Walkerdine, 1984); thus, at the Institute of Education (University of London), primary teacher training is sited within the Department of Child Development and Primary Education. What Donzelot (1980) called the 'psy complex' has great power both theoretically and as a force shaping children's lives, through the operation of health, welfare and legal policies and services. The surveillance of pre-school children by health staff is conducted within understandings of children as developmental projects (Mayall and Foster, 1989). If children truant from school, or do badly at school, the educational psychologist is called in to help; the school, as an institution designed for children, cannot be in question, so there must be something wrong psychologically with the child. As regards the disposal of children who come to the attention of welfare staff, it is psychologists and psychiatrists who are called in to explain and modify their behaviour and who are enlisted as expert witnesses in legal cases involving children (King and Piper, 1990; Haugli, 1993).

These powerful ideologies, implemented as they are through policies and services, are not only conceptually flawed, they serve to oppress children. The chapters in this book, using a range of topics and methods, work broadly within sociological frameworks, with the general aim of redressing the balance: of moving on conceptually and of using these reconceptualizations as bases for suggesting ways in which children's lives may be improved. The chapters focus on children as a social group within social contexts. They enquire what conceptualizing children as a social category allows us to understand of the generational relationships between the social group children and the social group adults — at home, at school, in the wider environment, in health service settings. A particular focus of attention is the interlinkages and interactions between gender and generation (Alanen, 1993 and 1994).

The chapters cite children's experience in their structural position; they take account of the proposition that instead of conceptualizing children as dependents subsumed within families and excluded (through adult protection and because of non-adult status) from social forces, we would do better to think of them as a social group, and to recognize that childhood is integrated into society, not only in that children participate in social events and social institutions but because: 'Childhood and the life conditions of children are fundamentally determined by the same economic, political and social forces which create the framework of adults' lives' (Qvortrup, 1991). Most of the chapters in this book are concerned with limits imposed on children, within a conceptual framework where, as Gerison Lansdown points out, concern for the natural vulnerabilities of childhood is displaced or augmented by concern for socially constructed vulnerabilities. The legal and social dependencies of childhood, combined with the power of developmental psychological frameworks, which are based on suspicion of children's competence, mean that, in most spheres, modern childhood in Western European countries is characterized by protection and exclusion (Engelbert, 1994).

In this book, policies and ideologies played out in adult expectations, assumptions and behaviours, and children's responses to them, are explicated and analyzed through a range of studies. Thus Virginia Morrow explores children's paid and unpaid work, given social expectations that children are not and should not be gainfully employed. Children's perspectives on the home and the school, are explored in the context of assumptions that these are environments not to be questioned by children (Mayall). Children may be commonly regarded as helpless victims of television but David Buckingham and his colleagues' study of their discourses about television indicates that they use it constructively and creatively to understand their social worlds. Lise Bird explores children's understandings of competence and ability, in the contexts of the social worlds of schools and of teachers' discourses. Gunilla Halldén studies understandings of the social worlds of the home through writings by children about their future families, and reveals, notably, the importance for them of power relationships within families. Colin Ward reflects on children's experiences of living in environments ordered for adults, and concludes that children's opportunities for active participation in domains beyond the home and the school have decreased over the years. His account of the hostility of the physical and social environments children are faced with can be seen as a metaphor for the hostility of adults more generally towards children, if they challenge adult social orders.

An important theme in these chapters is children's resistances to the impositions of adult-determined use of time and space. Children's days and where they spend time is mainly determined for them. In David Oldman's argument, most of children's time is ordered in the interests of adults (day-care, school, supervision out of school); children's time is organized in order to free adults for work, and to provide work for adults. The places where they spend time can also be understood as determined by adult interests. Adult care in institutions (if they are not at home) is deemed appropriate for both pre-school and school-age children. Indeed, the sight of a child on his/her own, out and about, is increasingly likely to invoke adult suspicion and questioning — why aren't you in school/with your Mum/at home? Absenting oneself from school has through the operation of welfare and police agencies been criminalized: truancy equals delinquency (Carlen *et al.*, 1992). Data presented here, and elsewhere, suggest that children not only question such constructions of where they should be and when, but act to resist, oppose, or find ways through gaps in adult ideologies, institutions and structures. Thus, children opt for the spaces adults do not designate as playspaces (Moore, 1986), they do truant from school, and watch more TV than they 'should'. They offend against adult ideologies of childhood innocence by displaying knowledge adults would rather they did not have, and by committing acts of violence (James and Jenks, 1994). If children have the good fortune to have a room of one's own, they describe its value as a space independent of adult control.

Whilst, therefore, it can reasonably be argued that there have been (in Western European countries) few organized political movements by children as a social group (but see, for example, Adams, 1991), it can be argued that children both recognize oppression and, individually or in small groups, respond to it; in some cases they take action against it. Thus, though Ann Oakley is surely correct in her analysis of differences between the genesis of women's studies (in a women's political movement) and of children's studies (to some extent in the adult-orchestrated children's rights movement), it does seem that the growing body of evidence from children, together with recon-sideration by adults, provides a basis for the development of a politicized sociology of childhood, which could enlist the support of children.

In the UK, a number of moves in recent years have forced children and their circumstances somewhat higher up the agenda — of some theorists and some practitioners. The UN Declaration of Children's Rights (signed by the UK in 1991) may not have high status here, or be implemented here, but it provides a basis for argument and for theorization (Rosenbaum and Newell, 1991; Alderson, 1992). More problematic and even ambiguous is the Children Act 1989, widely welcomed initially as a basis for upgrading children's rights to participate in decisions that materially affect their lives, more recently identified as leaning towards the subsuming of children within the family, and providing more support for parental opportunity for autonomous decision-making than for children's rights (Hendrick, 1994). The Children's Legal Centre and the Children's Rights Development Unit have provided data and analysis on children's status (Childright journal; CRDU, 1994).

These agencies have been not only useful but critical in counterbalancing public concern expressed by other groups. For there are currently growing problems with the proposition that children's rights should be fought for. These problems include: the ideology of protection of the vulnerable in social worlds regarded as ever more unsafe; the decline in the constituency of people with direct interest in children, since fewer and fewer adults live with children nowadays; the ageing of the population and the consequent social and economic problems politicians identify; and the fact that of all the social groups increasingly requiring resources, children do not have the right to canvass support through the ballot box. One may add that in some quarters children seem to be regarded as potentially dangerous; if they are allowed rights and freedom to act independently, they may do damage to the rights of others (such as parents) and to the social (and physical) fabric more generally. And the long-established tradition continues that if the innocence of children is corrupted through knowledge and experience they should not have, they may behave in socially undesirable ways (for example, Carpenter, quoted in Pinchbeck and Hewitt, 1973; Dobash *et al.*, 1986). A current example is the conflict on sex education in schools: between health educationalists who want children to learn about sex, and right-wing politicians who want them to remain ignorant and innocent.

Given these opposing tendencies — the upgrading of childhood as a topic of concern and its devaluing in political arenas — we may note the strategic importance of the international project which has recently completed five years of study on Childhood as a Social Phenomenon (CSP). This project, carried out in sixteen countries, has taken a macro approach to considering and reconsidering the status of children through study of the sociography of childhood (demography, family childhood), children's activities (at school and elsewhere, in employment and leisure), distributive justice within families and across generations (of societal economic, social and cultural resources), the economics of childhood (including the 'costs' of children and childhood, and children's contributions), the legal status of children (including the relationships between the state, parents and children, and the balance struck between protection and autonomy) (Qvortrup, 1991). The massive amount of data generated has been set out in sixteen country reports and fully analyzed and debated (Qvortrup, 1993; Qvortrup *et al.*, 1994; Heilio *et al.*, 1993); together these documents have provided thorough exposes of the structural and political situation of children, as expressed through the cultural norms of each country (as well as revealing significant gaps in our knowledge), and a range of provocative analyses and theoretical formulations of childhood as a social phenomenon. These form a seaworthy raft on which to embark on further voyages through difficult theoretical and policy-oriented channels — and oceans.

Notes on Issues in Sociological Theory

The chapters in this book have been put together to make them available to a wider audience: to add to the corpus of knowledge about childhood viewed, broadly, through sociological eyes (for example, James and Prout, 1990; Waksler, 1991). As suggested along the way, the chapters do or may serve a number of functions. Firstly, they provide theoretical discussions of ways forward in the sociology of childhood. Secondly, they provide, through empirical data, some insights into children's own experiences of, and resistances to the childhoods they are asked to live, which act as correctives to adult visions and ideologies, and may serve to help redefine what children 'are'. This function is partly of the 'thus I refute it' school — a table is proved to be (in an important sense) solid when you hit your hand against it, whatever philosophers may say about the nature of matter. It is partly a means of reconstructing notions of what children are in the light of their own evidence, as well as that of adults. Thirdly, these chapters, together with the growing body of research evidence, serve as thought-provokers and indicators for changes in social policies and practices affecting children: as regards their rights, their relationships with adults, the procedures for sorting out problems affecting them, the services offered to and available to them, the social institutions and environments which structure their lives.

Among many theoretical angles on childhood, some have emerged as particularly useful. Clearly, it has been fruitful to study children as actors — as interactive agents who engage with people, institutions, ideologies to forge a place for themselves in social worlds, and who, by demonstrating interactive skills, propose themselves as worthy of inclusion both as individuals and as a social group alongside adult individuals and groups. A critical task for sociology, as Alan Prout (1992) has suggested, is to consider how far interactionist perspectives run counter to, or lock into social constructionist approaches to children and childhood. Chapters in this book describe how children find themselves defined in certain ways and resist these definitions, or renegotiate them. Of particular interest, in this regard, would be many more studies of children's daily interactions with their parents and sibs in 'the home', which on the one hand imposes norms on children in the interests of reproducing normal people and on the other hand is the arena where some children have more scope than in any other setting to negotiate — because parents want them to be individuals, and because profound affective relationships may empower children to negotiate successfully.

Work on children as actors as they face up to adult understandings of children and childhood can be seen as part of the larger enterprise of teasing out the interrelationships of agency and structure. One of the purposes of this enterprise is a negative one: to avoid the negative corralling children and childhood into an enclosure marked: interesting (and even amusing) aspects of children's cultures. For whilst it is valuable in itself to document children's activities (children's worlds), it is important not to study them as a strange tribe on the other side of the river whose activities have no connection with the observer's social worlds. The positive aim of the study of agency/structure therefore is to show how children's activities affect and are affected by social structures. Through so doing, we can begin to see in what ways children belong to, and participate in, the social order, and how as a social group they relate to other social groups, and what is their contribution to the construction and reconstruction of the social fabric.

It seems therefore reasonable to argue that the sociological study of children is beginning to move onwards from what has been described, by analogy with women's studies, as stage one, in which children are added on (Oakley in this volume; Alanen, 1994). As Alanen notes, in the case of women, this first adding-on stage entailed including the variable 'gender' in all research designs, and in all debate about social issues, and it entailed showing how women fitted into and lived with male-devised social systems and structures. In the case of children, there has now been considerable work using both theoretical and empirical insights which provide us with better understanding of children's structural situation, and indeed oppression.

A further stage, as regards women, has required theoretical rethinking of their social positioning — of what positions they not only do hold, but could hold and might be enabled to hold. Crucial here has been the study of women's knowledge (Gilligan, 1993; Belenky *et al.*, 1996) and consideration of how the distinctive character of their knowledge provides them with distinctive experiences and interpretations of the social order, and could be enlisted to reshape the social order. Similarly, the attempt, however imperfect, to consider the social order taking account of children and of children's points of view, may be instructive. Theories that assume everyone to be adult, or which assume children solely or mainly as legitimate objects of adult socialization, will no longer do. Thus, we can and should take account of children not in some superficial sense as actors, but — as contributors to this book have shown — as moral interpreters of the worlds they engage with, capable of participating in shared decisions on important topics; as people responsible enough to be paid for their work, as discussants of moral values, as people with denied rights to social and physical space, indeed as participants in the division of labour at home and elsewhere. This taking account of the distinctive character of their knowledge and capabilities may lead us to reformulate social theory. Of particular interest here is the discussion by Priscilla Alderson of children's knowledge, which, she argues, embodies an ethic of care for other people and their opinions (just as, according to Carol Gilligan, most women's knowledge does); such knowledge provides a challenge to social theories and social institutions which place high value on lonely autonomy.

Study of children's participation in the division of labour presents a difficult and necessary challenge in the advancement of the sociology of childhood. As Margaret Stacey (1981) describes, sociological conceptualizations of the social order and the assertion of certain key themes were proposed through male viewpoints by the founding fathers and have been built on by sociological men since then. Certain concepts have acquired almost unchallengeable solidity and factual status over the years: for instance the division of the social order into the public and the private; definitions of work and leisure; ideas about what factors enable groups of people to function well — through study of organizations in the public domain. For the women's movement, it has been and remains a long struggle to challenge these structures and definitions. But study of women's daily lives: the character of their activities in and out of the home: has forced reconsideration of the social order and of definitions of work. As Ann Oakley says, if sociology had started from study of women's activities rather than of men's in the public domain, definitions and evaluations of 'work' would have been different, and the distinction between 'work' and 'leisure' might never have surfaced (since women don't have leisure!). Indeed, the division of social activities into public and private is itself problematic, viewed from the positioning of women, and still more of children. To the extent that structures of domination operate to control women and children in all social settings, the idea that one domain is more private than another is not self-evident and needs reconsideration.

Study of children's positioning within the division of labour is critical to understanding gender issues across generations. 'The question who does people work on children and how these activities are articulated the one to the other has to be made problematic at the level of the division of social labour, for children work and are worked on' (Stacey, 1981). Women's work with and for children may be regarded as altruistic, or as constituting oppression or abuse, in the home and in the range of health, welfare and education services and systems children are required to submit to. The debate continues as to whether women and children are linked by common oppression (see Oakley for discussion of Firestone), or whether women are better regarded as corrupted into the service of the social order as Smith (1988) argues; an example she pursues is the supportive behaviours required of mothers of school-age children. The proposition that children constitute a social group which has interests that cross-cut social settings, and whose interests conflict with those of adult groups may be a useful structure for reconsidering gender and generation issues within the home and elsewhere. As Alanen (1993) has argued, we need to investigate gender and generation in the relationships between women and children. In so doing we may reconsider the concept of mother-child alliances. Critical here is consideration of knowledge; for instance, there is work to be done on how mothers and children construct household norms and practices, including what kinds of knowledge are built up by mothers and children. Questions include: how are these inter-generational activities cross-cut by gender issues; what use is made by boys and by girls of the knowledge acquired at home, in the wider social worlds they negotiate with? And how far, therefore, does the concept of mother-child alliance hold, across gender; what are the processes involved in the modifying or cracking of such alliances, according to gender, as children engage with peer relationships, with school, street life, and with paid employment?

Empirical Studies — Issues and Methods

Empirical studies of childhood lives have a number of functions, alongside 'straight' theoretical debate. They can provide data that puts substance on critiques of developmental psychology and that provides positive help towards more appropriate formulations. Indeed one of the impetuses for the studies reported in the book, is the urge to consider whether, and to demonstrate that, children can do things that conventional visions in Western Europe think they cannot do; for instance, provide constructive critiques of what they see on television, construct relationships, understand families and power relationships within them, act responsibly in paid work, engage with adults in decision-making. Through empirical work, we can therefore increase our understanding of children's structural position, by studying their experiences of home life, school life, meetings with adults, such as teachers, employers, health staff, and attempts to construct domains apart from those proposed to them.

Empirical work provides demonstrations, as experienced by children, rather than adduced by adults, of the disadvantageous impacts of adult-devised social institutions and behaviours, whether intended or not, on children: how children are caught in the cross-fire of adults' various and varying interests; how children's interests conflict with those of adults. I cannot resist noting here, however, that telling things the way children see them (though the telling may be imperfect) also results in rather more cheering and optimistic accounts in some cases. The gloom induced by armchair theorizing — which can make childhood look shockingly oppressed, can be offset by hearing children's own perspectives. For though studies reveal that they do recognize oppression, they also seem to think they find some ways to mitigate it, or bolt-holes to escape it, temporarily. Like other oppressed people, children may be inadequately informed of the strength and pervasiveness of their oppression. Unfortunately it may be in part the knowledge that they will escape childhood through growing up which cheers; they will leave behind them the next generation to face the same music.

Collecting data from, with and/or for children raises a number of issues. All the authors of empirical studies in this book have devoted effort to discussing methodological and ethical issues: their choice of method, its drawbacks and advantages, the analysis of data, and the presentation of data. Gunilla Halldén asked children in school to write accounts of their future family, over a period of several weeks; both narratives and drawings were collected. Virginia Morrow also worked in school classrooms and asked children to write an essay about everyday life out of school. She also used group discussions with a small number of children. This was my main method too in the study of children's opportunities for health maintenance at home and school: children in twos and threes at school talked with me and with each other about their daily lives. I also used whole class brainstorms, and collected some data opportunistically and through observation, as a general helper in the classroom. David Buckingham and his colleagues also interviewed children in pairs or groups, and again kept the topics open, by encouraging them to set their own agendas for conversation. Priscilla Alderson's research took place in hospital settings and in children's homes; she interviewed children with or without other interested adults present — parents and health staff. Finally, Lise Bird took the most ethnographic approach: as a 'quasi-participant' in a primary school she took fieldnotes on children's activities and conversations and carried out some individual interviews; in a secondary school she and her colleagues acted as 'participant-observers' in science classes; they took part in the work, kept fieldnotes, audio-taped class sessions and interviewed some students.

Collecting data with and from anyone is fraught with problems, and each research project and each set of 'subjects' or 'objects' present different issues. But discussions about data collection with, from and for children tend to focus on the following perceived problems: children can't tell truth from fiction; children make things up to please the interviewer; children do not have enough experience or knowledge to comment on their experience, or indeed to report it usefully; children's accounts are themselves socially constructed, and what they say in conversation or tell you if you ask them is what they have been told by adults.

The short answer to all these proposed drawbacks is that they apply to adults too. All of us mix truth as we perceive it with invention. Adults too when interviewed tend to provide what the interviewer would like to hear. All accounts will be mediated through the teller's experience, and that range of experience is interesting in itself. All of us are of course influenced in what we say by those around us, and, again, it is of considerable interest if and how children's understandings of their social worlds are influenced by adults, and by other children.

The outstanding, linked, problems that remain when adults collect data from children are to do with power-relationships and interpretation. Although the researcher's relationship with the researched in general is conducted with more power on the researcher's side, both during data collection and in the analysis and use of data, it is possible to redress that balance somewhat, through enabling data-collection methods, and through including the researched in the later analysis and presentation phases. Women's research with and for women has provided examples. But whatever data-collection method is used, from pure ethnography to structured questionnaires, power lies with the researcher to interpret what she sees and hears. These issues are much more problematic where children are the researched. However much one may involve children in considering data, the presentation of it is likely to require analyses and interpretations, at least for some purposes, which do demand different knowledge than that generally available to children, in order to explicate children's social status and structural positioning. So there is an important respect in which research cannot be wholly for the children researched, even where the researcher puts aside her own career (writing academic papers). On the other hand, though the representation of children's views may be only partially accurate and may be mediated by the adult researcher's concerns and interests, the attempt must be made to forward children's interests, both theoretically and through attention to the structures which control their lives.

1   Women and Children First and Last: Parallels and Differences between Children's and Women's Studies*

Ann Oakley

This chapter considers the emerging field of childhood studies from the viewpoint of the established discipline of women's studies. Women and children are, of course, linked socially, but the development of these specialist academic studies also poses interesting methodological and political questions about the relationship between the status of women and children as social minority groups and their constitution as objects of the academic gaze. Are childhood and women's studies the *same* kinds of activities, or are they essentially different? What is the relationship between them? Are there insights that can be transferred from one to the other? Why are we studying children as a separate social group? Are these the same reasons as were used to justify the development of women's studies? Are they good reasons?

The first part of the chapter discusses in more detail the sociography of women and children's material and cultural position, and how this shapes the form of their personal and social relations with one another. The second part addresses the ways in which children and women have traditionally been constituted as objects of academic study. Lastly, the chapter considers the present phase of studying both children and women: the one in its infancy, the other, as some would argue, past its prime. Here I explore some of the ways in which studying children is like studying women, and some of the ways in which the two activities can be distinguished from one another.

The Social Status and Relations of Children and Women

Children are primarily women's business. Giving birth to children is what women do, though the cultural artefacts of hospitals, medical technology and obstetricians increasingly do not encourage us to remember this. Looking after children is also what women do, whether we call it childwork, or childcare, or childrearing, whether we speak of paid or unpaid work, and whether we frame our observation in the sexually egalitarian, though usually dishonest, language of 'parenthood' and 'parenting'. In these ways children are women's responsibility, though *childhood*, as I shall argue later, is much less so.

The close alliance of women and children has many different cultural representations. These run from the language of nineteenth century politicians, which spoke of the two groups almost as one (though more because women were regarded as less than adult than because anyone had given any particular thought to the actual competencies of children), through to the multiple, careful statistics of the Childhood as a Social Phenomenon project (Jensen and Saporiti, 1992). But statistics require interpretation; the same statistics can be invested with different meanings. Thus we read, for example, that virtually everywhere the birthrate is declining and virtually everywhere the paid employment of mothers is increasing. The link between these two phenomena can be stated in alternative ways: we may say either that women are choosing to invest less of their lives in mothering because they want to do something else with them, or that children control the form of women's labour power by winning the battle with employers and potential employers for ownership of women's time (Oldman, 1991). It seems clear that what frees mothers to work in the capitalist sense is not fathers but schools and other arrangements for out-of-home childcare. Educational and other institutions for children mediate the links between women's and children's lives. To be a mother in Switzerland, where school is a morning-only activity for most children, is quite different from being a mother in a country where school hours are regularly seven per day and some schools even make provision for after school care. Another, slightly more complex example of the relationship between women's and children's lives is the division of household labour: the fact that women's housework hours average twenty per week, those of girls six, of boys four, and of men three shows both that children are bound up with women's domestic oppression and that the development of masculinity can be defined as a progressive project for liberating men from housework (Frones *et al.*, 1990).

Whose Rights?

Children and women share certain crucial social characteristics. In the first place, *children and women are both members of social minority groups*. Membership of a social minority group results from the physical or cultural characteristics of individuals being used to single them out and to justify their receiving different and unequal treatment — in other words, collective discrimination (Hacker, 1969). Women and children are so constituted within a culture dominated by masculine power — in other words, patriarchy. One obvious manifestation of this situation is that both women and children are disadvantaged as citizens. The concept of citizenship, with its associated *de jure* and *de facto* rights and responsibilities, is a patriarchal one. Children did not have rights under the 1948 UN Declaration of Human Rights, which conceived of rights belonging to human beings who are adults; they needed their own codification of their own rights. It was a similar reasoning that caused the eighteenth century feminist Mary Wollstonecraft to write her *Vindication of the Rights of Woman* in 1798, and others to follow her example. Because these rights and responsibilities are not automatically conveyed to women and children, they will only be able to claim them as a result of consciously directed social change. Thus women in the past, and still now, have fought to be entitled to rights previously regarded as belonging only to men — rights such as the suffrage, participation in the paid labour force, and the right to bodily integrity. In today's children's rights movement, we see the same phenomenon, though complicated by the fact that it is largely not children but adults on their behalf who are claiming these rights. This attributed incapacity of children to act for themselves is, however, more than a complication, as I shall suggest later (see also Lansdown and Alderson in this volume).

Being Childlike

Deprivation of rights is only the most easily graspable aspect of minority group status. There are others which are less obvious but more fundamentally subversive in their effects. The first of these is the social construction of minority group members as less than adult, that is, as incapable of adult competencies and of behaving in adult ways. Over twenty years ago work by Rosenkrantz (Rosenkrantz *et al.*, 1968) and Broverman (Broverman *et al.*, 1970) demonstrated the ways in which cultural norms gender personality attributes so that qualities such as independence, rationality, intelligence, autonomy, and confidence belong to men, are seen as socially desirable, and are taken as standards of normal adulthood, against which gold standard women emerge as distinctly less adult, that is *as more childlike*, than men. This allegation does of course merit serious thought. What does it mean to criticize someone for being 'childlike'? Certainly in English the terms 'adultlike' and 'adultish' are not uttered as condemnations in the ways 'childlike' and 'childish' are.

Another ascribed attribute derived from their minority group status women may share with children is the tendency to adopt negatively critical and even hostile attitudes towards one another. This observation was first made in relation to ethnic minorities (Lewin, 1941), and then extended to throw light on the competitiveness — 'bitchiness' — women are noted on occasion to display to members of their own sex (Hacker, 1969; Miller, 1976). This can be seen as a psychological effect of discrimination and of marginality and the need to respect power relations and seek alliances with the dominant group. It may be that one reason for children's competitiveness with one another, represented in later childhood in the phenomenon of 'bullying', particularly at school, derives from *their* sense of exclusion and lack of power and consequent need to prove themselves superior to others of their group. Such an explanation would fit with the observations of Bettelheim (1971) and others about the links between providing children with a collective peer-focussed social environment, such as that available in the Israeli kibbutzim, on the one hand, and the development of personal identity in which peer attachments, rather than competitiveness, are a prominent motif, on the other.

In Their Best Interests

These shared characteristics of women and children — their status as social minority groups, their relative lack of rights and moral construction as non-adult — coalesce in the language which, more than any other, has been used to describe the position of both. That is the language of *'their best interests'*, according to which judgments about the welfare of women and children are based not on asking them what they want or need, but on what other people consider to be the case. It is a philosophy of exclusion and control dressed up as protection, and dependent on the notion that those who are protected must be so because they are deemed incapable of looking after themselves.

The exclusion of women and children from the paid labour force is a good example of the way the 'best interests' argument works. While the early excesses of capitalist industrial production in the UK and other countries inflicted long hours and appallingly health-damaging working conditions on factory labourers, the offence caused to the moral sensitivities of the middle-class male social reformers by women's and children's labour took precedence over consideration of the hardship these groups might undergo as a result of the withdrawal of the right to paid work (Hammond and Hammond, 1923). The process of restricting women's and children's labour was subject to cultural variation; in Finland and Sweden, for example, the motivation behind legislation to prohibit child labour was apparently principally that of eliminating the moral scourge of children idling on the streets (without, once again, any consideration of children's point of view) (Alanen and Bardy, 1991; Sandin, 1990). It is interesting to note that essentially the same debate is in progress today over child labour, with a conflict posed between the moral, protectionist perspective of the adult, and the potentially different, self-interested view of the child (Ward, 1990).

The legacy of the Victorian exclusion of women and children from industrial labour is evident today in the requirement that the main activity of children should be play — that childhood should be a time of fun and freedom — and that mothers should not work, that is, their commitment to paid labour is not expected to be the same as men's (though unpaid labour in the home and in caring for the old, the frail and the ill is quite alright, as it is not recognized as work — though here there is some cultural variation, with practices outside the UK generally viewing this more positively).

The Haven of the Home

For women and children, families and home life are the site of work — housework for women, school homework for children. Children and women are culturally represented as living in the 'haven' of the home, whereas men stride out into the marketplace of the world. The association of both women and children's labour with the home results in a similar invisibility (Qvortrup, 1985; and Oldman in this volume). The 'paternalistic marginal-ization' (Qvortrup and Christoffersen, 1990) of children and women is ex-pressed in terms of temporal and spatial restriction. Thus children have their own institutions and their own timetables, and within homes there are special spaces reserved for the being of a child. The same holds true of women: in their case the special space is the kitchen. Cultural norms prescribe both that each child ideally has her/his own room and that women ideally share bed-rooms with men, though this is not the case in upper-class households and is a relatively recent historical invention both architecturally and morally (Oakley, 1974).

But women and children's ideological restriction to the domestic sphere also results in a shared material deprivation. Women are more likely to live in poverty than men, and children are more likely to live in poverty than adults. Families with children are generally the poorest households, and fami-lies consisting of a mother and a child or children alone the poorest of all. It has often been pointed out that the realities of many children's lives uncover the empty rhetoric of the *political valorization* of children; children may be precious, worthy of protection, both in themselves and because they repre-sent the future, but in many countries they are clearly not worth the financial and policy investment required to ensure even adequate living conditions. In this respect, the position of children is the same as that of women, who are put on another kind of idealistic pedestal, but not seen as worth the moral and economic investment of equitable living conditions.

Social Problems

Taking these material inequalities of minority groups together with the pater-nalistic language of 'their best interests', we can see how another common characteristic of women and children is derived: their constitution as a *social problem*. In the nineteenth and early twentieth century politicians and pro-fessionals of various kinds were widely concerned with something called 'the woman problem' (O'Neill, 1969). Whilst particular groups of women were variously considered to be a problem — the unmarried or the married, the sexually active or the sexually frigid, the educated or the uneducated, the working or the idle — the range of these categories reveals the fact that it was basically *women themselves* who were seen as the problem. In the same way, particular groups of children are seen as problematic today: those who are abused by their parents, or who might be; those who do not attend school, or who do not meet the standards of behaviour or attainment expected of them at school; those who fail to correspond to the charts of child development and growth beloved of paediatricians and child psychologists; those who eat the wrong food, smoke, drink, consume drugs, have sexual intercourse before they ought to, fail to use contraception, or become parents before they should; those who are not able-bodied or able-minded and who challenge the facile logic of 'integration'; those in care who are not cared for, and those at home who might not be; those whose mental health may be threatened by parental divorce or separation or by its opposite; children antagonistic to, or even criminally subversive of, adult authority. There are, again, so many categories of children who pose problems that we are forced to conclude that it is *children themselves* who are seen as the problem.

The Problem of 'The' Family

A major difficulty confronting those who wish to chart the experiences of being a child is that these are hidden in the ideological apparatus of 'the family'. This is the same for women. Indeed, the development of academic women's studies has very largely been the project of liberating women from 'the' family. But those who want to find out what goes on in families start with the handicap imposed by cultural thinking. According to this, 'the family' really exists and can be seen all around us in the form of idealized clones. 'The' family exists on the backs of cornflakes packets (Oakley, 1982), and in the medium of official statistics, which treat the family as the unit of analysis, and so deny the existence of real differences between *individuals* within families (Oakley and Oakley, 1979). A good example of this is the difficulty of deducing the living circumstances of children from official statistical data on families. It has been shown that using the family as the unit of observation results in an overestimate of the numbers of children without siblings compared to the estimate derived from using children themselves as the unit of observation (Qvortrup and Christoffersen, 1990). Within the rubric of women's studies, the critique of the tradition of studying families rather than people has given rise to a substantial body of work on the ways in which resources in households are actually and unevenly distributed (Brannen and Wilson, 1987). Though such work opens 'the black box' of the family to make *women* visible, it has done little to expose *generational* inequalities, including the experiences of children within families.

Among the most misleading myths of the twentieth century is this one; that everyone lives in families, and that these are happy, successfully functioning, democratic, supportive places, in which we may all retreat to share our secrets and replenish our energies for the harsh realities of the public world. Families may be like this for some people, but these families are the exceptions proving the rule. The rule is that within families power relations are unequal, resources are not equally shared, and frank or covert physical or emotional abuse often takes place. These features of family life affect women and children more than men.

In other words, a comparative sociography of children and women conveys a picture of *mutual dependence* and *interdependence* and *mutual oppression*. The term 'oppression' is a technical one: it describes the position of minority groups within a capitalist and patriarchal structure. The embeddedness of children and women within *each other's* lives has consequences for their structural and personal relations with one another. These have been studied over the past twenty years in the case of women, for example, in that area of work which goes beyond the moral dogma of the perfect, and perfectly self-denying mother, to ask why women want to become mothers (or not), how mothers experience children, and what their relationships with children are like (Boulton, 1983; Oakley, 1979; Rothman, 1989). But the counter to this — how children experience mothers — has been little explored. Indeed, it is one of many questions few have thought fit to ask them.

Children and Women as Objects of Study

It is important to outline some of these common features of women and children's position because these constitute the *framework* within which women and children are studied. The next section of the chapter considers some of the parallels and differences between women and children as objects of study, and as the focus of the gaze of researchers who may be conscious of the legacy of discrimination but are less sure what to do about it.

Down with Childhood

The academic study of women was born out of the politics of the women's movement. Texts such as those by Firestone, Mitchell and Greer represented the intellectual pole of second wave feminism; the political movement which shifted the argument about women's position from liberal equal rights claims to the more revolutionary aim of liberation and the removal of gender as a factor structuring social life. After these initial texts came a veritable industry of books about women (see Oakley, 1991).

When Shulamith Firestone published her radical text *The Dialectic of Sex* (1972), she included a chapter called 'Down with childhood'. In this she drew on historical work to argue that childhood was invented as an adjunct to the nuclear family, and that both are equally oppressive to women. But if childhood is oppressive, so too, according to Firestone, is childbearing. She characterized this as 'barbaric', and recommended its removal to the laboratory of the IVF specialists. Two years before Firestone, Juliet Mitchell in *Woman's*

Estate (1971) contended that reproduction is one of the four structures through which the oppression of women is achieved and maintained; and a year before her, Germaine Greer in *The Female Eunuch* (1970) discussed sex and gynaecology but not childbirth or the lived realities of childcare, referred to the child as 'he', and fantasized unhelpfully about a farm in Calabria where the children of clever women like her might be raised by local peasant families to avoid the traps of the isolated nuclear bourgeois family, and so that their mothers would be free to write books and engage in other similarly liberated pursuits.

The role of politics is highly relevant to an understanding of the parallels and differences between women's studies and children's studies because it establishes *a crucial difference*. Women's studies grew directly out of the political movement for women's liberation; it emerged out of the politics of experience. But children's studies are not rooted in the same way in the movement of children to claim their own liberation. Although there are some instances of children acting politically to secure their rights (Adams, 1991), the children's rights movement is not a political movement initiated primarily by children themselves. By and large, it is adults who are making representations on behalf of children — in their 'best interests' to re-use the traditional phrase. Children are coming to the fore in adults' minds, but the danger is that adults may continue to be the protectors of children, the representers of their interests, rather than the facilitators or active seekers out of children's own perspectives and voices. (The work of Priscilla Alderson, in this volume, is a notable exception here.) Because of the power relations involved, it is likely to be men more than women who will defend children's rights. There is a parallel here with the issue of fetal rights, which I shall come back to later.

Stages of Study

The sociologist Sylvia Walby (1988) has identified four stages in the development of academic knowledge relating to the position of women. First, there is the *virtually total neglect of women's position*. This includes their treatment in brief asides and footnotes, and tends to be associated with loose, unscientific attributions to biological factors of social differences between men and women. In the next stage, there is much *criticism* of traditional approaches, particularly of the determinist nature of sex differences, and many observations are restated as assumptions and then as research questions, that is questions which can only be answered by appropriate empirical inquiry. The third stage is the *additive* one: women are added in, or on, as a special case, in order to compensate for their previous omission. In the fourth stage the additive response passes into an integrative one, and there is commitment instead *to integrate the position of women fully* into the central questions and concerns of different academic disciplines.

Walby's schema is an evolutionary one, and has some of the same problems as all evolutionary descriptions. But the parallels with children's studies are clear: children's studies is at stages 1 and 2 as described by Walby. Academics are asking questions about *where children are* in the academic knowledge of social life, and pointing to some of the reasons for their absences, in particular the close links that exist between dominant theoretical and explanatory paradigms and the omission of children as active subjects. If this is where children's studies are at, then perhaps it is possible, by continuing the parallel with how women's studies developed, to identify some of the *critical questions* that are likely to arise in the next stages of work. I shall suggest three, and say a bit about each before moving onto some concrete questions about the activity of studying children, that is, how as researchers we can relate to children as the objects of our study.

'That Strange Ungendered Isolate, the Child'

The first issue is the danger of treating children as a *homogenous group*. The redundant nature of Freud's question about what women want has been clear for some time: women do not all want the same thing, nor can their social positions all be represented in the same way. Class and ethnicity cross-cut systems of sex and gender differentiation, and these are intermeshed with other discriminations relating to sexual orientation and bodily disability. Even feminism itself, once constituted as a monolithic text, has been broken down into 'feminisms' (Barrett, 1980). In exactly the same way children are not one group but many. Children are also two groups: male and female. Judith Ennew (1994) speaks of 'that strange ungendered isolate, the child', and some contemporary work in the field of childhood studies, particularly the larger scale quantitative work, speaks of children as an ungendered group (see Qvortrup, 1994), though other studies seek to highlight gender as a necessarily crucial variable (see, for example, James, 1993; Prout, 1987; Bird, in this volume). Carolyn Steedman in *The Tidy House* (1982) uses girls' school stories to isolate some of the ways in which children's knowledge of the adult world is fundamentally gendered. In Sweden, Gunilla Halldén (see Halldén, in this volume) has continued this tradition of work. Gender differences in parenting and socialization practices (Walkerdine and Lucey, 1989), and in the constructed subjectivity of children at school (Urwin, 1984) are other themes. However, these works tend to be classed as about women rather than about children; it is as though the very mention of gender signals a preoccupation with the construction of womanhood rather than childhood.

But any ungendering of children is particularly striking by comparison with women's studies, which strives to bring to our attention precisely those ways in which the constitution of femininity is rooted in the gendering of childhood. How else, indeed, was women's studies to contend biological determinism other than by identifying the ways in which the cultural artefact of gender imposed on children's biology to make them little boys and little girls? (Belotti, 1975). There are a variety of reasons why children's studies should tend to neglect the effect of gender at this stage of its work. One reason is the *methodological* requirement imposed by the early stage of the work itself — the necessity of emphasizing children's status as a homogenous group in order to make them visible at all. This is what happened in women's studies. The second reason is slightly more sinister. Because women's studies neglected *children* (Alanen, 1994), there may be a contrary impulse among male academics studying children to neglect *gender*. To go back to the beginning of this sentence, it is not entirely true to say that women's studies neglected children. What happened was that the deconstruction of notions of 'the family', and the uncovering of biases in theoretical assumptions made about women, resulted in an emphasis on *women's* experiences of children rather than on *children's* experiences of women (or of anything else). Children came to be represented as a *problem* to women. This reflected the political concerns within the women's movement to do with freeing women from compulsory motherhood and childcare work. From both an academic and a political point of view, the children-as-a-problem perspective came to be revised later, as it became obvious that women needed to find ways of representing motherhood as a cultural strength rather than a biological weakness and imposed social necessity (Oakley, 1986).

Attention to gender has an important role to play in the 'denaturalizing' of the phenomenon of childhood. Alanen (1994) has pointed out that historical chronicity and relativity, as represented, for example, in Aries' *Centuries of Childhood* (1979), do not really do this adequately. It is perfectly possible for 'the natural child' to exist in all socially changing eras of history.

Theorizing About Children and Childhood

Following the chronology of what happened in women's studies, the second question awaiting the next phase of children's studies is a *conceptual* and *theoretical* one. Put simply, it is this: how far does the available theoretical and conceptual language for discussing and studying children constrain what it is possible to know? Until recently, there has been little genuine *sociological* thinking about children and childhood (Alanen, 1994). The dominant theoretical perspective of most work derives either from psychological notions of individual development, in which children are seen as essentially 'pre-social', or from notions of socialization, in which children's status as 'anti-social' requires the imposition on them of social rules and mores. In both these strands of theories about children, the emphasis is *not on what children are*, but on *what they are not*. Further, the overemphasis on childhood as an individual process unfolded from within has tended to neglect the impact on children and childhood of social and cultural contexts. Grand overarching abstract generalizations substitute for empirical studies of children in their everyday environments (Skolnick, 1975). We learn not about children's perspectives, but about *adults' concepts of childhood*. This is why the assumption of children's non-competence is generic to all such theories, so that it becomes their prime distinguishing feature (May and Strong, 1980). In this sense, most work on the concept of childhood is adultist. As others have pointed out, it is also overwhelmingly classist (Ennew, 1994), and tends to present a masculine (Skolnick, 1975) view of who children are and will become.

If children have no place of their own in theory, and do not give rise to their own concepts, their value is not in *being* but in *becoming* — in their status as would-be adults. The sociologist Ronald Frankenburg has pointed out the derogatory tone of the concept of 'adolescence'. This labels teenagers as people who are *becoming* adults. Frankenburg (1992) suggests that, by analogy with this, adults ought to describe themselves as 'mortescents'. The primary determinant of concepts of childhood and theories about children is the cultural emphasis on adulthood as a project of individual identity. The result of this, from children's point of view, is often an uncomfortable fitting of their experiences into a framework not derived from them. Priscilla Alderson (1993) gives the example of a small boy's love for his mother, which may be transformed from rational personal motive to mindless biological instinct by being given the label of an Oedipus complex — a term which is likely to be pretty meaningless to the child. Many other similar examples could be quoted of this 'Icarus syndrome' — the tendency for people to take a quick look at a few data and then take flight towards general theories which are consequently only tenuously based on the evidence. Indeed, it would seem that theories about children are particularly *unlikely* to be revised in the light of new evidence. Piaget's theories about the unfolding cognitive development of children provide a good example of a relatively inflexible theoretical position which has been challenged by a good deal of evidence (see Morss, 1990), but which continues to survive substantially intact and even to inform important policies regarding children, for instance those relating to the age at which children can meaningfully be said to consent to health care treatments of various kinds (Nicholson, 1986). Similarly Kohlberg's work on children's moral development has been criticized by researchers who do not find children thinking in this way (Kohlberg, 1981). The fact that these moral development theories derive from a particular world view — that of men — has been highlighted by data provided by women about *their* moral thinking and choices (Gilligan, 1982; Belenky *et al.*, 1986) — and half of all children can be described only as little women.

Sociologies Of or For?

A third issue awaiting studiers of children concerns the preposition it is appropriate to use when describing studies in this area. Is what is being done *work about* or *on* children, or is it in some sense *for* children?

Here we key into the debate taken forward within sociology particularly by Dorothy Smith (1988). In an influential paper which is now more than a decade old, Smith pointed out a problem with the simple critical or additive approach to the mixed invisibility and overvisibility of women in sociology. There is, she said, 'a persistent difficulty that does not yield to the critique of standard themes and topics. In any of the many ways we might do a sociology of women, women remain the objects of study . . . By insisting that women be entered into sociology as its subjects, we find that we cannot escape how it transforms us into objects. As women we become objects to ourselves as subjects' (Smith, 1979, p. 159). In other words, what happens with the entry of women as a minority group into academic sociological discourse is that the centrality of subjectivity is reduced to the function of 'objective' research data. This, in Smith's view, exposes fundamental problems to do with the organization and representation of knowledge in a capitalist social structure. However, it is possible to take remedial action to shift a sociology *of* women into a sociology *for* women. A sociology for women is not simply an ideological position on women's oppression, and the shaping of research data to fit this position. It is a method that 'creates the space for an absent subject, and an absent experience that is to be filled with the presence and spoken experience of actual women speaking of and in the actualities of their everyday worlds' (Smith, 1988, p. 107). It is thus essential to preserve 'the presence of subjects as knowers and as actors', and to ensure that subjects are not transformed into objects of study by the use of 'conceptual devices' for eliminating their active presence (*ibid*, p. 105).

Children as the Researched

It is easier to see how Smith's recommendations can be made concrete in certain forms of social research than in others. For example, small-scale in-depth studies of women's experiences of academic life, or of power relations in the household, or some other similarly researchable topic, are relatively easily amenable to the injunction to start, continue and end as researchers with the standpoint of those women who form the population being researched (although steps will usually need to be taken to reduce the potential bias of most researchers being white and middle class). But it is much less easy to see how her approach relates to other research areas. For example, research on the effectiveness and appropriateness of different forms of health care requires larger numbers, some method of comparing groups which must of necessity not be based on the preferences of research participants, and some summary quantification of responses in which the finely tuned sensitivities of the subjective narrative can scarcely be represented. However, if it is hard to see how Smith's recommendations would apply to some areas of research on, and for, women, then how much harder it is to see how the same strictures might apply to the study of children. What would it *really* mean to study the world from the standpoints of children both as knowers and as actors? Are there particular problems to do with children's status as research participants, or are they just like adults? Leaving aside the unhelpful rigidity of Piagetian developmental stages, are there nonetheless some *age-imposed constraints* on the extent to which children can become full members of the research process?

We already have the beginnings of the answers to some of these questions. One answer is that children are not a homogenous group. Within the age range 0–16 years, there are important differences from a research point of view. Older 'children' can be treated as adults, and very young children cannot verbally express a point of view. This is a problem for research using spoken words as data. However, in between these ages we need to beware of the tendency to fall back on the argument about biological differences. Children *are* biologically different from adults, but biology is socially constructed. This is, of course, a powerful lesson learnt from women's studies (Birke, 1986). In relation to the notion of children's incompetence as research subjects, the notion that parents have to act as proxy interviewees for children has already been discarded by a good many pieces of research. Berry Mayall (1994) has shown how children as young as 5 can take part in data-gathering exercises concerned with the topic of health care across the settings of home, school and the formal health services. As a result of the information conveyed by these and older children, Mayall has built up a picture of the ways in which what to teachers is a *child-centred* environment — the school — appears to children themselves *adult-centred*. Children have to go to school; they have no choice about it. Through children's eyes schools demand conformity and the abdication of autonomy and control. They are even sometimes described by children as positively health-damaging. These child-centred perspectives on schooling build on the work of others, for example Holt's child-centred critique of adult learning theories (Holt, 1969), or work demonstrating that the amazing perceptual skills of young children actually tend to be wiped out by the imposition (through formal schooling) of more abstract ways of thought (Skolnick, 1975). There are also studies such as Tizard and Hughes' (1984) study of learning at home, which demonstrates on the basis of tape-recorded conversations between 4-year-old girls and their mothers how much of an informal curriculum of knowledge is transmitted in 'ordinary' domestic discourse, and how the active role of children in this as initiator and pursuer of questions they want answered can be contrasted with the more regulated and less autonomous role of the school child.

The idea that children can contribute meaningful research data conflicts with '*adultist*' views of children as less than competent to make sense of the adult world. Of course, one problem is that children, if given the chance, may not make sense of the adult world in the same way that adults would. For example, a study of children's consent to health care (Alderson, 1993) demonstrates both the *resistance* on the part of some professionals and parents to wanting to see children as competent, and the extent to which even young children can show an *understanding* of the balance of benefits and hazards to be considered when deciding to undergo a particular course of treatment. This ability of children meaningfully to consent to treatment extends to research. In the USA in 1976, researchers wanted to test the effectiveness on children of a flu vaccine. They explained to 6 and 9-year-old children at school the study they wanted to do, and invited them to ask questions. In a non-directive question-and-answer session, the 9-year-olds asked all the questions about the risks and benefits of the vaccination and about the study that the researchers had thought of and considered important (and which they would have put into any written document for adults). After having asked their questions, 54 per cent of the children agreed to take part in the study. The remainder either disagreed or were uncertain. The parents of these children were asked to consent on their behalf; on this basis a further 15 per cent of children were enrolled in the study (Lewis *et al.*, 1978). These findings on consent rates suggest that if children are asked for their consent to be research subjects, a considerable proportion may say no, and that if parental consent is taken as a proxy, some children will be enrolled in research against their will. Interestingly, research on medical ethics committees and proposals for research on children show that a policy of asking for children's own consent to research is almost unknown; in one study, 18 per cent of committees did not even require consent from parents (Nicholson, 1986). Furthermore, the presence on these committees of an expert on children such as a paediatrician made it *more* and not *less* likely that research proposals would pass through these committees unchanged. It would seem that experts on children may be precisely that — in other words, advocates of research *on* children, rather than defenders of children's interests in taking part in research which is *for* them. The best way to defend the development of children's studies for children is to enrol them fully in the research process. Again, there are examples of good practice. For example, in Glasgow, Helen Roberts and colleagues have worked with teenagers as sources of information about childhood accidents, both talking with them about their views as to factors affecting these in the present, and asking them to reflect on the safety and danger of their own childhood environments (Roberts *et al.*, 1992).

The consensus that emerges from studies exploring children's perspectives is that the major issues of the researcher-researched relationship are *essentially the same* with children as they are with adults. These issues include the need to be aware of and respect the imbalanced *power relations* of the researcher vis-à-vis the researched, the importance of distinguishing '*private*' from '*public*' accounts, and the need to handle controversial and or personal topics with *sensitivity*. Anne Solberg (1992) has noted the importance, when interviewing children, of *not* using 'parentist' language, that is, not transferring to one's role as researcher the ways that as a mother or a father one would talk to children. Studying primary school children's AIDS-related health knowledge in London schools, Clare Farquhar (1989) noted that attention to the power dimension of research when combined with the disparity in size between children and adults, meant that she had to attend carefully to her *physical position* when talking to children, ensuring, for example, that she and they were on the same level so that the children did not have to look up at her. There may be particular topic areas, for example research on traffic accidents, where taking account of disparities in size is particularly important (Sandels, 1975). But at the same time it is also important to beware of capturing children as research subjects frozen in their biological modes at certain ages. Cross-sectional data on 4-year-olds or 8-year-olds, for instance, can answer certain questions about the perceptions of the social world and capacities to provide research data characterizing these age groups, but we also badly need *longitudinal* studies which allow children to chart their own changing paths through and out of childhood, and thus to document the ways in which their perceptions and research competencies alter with age.

Most supposed differences between children and adults as research subjects disappear on closer inspection. Even as regards size and age disparities, the issues that are highlighted in thinking about research in the area of children's studies are not a particular class of issues: they are questions to which all *good* researchers will attend in conducting their research in both a scientific and a moral manner. We are once again brought back to the parallels with women's studies. Many of the issues to which feminist researchers have drawn attention have simply been insufficiently attended to by masculinist research; that is, mainstream (malestream) research has tended to skirt over, or to ignore, the *ethical* and *social* dimensions of research. Because of this, it has been argued that research in the field of women's studies is likely not only to be achieving *higher ethical standards* than most research, but also to be fulfilling that function on behalf of research in general (Oakley, 1992). Relevant ethical issues here include the need *fully to explain research* to potential participants; the importance of attending to congruencies or discongruencies between the *class, ethnicity and gender* of researchers and researched; the *lack of fit* between the 'mechanical model' of interviews as data-collecting activities and the real reciprocal relationships of researchers and researched; and the desirability, which flows from this, of guarding against the *exploitation of 'pseudo friendship'* developed in the interview situation.

Because of the moral base from which it starts, this attention to the requirements of 'good' research is likely to be extended to children's studies. But there are other practical questions that need to be asked. For example, can children meaningfully be asked *to set research agendas* as well as to answer researchers' questions? Flowing from a commitment to a sociology *for* children, what responsibility might researchers have to take back to children their interpretations of research data, so that the findings of research become a genuinely consultative product? In her book *The Tidy House*, based on the stories told by three 8-year-old working class girls about the families they will live in one day, Carolyn Steedman draws attention to this important aspect of research on children.

> It is extremely important not to confuse our appreciation and under-
> standing of (the children's) text with their consciousness and motiva-
> tion. The three girls wrote the story because they were expected to
> and because they enjoyed doing it. They did not *set out* to reveal
> what we may come to see as the message of *The Tidy House*. In this
> adult sense, they were *not* motivated to convey something to an
> audience by use of the written word. We can, I think, with perfect
> propriety, set the children to one side and examine their text for
> evidence of the huge mythologies of love and sex that inform our
> culture and of the way in which working class girls become working
> class women, just as we might watch children's play and find it
> revelatory. But it would be a grave mistake to *involve* children in our
> discoveries and theories. . . . (Steedman, 1982, p. 120)

But is it a grave mistake, and, if so, then what steps need to be taken to avoid
making it? Is a repetitive disclaimer to the effect that this is *our* interpretation rather than *theirs* really sufficient?

Critical Differences: To Conclude

These questions will be critical in the next stages of work in children's
studies. This chapter ends by focussing on a few critical *differences* that may
exist between children's studies and women's studies.

The Common Experience of Childhood

One difference is that we have all been children somewhere in our pasts, but
we have not all been women. Childhood is not only something to be studied,
it is something *we all hold within us*: a set of memories, a collection of ideas.
Childhood may be a repository of happy, garden-of-Eden memories, in accord
with the cultural dictum that childhood must above all be *fun*, and/or it can
be remembered as a nightmare of *unhappiness* in line with recent discoveries
about the nasty things that are likely to happen to children in even the most
ordinary families. Our own childhoods were lived by us and are variously
remembered, though usually not in a linear way. Memories are filtered through
the lens of how we have learnt as adults to think of childhood. In studying
children, therefore, there is a sense in which we are likely to be studying *the
child within ourselves*. In his book *The Child in the City* Colin Ward (1990)
refers to Ernest Schachtel's essay 'On memory and childhood amnesia'
(Schachtel, 1947). In this Schachtel observes that it is difficult for adults to
experience the experiences of childhood because by then one's whole way
of experiencing things has changed. For adults many experiences are familiar,
even over-familiar. For children everything is new. Schachtel says that he
learnt from the anthropologist Ruth Benedict that women recall much more

about their lives before the age of 6 than men do. He suggests that the forgetting of childhood is more common when there are radical cultural discontinuities between childhood and adulthood. In Western culture, these discontinuities are more marked for men than for women, who remain, as we have noted, from one point of view, childlike in their sharing with children of the status of a minority group. Historically, boys, and, within that group, upper class boys, had their childhoods long before girls and working-class children (Firestone, 1972). Feminist psychoanalytic theory (Chodorow, 1978) would also suggest that women's continuity with childhood is greater because the gendering of parenting requires no severance for them of their bonds with mothers akin to those boys must make in order to become men. But whether it is true or not, the gendering of childhood memories is both a *testable hypothesis* and a way of reminding ourselves of our own potential *individual* investments in the academic representation of childhood.

A Question of Politics

Another difference between children's and women's studies concerns the link between political activity and academic work mentioned earlier. Both women's studies and the women's movement originated in *a point of rupture* between women's experiences and social forms of consciousness (Smith, 1979). It was a subjective realization of women's material position which turned them into a political force *and* generated the questions of academic enquiry. Is this the case with children? It is certainly true that there is a point of rupture within the *adult* consciousness; *adults* can perceive the dislocation of experienced world and socially formed consciousness on behalf of children, responding perhaps also in some way to their own interior half-remembered childhoods. But it may also be — and this is a common theme in both novels and auto-biographies — that children experience the rupture of who they feel themselves to be in their everyday lives and who they are expected to be. This, indeed, is one of the principal dynamics behind what adults perceive as children's naughtiness and bad behaviour. Adult society asks children to conform. In so doing, it effectively defuses the revolutionary potential of children's ways of seeing. Once again, the parallels with women's situation emerge. But in the case of children, such is their oppression that we know little, yet, about what they think. The uncovering of children's own perspectives and positions is complicated by the power relations of those who claim to be working on their behalf. For instance, as David Oldman has argued, any statement about children's rights is likely to be infused by the interests of those who work with, or for, children, and expressed in terms of particular professional ideologies. Oldman argues that the 'clamour' for children's rights is partly 'a cri de coeur from workers in bureaucratic organizations seeking some redress from the alienating consequences of the restrictive and half-understood complexities of their work with children' (Oldman, 1991, p. 48).

This is one of the things that the 'clamour' for children's rights is also about, but there are others. The example of the debate about fetal rights is instructive here. Doctors in North America, in the UK and elsewhere in Europe, are increasingly using the argument about the best interests of the fetus, and the fetus's rights to life and to whatever kind of birth doctors consider best for them, to override the standpoint and wishes of mothers (Rothman, 1989). The fetal rights debate uses the language of paternalism and protection to drive a misogynist wedge between children and mothers as the bearers of children. As most fetuses go on to become children, we may well see the arguments deployed in discussions of fetal rights extended in future to children's rights. Both the argument that fetuses who are not separate beings have rights, and the notion that the rights of children and their mothers may in certain instances conflict, draws attention to the inappropriateness of the traditional language of rights in framing and arbitrating the relative social positions of mothers and children. The language of rights describes a particular way of viewing the world in which human beings *are* seen as separable from one another rather than as joined in some collective whole. It also suggests that general principles can be used to determine the precedence of one person's position over that of another. But these ways of thinking are not the way many people think about rights. As the work of Carol Gilligan (Gilligan, 1982), and of Mary Belenky and others (Belenky *et al.*, 1986) has shown, the way people, notably women, define moral rules is complex and situation-dependent rather than simple, abstract, and easily generalizable.

Who Owns Children?

This leads to another significant difference between children's and women's studies. The issue of who owns women is no longer really contended. At least it has been reduced to theoretical debates about the roles of men in the form of patriarchy and of the state under the guise of capitalism (Barrett, 1980). But the issue of *who owns children* remains a live issue. Oldman (1991) points out how childworkers, in grappling to understand their work with children, speak the language of children's rights, and in so doing lay some claim to the ownership of legitimate and valid knowledge about children. In this sense social workers, health visitors (public health nurses), paediatricians, psychologists, psychoanalysts, nutritionists, teachers, mothers and fathers all have a stake in the business of knowing about children. Each of these groups is likely to focus on particular aspects of children. For example, health workers overwhelmingly consider children as a product whose physical and psychological perfection must be strived for, whilst mothers view children as active constructors of their own concepts of chiidhood (Mayall and Foster, 1989). The medical emphasis on bodily quantification results both in a construction of children as weights and measures who do, or do not, conform to the formulae of growth charts, and an appeal to the moral nature of children as wonderful which is supposed to overlie the ways in which real children are less than this (Davis and Strong, 1976). The point of children's studies is critically to examine these perspectives and measure them against the knowledge about children supplied by children themselves. But it is also essentially for the practitioners of children's studies to consider the *ultimate goal* of their exercise. Is it (to return to the parallel with women's studies) to *provide knowledge* capable of being used *by children* in their struggle for some notion of their civil rights? Or is it to *advance the academic positions* of researchers, who can build on their work in children's studies their own chances of promotion and a claim to be the developers of a new specialism to join all the others that already exist and that segment children's lives and minds and bodies between different professional groups?

The Dialectics of Childhood

In *The Dialectics of Sex*, Shulamith Firestone concludes, not surprisingly, that children and women are locked together in a mutual oppression which does not encourage either group to behave particularly well towards one another. But, whereas women are capable of stating their own political importance, children are usually considered incapable of this. Who then should speak on behalf of children? Firestone (1972) says:

> ... it is up to feminist (ex-child and still oppressed child-women) revolutionaries to do so. We must include the oppression of children in any programme for feminist revolution or we will be subject to the same failing of which we have so often accused men; of not having gone deep enough in our analysis, of having missed an important substratum of oppression merely because it didn't directly concern *us*. I say this knowing full well that many women are sick and tired of being lumped together with children ... It is only that we have developed, in our long period of related sufferings, a certain compassion and understanding for them that there is no reason to lose now ... But we will go further: our final step must be the elimination of the very conditions of femininity and childhood themselves that are now conducive to this alliance of the oppressed, clearing the way for a fully human condition. (pp. 101–2)

Firestone's forceful words draw attention to something which is very crucial. There is an important sense in which children's rights and adults' rights do conflict. There is also an important sense in which women's rights are at odds with those that men claim. But the critical point here is the social and economic fabric within which the rights of different groups are set against one another. In this, and with so much else, the answer lies in the generation of a different kind of society — one whose structures do not have to deprive some people of freedom in order to give it to others.

Notes

* An earlier version of this chapter was presented at the International Conference on Childhood as a Social Phenomenon Lessons from an International Project, held in Billund, Denmark, 24–26 September 1992, (Qvortrup, 1993).

2   Children's Rights

Gerison Lansdown

Traditionally in our society, as in most if not all others, children are viewed as the property of their parents, who are invested with rights seen as necessary to carry out their duties. However, during the course of this century we have begun to witness a fundamental change in attitudes towards parent/child relationships. First has been a growing recognition that parents' rights over their children are not inviolable, and that the state has a right to intervene to protect children's interests. Our legislation marks those changes. Until the divorce law reforms in the 1970s, decisions about children were based on the guilt or otherwise of the parent: the guilty partner lost custody regardless of the impact on the child. Now, however, the welfare of the child must be the paramount consideration in decisions taken by the court under the Children Act 1989. We have also seen the growing recognition that parents are capable of harming and abusing their children. This knowledge is now so commonplace it is difficult to comprehend the shock of the Maria Colwell case when it first hit the headlines, shattering comfortable assumptions about the nature of family life. It is now clearly accepted that children have a right to be protected from such harm and that the state has a responsibility to intervene to provide that protection. The other major change has been the recognition that parents do not have sole responsibility for their children. The state is now acknowledged to have a key role to play in supporting parents. The introduction of universal child benefits and full-time education from the age of 5, free health care and, in particular, the provision for children of regular developmental health checks, the school health service, dental and optical care, all attest to a level of concern current in our society for the general well-being and protection of our children. Whether that level of concern goes far enough is a matter for political debate which I will not pursue here. But the central point is that we do have a broad consensus that neither the rights nor the responsibilities of parenthood are total or absolute although there are fundamental differences of opinion about where the lines should be drawn.

It is also important to recognize that our perceptions of childhood undergo constant change and are in many ways ambivalent and contradictory. For many adults, childhood is imbued with a rather romanticized notion of innocence — a period free from responsibility or conflict and dominated by fantasy, play and opportunity. Yet for many children of all cultures and classes the dominating feature of childhood is that of powerlessness and lack of control over what happens to them. Some adults perceive children as essentially irrational, irresponsible and incapable of making informed choices on matters of concern to them and to a large extent our legislation still reflects this view — the Children Act being a notable exception.

There are widely varying views of the capacity of children to undertake employment, be left alone, play unaccompanied, participate fully in the democratic processes, choose a religion. And these views are not static; for instance, in 1971 80 per cent of 7–8-year-olds were allowed to go to school alone, but by 1990 the figure had fallen to 9 per cent (Hillman *et al.*, 1990). Certainly when I was growing up in the 1950s it was common for young children to be granted considerably more unsupervised activity than is acceptable today. Similarly with employment: our current legislation, deriving from the 1920s, set 13 years as the lower age limit for part-time employment but there is now pressure from the European Community to raise this to 15 or even 16 years. So the concept of what is a child varies within different cultures, different social groups and at different points in history.

However, there is a degree of consistency inherent in both the traditional view of parental rights and the current recognition of a degree of partnership between the parent and the state: children are perceived as vulnerable and in need of protection. Whatever boundaries of childhood are drawn, they are, as a group of people, comparatively more vulnerable than adults and therefore require special measures to protect and promote their needs. What has been substantially lacking from the debate has been any real recognition that children have rights and not just needs.

I would like to begin by exploring the implications of a protective model of adult relationships towards children and to argue the importance of developing a rights analysis within which to create the necessary framework for change to diminish the harmful consequences of vulnerability.

Children are vulnerable. What does this mean? I would argue that their vulnerability is twofold.

Inherent Vulnerability
The very fact of their physical weakness, immaturity, lack of knowledge and experience renders children dependent on the adults around them. For very young children their survival depends on the quality of care and commitment provided for them by the adults who have responsibility for them. They need shelter, food, education, health care, affection and protection and their survival is dependent on the willingness and capacity of adults to meet these needs. Clearly the degree of vulnerability diminishes rapidly as they grow older and become better able to exercise responsibility for themselves.

Structural Vulnerability

Children are also vulnerable because of their complete lack of political and economic power and their lack of civil rights in our society. This aspect of childhood derives from historical attitudes and presumptions about the nature of childhood. It is a social and political construct and not an inherent or inevitable consequence of childhood itself. Children have, in general, no access to money, no right to vote, no right to express an opinion or be taken seriously, no access to the courts, no rights — except within the framework of the Children Act — to challenge decisions made on their behalf, no right to make choices about their education, within families they have no legal right to physical integrity — parents are at liberty to hit them if doing so falls within the boundaries of 'reasonable chastisement' — and they have no formal voice in society at all.

The relationship between inherent and structural vulnerability is obviously heavily determined by cultural attitudes. I would argue that there is a tendency to rely too heavily on a presumption of children's biological and psychological vulnerability in developing our law, policy and practice, and insufficient focus on the extent to which their lack of civil status creates that vulnerability.

It is useful to look at the position of women as an analogy (see Oakley in this volume). Traditionally, women and children have been cast together as weak and vulnerable members of our society. Women were perceived as needing male protection in the shape of a father or husband, both because of their physical lack of strength and because they were intellectually and emotionally unfit to take full responsibility for themselves. This perception of women was used for many years to justify their continued social status as the property of men.

In other words, their presumed inherent vulnerability was the excuse for failing to tackle their structural vulnerability. Once the battles to remove those structural factors began in the right to vote, the right to own property, the right to custody of children, the right to refuse sex within marriage, the right to physical integrity and freedom from assault, the right to equal pay, not to be discriminated against, the right to privacy — the view of women as being intrinsically in need of protection began to be eroded. Women have a long way to go before achieving full equality with men, but our attitudes in respect of civil rights for women on the principle of equality have shifted dramatically over the past 100 years.

If we are to enhance children's status in society, it will be necessary to achieve a comparable change with that achieved for women. Achieving such a major shift in our fundamental attitudes towards children would necessitate changes in law, policy and practice in both the public and private sphere. In this context the ratification of the UN Convention on the Rights of the Child is of major significance.

The UN Convention on the Rights of the Child, which was adopted by the General Assembly in 1989, represents a turning point in the international movement on behalf of children's rights, in two respects. Firstly, it provides a comprehensive framework which addresses rights relating not only to children's need for care, protection and adequate provision but also for participation. Secondly, a Convention is binding, requiring an active decision by the member states to ratify it. Until the Convention on the Rights of the Child was adopted, there was no binding international instrument which brought together states' obligations towards children.

It has now been ratified by 156 countries (March 1994). By ratifying, a government is signifying its intention to comply with the provisions in the Convention and, having agreed to be bound by it, is required to report to a UN Committee on the Rights of the Child on progress towards implementation, initially within two years and subsequently every five years.

The UK Government ratified the Convention on 16 December 1991 and is now required to ensure that we meet the standards it embodies for all children. The Government reported to the UN Committee on the Rights of the Child on our progress in January 1994.

The Convention is a very wide-ranging treaty and has application for all children under the age of 18 years. The principles it contains can be broken down into three main categories — provision, protection and participation.

> The **provision** Articles recognize the social rights of children to minimum standards of health, education, social security, physical care, family life, play, recreation, culture and leisure.

> The **protection** Articles identify the rights of children to be safe from discrimination, physical and sexual abuse, exploitation, substance abuse, injustice and conflict.

> The **participation** Articles are to do with civil and political rights. They acknowledge the rights of children to a name and identity, to be consulted and to be taken account of, to physical integrity, to access to information, to freedom of speech and opinion, and to challenge decisions made on their behalf.

It is that third set of principles, which, if fully respected, would represent a significant shift in the recognition of children as participants in society and which pose a substantial threat to the traditional boundaries between adults and children.

I shall look here at two key articles in the Convention which in some ways expose the inherent tension between a view of children on the one hand, as dependent on adult protection and incapable of taking responsibility for their own decision-making, and on the other, as people with basic civil rights including the right to participate fully in decisions that affect their lives.

The first is Article 12 which states that

States parties shall assure to the child who is capable of forming his or her own views the right to express those views freely in all matters affecting the child, the views of the child being given due weight in accordance with the age and maturity of the child.

and

For this purpose, the child shall, in particular, be provided with the opportunity to be heard in an judicial and administrative procedures affecting the child.

This principle is fundamental both to the Convention and to any recognition of children as people with a right to be heard. It sounds self-evident and rather innocuous but has profound implications if we are to take it seriously. We are very far from complying fully with it at present.

The Children Act in England and Wales incorporates the principle, requiring that children's wishes and feelings are considered when decisions which affect them are being made. The recent cases of children applying to court for judgments about where they live and who with are positive examples of the application of this right.

It is interesting to witness the response to these cases in the media. The Children Act has been labelled as a 'Brats Charter' which will herald the break-up of the family. Many people are profoundly threatened by the notion that children have formal rights to have their views heard in the judicial system. Nevertheless, the rights do exist in the law and are being used increasingly now by children.

But it is a different matter when we look at the education system where there is no duty whatsoever to listen to or take seriously children's views. It is interesting to note that before ratification in this country the Department of Education and Science claimed that it fully complied with the Convention and that there was therefore no action required to achieve compliance. Yet there is no obligation to hear children's views when decisions about school choice are being made and no right to be heard even when suspended from school. There has been a great deal of debate in recent months over, in particular, the provisions in the Education Act 1993 to move further towards a system of grant maintained schools, controversies over testing, parent's charters, parent's choice, the proposed reduction in levels of teacher training for nursery and primary teachers. Nowhere in any of that discussion has a voice been heard from children — their right to education, their right to be heard, to participate in discussion about testing and the National Curriculum, bullying in the playground, how schools are run. Very few schools have school councils and even fewer operate on the basis of mutual respect for pupils and teachers. Children have a right to be seen as the consumer and not just the product of education. The Government has consistently refused to consider this issue. They argue on the one hand that these rights are covered by the

Children Act, which they are patently not, and on the other, that such rights are inappropriate and potentially dangerous, a view which is in flagrant breach of the Convention to which they are bound by international law.

There is no obligation written into health legislation to listen to children and take account of their views. The Gillick principle affirmed the right of a 'competent' child to make decisions on her own behalf in relation to treatment (Gillick v. West Norfolk and Wisbech AHA 3 AU ER 402, 1985). This judgment makes clear that involving children in decisions about their medical care is an issue for all children of sufficient understanding regardless of age. However, this principle has been seriously eroded by the Court of Appeal decision in the case of a 16-year old anorexic woman (re W.A. Minor: Consent to Treatment 1 FLR1, 1993). This judgment has also challenged the statutory right, contained in the Family Law Reform Act 1969, of 16–17-year-olds in England and Wales to any degree of self-determination with regard to treatment. The interpretation given was that the right to consent does not include the right to refuse consent. Where a young person wishes to refuse consent to treatment his/her wishes can be overruled irrespective of the competence of the young person in question. This decision has profound implications for the rights of *all* young people to autonomy and self-determination. Clearly, there was concern in the case that the young woman's life was at risk but this risk could have been dealt with more appropriately under the Mental Health Act on the basis of the individual circumstances concerned.

Nor is there any requirement in Britain to take account of the views of children within the family. In Finland, there is a requirement written into their equivalent of the Children Act that parents must consult with children in reaching any major decision affecting them, subject to the child's age and understanding. Similar provisions exist in Germany, Sweden and Norway. In Scotland, the Scottish Law Commission in a recent consultation on proposals for family law found that there was widespread support for comparable provision here. However, to date there is no such requirement in law.

In Britain, we have a long way to go before we could claim to be fulfilling the standards required by Article 12. At the Children's Rights Development Unit, we have been undertaking a series of consultations with young people in the last few months over how far they feel their rights to participation are respected. The view which comes across with remarkable consistency is that they do not feel they are valued, listened to, taken seriously. Despite the requirements of the Children Act, it is also clear that children looked after by the local authority continue to experience a sense of impotence and alienation from the system and that little has improved since the Act's implementation. We do not have a culture of listening to children. Serious application of the principle would require that we:

- ensure that children have adequate information appropriate to their age with which to form opinions. For example children in a hospital setting need to be informed about who is responsible for telling them what is happening, what the implications of treatment are, side effects, options that are available, implications of not having the treatment, whether it will hurt, how long it will take (see Alderson in this volume);

- provide them with real opportunities to express their views and explore options open to them. This requires a serious commitment to respecting children and their right to participate in matters of importance to them, whether they are in school, in care or in hospital. It is imperative to make the time necessary to ensure that children have ample opportunity to explore the issues facing them. Their doubts, anxieties, confusions must be addressed if they are going to be effectively involved. In assessing a young person's competence to be involved in decisions, it is important to consider the young person's own views about their competence. The ability of a child to make decisions on her own behalf depends on the child herself but also on how much she is informed and respected by others concerned;

- listen to those views and consider them with respect and seriousness and tell children how their views will be considered. There is obviously no point in listening to a child's views if you have no intention of taking them seriously. It is necessary to be clear about what aspects of the child's care or education or health or play, he/she can be involved in. In order to allow children to be involved in decisions about themselves, adults need to be prepared to listen and respect them and speak in partnership with them, not as substitutes for them;

- let them know the outcome of any decision and, if that decision is contrary to the child's wishes, ensure that the reasons are fully explained;

- provide children using public services with effective, accessible and genuine avenues of complaint, backed up by access to independent advocacy for situations where children feels they have been mistreated or ignored or abused in any way. In Lothian, the social work, education and health authorities have joined together to produce a Children's Charter which sets out a shared statement of principles, backed up with details of entitlements within each of their services. Every child has been given information about the Charter, which also introduces an independent Adjudicator to whom they can go if they feel that the principles or entitlements are not being respected.

The Convention therefore imposes a duty on those with parental responsibility to involve children in decisions that affect their lives in accordance with their age and understanding. It therefore sets up a model of participation. It also imposes a duty to act in the child's best interests.

The second Key Article I wish to examine is Article 3:

In all actions concerning children, whether undertaken by public or private social welfare institutions, courts of law, administrative authorities or legislative bodies, the best interests of the child shall be a primary consideration.

This principle clearly locates adults as having responsibility for the welfare of children. I would like to examine this article firstly to see how far it is recognized in British law as a principle governing decisions affecting children and secondly to look at the implications of the principle itself.

This principle is central to the Children Act in England and Wales, with its requirement that the child's welfare must be paramount consideration. However, the Children Act and the paramountcy of the child's welfare applies only to courts considering matters about a child's upbringing. Not all courts of law in the UK are subject to such a principle. Examples are tribunals hearing immigration and nationality appeals and all the tribunals operating in the education system on school choice, special needs, school exclusions. The case last year where a mother was imprisoned whilst awaiting deportation and her three children, all of them British citizens and one of them a baby, were taken into care, exposes the harsh realities of legislation which takes no account of a child's welfare. Outside the courts too the concept of best interests is notably absent. There is no best interests principle in education law. There is no requirement on schools, local authorities or governing bodies to take account of either an individual child's welfare when making decisions about that child or of children as a group. This means that decisions to exclude a child, or to withdraw special support services, to close a school, to change the admissions criteria, to introduce a compulsory uniform, to stream, not to accept children with special needs, to operate their disciplinary procedures or to publish league tables do not have to be made with reference to the child's or to children's best interests. Other considerations such as economy, parental choice, prestige of the school or efficiency can all take precedence.

Similarly, there is no best interests principle governing the provision of health services or health care. There is no-one with any statutory responsibility for ensuring that the particular interests of children are protected when such decisions are made or that considerations for the health of children take precedence over those of 'efficiency' or 'economy'.

Likewise, if we look at planning and environmental issues, considerations relating to children are not even part of the agenda. If we were to take seriously the duty described in Article 3, it would be necessary to look at the implications for children when a new road was being proposed — what would be the implications for their health arising from noise pollution, lead pollution, poorer access to play facilities, decreased mobility and ability to move around within the local environment. How far are children's best interests considered in the housing developments we see around all our cities — with their lack of play facilities, lack of pavements, dangerous road crossings and so on.

There are two issues which need to be noted. Firstly, it is clear that apart from the Children Act, the concept of the welfare of the child is absent from our legislation. Children's welfare is not central to decisions made throughout society. Clearly many professionals working with children would argue, with justification, that they operate on a day-to-day basis with that principle as central to their work. However, because of children's lack of civil status, they themselves have no means of ensuring that their interests are heard and therefore, without a principled legislative framework to back it up, there is no guarantee that their interests will be considered or that there will be any means of redress in the event of a failure to do so.

Secondly, the operation of a best interests principle should not be seen as inherently beneficial to children. It can be, on the contrary, a powerful tool in the hands of adults, which can be used to justify any of their actions and to overrule the wishes and feelings of children. It is extremely difficult for any adult to determine the best interests of a child. Most parents have at some time been in conflict with a partner over what is best for their child — for example, as regards the day-to-day decisions about bedtimes, staying out, discipline and so on. Therefore, whilst it is necessary for adults in whom the responsibility for children or for aspects of their lives is vested, to pay heed to their welfare in making those decisions, it is also necessary for there to be clear, explicit and formal channels for children to have the opportunity to challenge the operation of the welfare principle where they consider that it has been wrongly applied or applied without any consideration of their views.

Even more important, is the recognition that children have basic civil rights — the right to be listened to and taken seriously, the right to freedom of expression, the right to freedom of conscience, the right to physical integrity. If one accepts these principles as given, then they form the principled framework against which the concept of best interests can be tested. Without it, the rights of the child can be subjugated to personal prejudice, an unwillingness to resolve conflict, lack of any consideration of the child's perspective or simply a battle for power in which the adult is invariably the stronger.

As a useful illustration, we can look at decisions made in the context of adoption. In practice, a welfare model is used to make decisions in respect of permanent placements for children. Another approach would be to construct a set of principles based on the rights in the UN Convention which would form the framework within which decisions should be tested. For example all children have the right to their identity, a right to name, nationality and to know and be cared for by parents, the right to enjoy their own culture, language and religion, the right not to be separated from parents unless necessary for their best interests and if separated, the right to remain in contact, the right to be involved in any decisions that are made and to have their views taken seriously. If social workers were to examine the circumstances of an individual child requiring placement, this framework would provide a coherent structure against which to judge the welfare of the child. Without it, many decisions are made in the name of a woolly concept of best interests incapable of being tested or monitored. If, on the other hand, these principles were acknowledged, the child would have the opportunity to challenge decisions if he/she felt that his/her rights had not been properly considered or respected.

In recent years, there has been a great deal of focus by childcare practitioners, lawyers and policemen on the issue of the protection and welfare of children. The application of a welfare principle which fails to address the right of children to participate in decisions which affect them is to undermine their capacity for self-determination. The welfare principle serves to perpetuate the structural vulnerability of childhood rather than seek to provide children with greater opportunities for taking control of their own lives. For example, the children abused over many years in residential care in Leicestershire (Kirkwood, 1993) and Staffordshire (Levy and Kaahan, 1991) provide a telling illustration of the powerlessness and vulnerability of children where those fundamental civil rights are not respected. If these structural rights were addressed the potential for abuse deriving from children's inherent vulnerability would be substantially diminished. Unless there is recognition in our legislation and in the policy and practice that flows from it that children are people and that they have rights which must be respected and upheld, then their inherent vulnerability will continue to be compounded by their lack of civil status.

However, the case for children's rights is not uncontroversial. We have witnessed this year a profound backlash against the idea that children have a right to greater levels of participation. It has been argued that it is not appropriate to give children rights, but that what we need to focus on is teaching them about responsibility. Children have been portrayed as lacking morality, as being out of control and lacking the experience on which to draw for effective participation. In the wake of ratification of the Convention and following the implementation of the Children Act, there has been considerable debate about the balance between parents' and children's rights. Some argue, for example, that the Children Act moves too far towards promoting parent's rights at the expense of children's. Others, an increasingly vocal lobby, argue that the promotion of children's rights obstructs parental rights and family life.

In order to analyze the conflict between parental and children's rights, it is perhaps useful to examine the derivation of the rights involved. Parental rights, as defined by Lord Scarman in the Gillick judgment, derive from their responsibilities to promote the child's welfare and are limited by that responsibility. The Convention in Article 5 describes parents' rights and responsibilities in terms of the provision of appropriate direction and guidance to the child in the exercise of their rights and in a manner consistent with the evolving capacity of the child. Both the Convention and the Gillick judgment, therefore, impose very clear boundaries on parental rights. They exist only in so far as they are necessary for the protection, welfare and promotion of the child's rights. As soon as the child acquires the capacity to exercise those rights independently, the right of the parents to exercise their responsibility recedes. Where there is conflict, it is not actually a conflict between the rights of parents and the rights of children. It is perhaps more usefully described as conflict between the adults' responsibility for the protection of the child and the child's pursuit of the right to participation and to self-determination, the rights to be listened to and taken seriously. In other words it is a conflict between, on the one hand, the child's right to be protected and, on the other, the child's right to have a voice. Such a construction does not in any way remove the dilemmas and difficulties inherent in resolving conflict between adults and children but it does provide a more valid framework within which to understand that conflict. It also locates the resolution of the conflict within the need to find a solution best for that child.

Recently, we have witnessed a vocal re-emergence of this debate in the controversy over the right of a childminder, with a parent's permission, to smack a child (*The Guardian*, 12 February 1994). This issue provides a useful illustration of the conflict. If one accepts that children are people with social and civil rights comparable with those of adults, then they should be afforded the same rights to physical integrity as adults. In other words, they should have the right, which adults in our society take for granted, not to be touched without consent, assaulted or hurt. However, the debate is invariably framed in the context of the right of the parent to exercise whatever discipline they consider necessary or appropriate and not in terms of the right of the child not to be hit. It is important to construct this issue in terms of the civil rights of the child and not merely in terms of protection or welfare of children. Protection imposes a duty on adults to behave in particular ways towards children but many parents defend the use of corporal punishment in terms of the protection of the child. If the argument is cast in terms of the child's right to physical integrity, the issue starts with the child and becomes a clear matter of principle. The social and legal endorsement of hitting children is one of the most symbolic indications of their low status in our society and until we cease to endorse it as legitimate punishment, we will continue to violate the Convention and perpetuate children's vulnerability to the abuse of adults.

The model we tend to work with in respect of children starts with a presumption of protection at birth with a gradual move towards self-determination on the part of a child as she or he demonstrates a capacity to make decisions in her or his own right. In other words, the child has to 'earn' the right to self-determination. There is an alternative approach which is the model adopted for adults in a democratic and participative society — that is, that we begin with a presumption of self-determination and only where it is clearly not in the child's best interest or where it would impinge on another's rights would it be justifiable to override or deny the child that civil right. Such an approach places the onus on the adult to justify the intervention rather than on the child to fight the case for a right to participate in decisions concerning her own life. Clearly, the smaller the child, the greater the need to intervene. Even so, we have evidence of this philosophy employed with tiny babies; thus the shift to demand-led feeding from the routine of four-hourly feeds is an example of allowing the child to determine and control the meeting of need.

Adults do have clear responsibilities for the protection and welfare of children. In the childcare sphere that responsibility is bounded by the requirement to act in the child's best interests. In other spheres, both private and public, there is not even this constraint on behaviour or actions. What needs to be recognized, however, is that children have civil rights which must form the framework against which decisions and judgments are made. A presumption of competence should prevail and where it is overridden all actions should be tested against the promotion and respect for those rights.

3 Researching Children's Rights to Integrity

Priscilla Alderson

This chapter considers how concepts of rights were originally based on values of rationality, independence and freedom. Since these characteristics are identified with adulthood rather than with childhood, they contribute to common assumptions that children should be denied civil rights; instead the child's need for protection is usually emphasized. As Gerison Lansdown has argued in this volume, civil rights can conflict with protection rights, especially when the person concerned is perceived to be immature. Civil or participation rights will be taken here to include rights to have information, to exercise autonomy and choice, and rights to physical and mental integrity. Gerison Lansdown's point about tensions between inherent, inevitable vulnerability in children and structural vulnerabilities imposed on them through social beliefs will be further considered in this chapter. The tensions will be discussed in relation to recent cases about children's rights to have access to medical information and to share in decisions about their health treatment. The impact on research of current beliefs about childhood is considered, with the need for researchers to examine their own values when researching children's rights.

The previous chapter discussed tensions between children's rights to participation and to protection. This tension can be at its most extreme in decisions about children's health care.

The idea of children's rights to integrity raises the following questions:

Do or can children have integrity?
If so, what do any rights to integrity, which they may have, mean and entail?
What pressures and beliefs encourage or restrict respect for such rights?

The questions will be considered mainly in relation to the rights of children using the health services; health rights offer the most graphic examples of respect or disrespect for rights to physical and mental integrity.

Priscilla Alderson

Three Models of Integrity

From a range of definitions of integrity, three meanings or models contribute to the understanding of children's health care rights: physical, mental and personal integrity. The simplest model is the idea of physical integrity which should not be violated. This is the basis of Anglo-American law on battery and assault. In principle, even touching people without their consent is illegal. There are exceptions, such as giving medical help in an emergency to save life. However, most of the exceptions, which are gradually being eroded, have affected groups commonly thought to be inferior, who do or did not have civil rights such as the right to vote: women, children, criminals, the insane. In the UK, sixty years after getting the vote, women obtained legal protection from rape within marriage; slowly their rights to physical integrity are being strengthened.

Anglo-American legal concern for physical integrity has been summarized as, 'Every human being of adult years and sound mind has a fundamental right to determine what shall be done with his own body' (Cardozo, 1914). The mention of 'adult years' is significant. Children are the only group of people in the UK who still do not have legal protection from physical assault, since parents can still inflict physical punishment (Newell, 1989). Children are also the group most subject to routine invasive investigations, and interventions such as immunization, through child health surveillance programmes.

The second model, mental integrity, also carries notions of a territory, in this case the mind, which others should not invade or seek to control. The right to vote gives clear examples of ways in which the law protects voters, who by definition have unconditional rights of choice, from mental pressures such as bribery or coercion. Similarly, medical researchers are required to exert no mental pressure on people they ask to take part in their projects, but to respect their integrity: 'The voluntary consent of the human subject is absolutely essential . . . free power of choice, without the intervention of force, fraud, deceit, duress, overreaching, or other ulterior form of constraint or coercion' (*Nuremberg Code*, 1947). These safeguards were advocated in the belief that ultimately the only sure protection from abuse can be exerted by the person concerned; no-one else can wholly be relied on.

The *Nuremberg Code* also stated the belief that ordinary people had the ability to make wise decisions, even in esoteric matters: they can have 'sufficient knowledge and comprehension of the elements of the subject matter involved as to enable (them) to make an understanding and enlightened decision'. Informed and voluntary consent is here seen as the key to ensure protection of each person's physical and mental integrity. Children were specifically excluded, as being incapable of making informed, unpressured decisions. Implicitly, their minds are envisaged as too unformed or too nebulous to be able to resist mental pressures.

The third model, personal integrity, moves on from mainly negative concepts of protecting territory against violation, to more positive examination of what lies within the boundaries: the countless aspects of each personality interrelate and integrate to form each unique whole — the person with integrity. Adults are generally assumed to have achieved this, and to be their 'own man', or 'own woman', but children are often assumed to be going through a long process of socialization or development towards this goal.

In the literature relevant to 'children's integrity', this actual phrase is almost entirely absent; it is assumed that the child's personality is too partial and fragmented to form an integrated whole. If common assumptions about adult and child integrity were expressed in visual terms, these could be as two circles. The adult one would have a firm, thick circumference, signifying a clear sense of self as distinct from other, around an intricate, sharply delineated network pattern, illustrating the complex, unique relations developed between sensation, memory, foresight and countless other factors. The child's circle would be a dotted line, symbolizing the weak sense of self, as theorized, for example, by Freud and Piaget, around blank spaces and fuzzy pale shapes — the fragmented rudimentary features of the emerging personality.

The circles illustrate two points. Firstly, if the child has little sense of self versus other, then invading the child's body or mind, crossing the dotted line, hardly matters. Indeed, crossing between the dots is not really crossing anything and hardly constitutes an action; if there is no real self, there cannot be any real invasion, or integrity to violate. From among countless examples, nudity on television illustrates this point. One half-hour documentary about a 5-year-old physically disabled and mentally very alert boy showed him crawling naked and fully exposed. It was implied that he and his peers at school would not see the film, or would not understand or remember it, or would not consider it an invasion of privacy. Adults' privacy and dignity could not be ignored in this way. Secondly, if the child's personality is nebulous and fragmented, then children cannot possibly make informed or wise decisions about their own welfare; they cannot have the requisite sense of self, or of harm or benefit to it, or of time, and of past and future interests. Adults must decide for them until children's personality is sufficiently developed and integrated. Although usually held unconsciously, this cloudy vision of the child seems to underlie much academic, professional and public thinking about children's rights. The usual emphasis is on providing resources, and on protecting children from themselves and any danger which allowing them freedom to choose might threaten.

Autonomy rights of self-determination are usually set in opposition to protection rights from harm and abuse. Autonomous persons are assumed to be able to protect themselves; children are assumed to need protection by others. Yet as Plant (1992) has shown, the two rights meet, for example in the protection of civil rights through the law and order services. The difference between adult and child protection is that adults' freedom of choice is protected, whereas children's choices tend to be overridden by 'protective' adults.

Health care provides many examples of children being treated and immunized against their will, their physical integrity literally being violated, in efforts to protect their body and mind from disease or disability.

'Autonomy' is commonly used to express a well developed sense of self, and personal rights to self-determination, independence, non-interference and freedom of choice. 'Integrity' has been used here to express similar concepts, but also to convey, more clearly than perhaps 'autonomy' does, questions about the intricacy of the autonomous person, the uniqueness of each individual person, and the crucial issues of invasion and violation.

Researching Children's Rights to Integrity

Beliefs about childhood and integrity raise many questions for research. How far are childhood and integrity assumed to be mutually exclusive? What are the origins of these assumptions, and what logic and evidence support them? How do models of integrity fit empirical evidence about children in the 1990s? What are the problems and complexities of defining and assessing children's integrity? What are the risks and benefits of trying to respect it? What do children and the adults caring for them think about these questions?

There is growing international recognition of children's rights to information, expression and participation, as the previous chapter showed. The Children's Rights Development Unit's Reports about implementing the articles in the 1989 *United Nations Convention on the Rights of the Child* give evidence on a macro scale of how far we have to go in the UK before these rights are widely respected. Researchers can also contribute evidence on a micro level of individual children and adults negotiating choices about how best to respect each child's integrity.

Empirical examples illustrate how children's rights may be caught within conflicting values about integrity: the present interests of the child may be set against the putative interests of the future adult, and also against the personal integrity of the parents and of doctors who advise a certain course of treatment. How can children's choices, when they conflict with adults' views about the child's best interest, be respected without denigrating the clinician's judgment, or the parents' moral concern? Another crossroads of conflict concerns choices between respecting children's rights to be informed and to share in making personal decisions if they wish to, against any rights they have to protection from distressing knowledge (such as about terminal illness or dangerous treatment), or from the potential anxiety and guilt attending serious and complex decision-making.

In the case of young children with life-threatening disease facing dangerous and painful treatment, the adults caring for them have to resolve such dilemmas as: Should the child be given honest information or protected from it? The problem here is that a child who is protected by silence is unable to share in making informed decisions. Unless the severity of the illness is explained, the treatment can seem far worse than the disease. It is then quite rational for the child to refuse treatment. Should treatment then be enforced on a resisting child? This would violate physical and mental integrity, yet the intention would be to protect the child from destructive disease. Should young children have the right to make choices about serious, complex treatment, or the right to be protected from the burdens of decision-making, which adults should shoulder for them? If they are excluded from being informed and involved in decision-making, then there is the risk that treatment will be imposed on bewildered, fearful and resisting children; so attempts to protect children from one risk can expose them to another risk. Empirical research can provide many examples of such conflicts, and of theoretical and practical means of resolving some of these problems.

A further contribution from researchers is to examine layers of meaning and interpretation, and the researcher's own motives and reactions. The study of babies and children, for example, is:

> a venture in self-reflection . . . Scientists studying babies do not sim-
> ply measure and calculate, they take part in a debate about the moral
> status of human life which stretches back through countless centuries
> of poetry and religious teaching . . . Scientific observations about
> babies are more like mirrors which reflect back the preoccupations
> and visions of those who study them like windows opening directly
> on to the foundations of the mind. (Bradley, 1989)

As Bradley notes, an example of unexamined assumptions is provided by Bowlby, when studying 'maternal deprivation', who assumed that the ideal mother-baby relationship mirrors an ideal of the ever-attendant-wife-and-gratified-husband relationship (Bowlby, 1964). Piaget envisaged the young child as a lonely scientist struggling to solve intellectual problems, isolated from social and emotional ties. Researchers project their own dreams onto their work, as when they perceive the human body in terms of clocks, pumps, computers or malleable genes (Merchant, 1982). Adults' perceptions of children are inevitably context-bound, partial and disputed, influenced by their time and place. So also are children's perceptions of their own abilities (Solberg, 1990).

Research can investigate how beliefs about children's integrity have changed over the decades. This work need not be simply relativist, or suggest that all beliefs are transient or arbitrary; some are constant, others become refined. Beliefs can also be examined in the light of moral values, such as what it means to avoid harming children, and how ideas of 'harm' change through history (Hardyment 1984). Repressive under-estimation of children's capacity and their desire for respect can be examined, as well as over-high expectations and oppressive demands on children. Research can usefully show the wide range of children's varying needs, and ways in which adult-defined 'best interests' complement or conflict with children's views of their own rights and needs.

Research about rights can include study of the meaning of the term 'rights', intrinsic contradictions and limitations within concepts of rights. Rights theories have disadvantages (Midgley, 1981 and 1989). They are only models which change over time, and are partial tools to help us to understand some aspects of conflicts. Slogans about rights tend to be based on selfish individualism, and a take-it-or-leave-it pattern of relating, which resolves conflict by ending contact (Pfeffer and Coote, 1991). This model does not allow, for example, for trust and loving interdependence between child and parents, or uncertainty about what is best for the child. Rights theories are useful for clarifying respect for children's growing independence, but they need to be complemented by other theories which appreciate child-adult interdependence; these can be examined in practice through research. Rights theories are useful at a political level, such as when generally regulating contracts and relations between patients and doctors. But rights theories are too impersonal and confrontational to explain all the varied, complex relationships between children and parents or caring professionals. Historical and philosophical discussion about rights tends to be adult-centric in traditions set by Locke (1924) and Kant (1948) which identify autonomy with adulthood. Empirical studies of children today can examine whether they exercise autonomy rights and, if so, how adults respond and how child-adult relationships are affected.

Do or Can Children Have Integrity?

Integrity is here taken to mean an integrated, coherent and distinct personality, with a sense of self and of personal relations with others through which one's own integrity can be enriched or threatened. Locke described this kind of personal awareness as self-consciousness: 'that consciousness which is inseparable from thinking, and as it seems to me, essential to it; it being impossible for anyone to perceive without perceiving that he does perceive. When we see, hear, smell, taste, feel, medietate, or will anything, we know that we do so' (Locke, 1924, Bk II, p. 27). Since babies see and hear and interpret each one in a distinctive way, Locke's discussion of integrity presents valuable hypotheses for research into the development of integrity in early childhood.

As stated in the opening sentence, early concepts of rights concerned non-interference with personal autonomy, the right of rational man to run his own life because his pure reason enabled him to make correct judgments (Locke, 1924; Kant, 1948). Women, children and non-property-owning men were excluded from having rights to independence because of their economic dependence; women's and children's presumed irrationality was thought to prevent them from rising above feeling and need in order to make truly free judgments (Grimshaw, 1986).

Philosophers' premises about rationality and autonomy have strongly influenced cognitive and moral psychology and medical ethics. Freud's work

(1914) on the 'narcissistic infant' was continued by Piaget (1932) on the 'ego-centric child', Erikson (1971) on the adolescent's need for isolation ('in order to become conscious of one's ego, it is necessary to liberate oneself from the thought and will of others') and Kohlberg (1981) on the goal of impersonal morality. Piaget based his theories of egocentrism on evidence from his mountain test, in which he asked children to point to a spot among three model mountains which could not be seen from another spot. He found them unable to do so until they were about seven years old, and from this he inferred that they were incapable of understanding another person's point of view (Piaget, 1924). If you believe that a child is not able to distinguish between the views held by herself and by others, then you are likely to assume that the child has little sense of personal identity, or of an integrity which could be invaded.

A recent example of disbelief in children's integrity or ability to decide their own interests, and therefore their need for invasive protection by adults who decide for them, was given by two bioethicists (Buchanan and Brock, 1989). Writing on 'incompetents' and referring to Piaget's mountain test, they stated:

> Role-taking skills are also thought to be necessary to enable a child to consider as potentially valid both a position presented to him or her by the physician and his or her own, different position, so that the alternatives can be weighed against each other. These skills are undergoing substantial development in the 8 to 11 age period, and are often quite well developed by 12 to 14.

The authors continue with an elaborate analysis of competent thinking, as a set of mechanistic skills, isolated from experience, feeling and the social context. The skills include the ability to concentrate,

> to weigh more than one treatment alternative and set of risks simul-taneously (i.e. cognitive complexity), ability to abstract or hypoth-esise as yet non-existent risks and alternatives, and ability to employ inductive and deductive reasoning . . . and abstract concepts in prob-lem solving.

These philosophers label young children as 'incompetents' because they are thought to be incapable of 'cognitive complexity', to have unstable, transient values, no real concept of 'the good', of death, of their future, or their likely future values.

Enlightenment concepts of autonomy emphasize the thick band around the person who must be left to make personal decisions without interference. These concepts were highly developed by Kant, who perceived himself as dependent on no-one — presumably he was oblivious of the servants who served his food and washed his clothes. Philosophers still cling to isolationist visions. These are criticized in recent work, mainly by women who advance theories of interdependence which can enrich personal integrity (Benhabib, 1987). In this second view the personality has a distinct (though not necessarily thick) circumference. It also has areas of overlap, and a partly shared identity with other close people.

Attached and Detached Models

Through empirical studies, Gilligan (1982) identified two contrasting and commonly held models of human development and relationships. She termed the model which men tend to adopt: that values independence and avoids intimacy as the detached approach. Women tend to adopt the attached approach which values intimacy and fears isolation. The differences are associated with gender but not exclusively.

Gilligan's analysis illuminates how researchers' basic assumptions crucially influence their analyses of their data. Those who assume that integrity is threatened by approaches from others divide personal decisions sharply into autonomous ones made by the person concerned in lonely independence (Faden and Beauchamp, 1986), and non-autonomous ones, made by or strongly influenced by others. For example, in a study of decision-making preferences of children with cancer, psychologists Ellis and Leventhal (1993) concluded:

> Children prefer to be fully informed about their disease and its treatment. However, this study suggests that, with the exception of terminally ill teenagers, children do not want to make decisions about their treatment. The current trend towards increased decision-making responsibility in children is contrary to the preferences of both patients and their parents. (p. 283)

Yet the authors described how, (a) '10 per cent of children considered their treatment very much their own decisions, but 98 per cent agreed with their treatment'; and (b) 'the majority of adolescents wanted to make their own decisions about palliative therapy and participation in drug trials'. Point (a) assumes that a decision is only 'very much their own' if the person disagrees with others and decides in lonely autonomy. Point (b) assumes that decisions about palliation and drug trials are separate from 'decisions about treatment', although the different kinds of decisions are frequently integral to one another. Instead of thinking in dichotomies, people who think in complementary ways recognize the value of shared decisions, where children feel able to accept proposed treatment as 'very much their own' decision, not something forced onto them despite their resistance.

The cancer paper illustrates the gradual trend nowadays towards professionals sharing more information with patients, but not yet being very willing to share decisions with them. To share information can increase professionals' power by giving them a stronger hold over the way patients conceptualize their disease and treatment in medicalized models and value systems. In contrast, to share control over decisions can decrease professionals' power. In cases of dependence and clear discrepancies of power, such as between doctors and patients or adults and children, besides examining personal philosophy and imagery, researchers also need to examine the play of power and interests. Much research on informed consent is carried out by hospital psychologists, who are also at times responsible for informing and supporting patients. It is in their interests to assess how effectively they ensure that patients recall and recount the professional information, and to argue for the need to maintain and extend this remit.

Cancer patients are particularly likely to be anxious about taking on responsibility for treatment decisions because of the great fear associated with this particular disease (Sontag, 1983), and for fear of being abandoned by professionals who have power to save life, or to provide palliation and pain relief in the later stages of the disease. For these reasons, adopting a model of integrity as either lonely, inviolable autonomy, or as a state of being a whole person (body, mind, emotions, spirit) fully experienced through relationships of respect and care, is crucial when formulating research questions. The assumed model affects the replies elicited in studies such as the cancer one just cited. Whether the model is explicit or not it can be influential, perhaps more so if held sub-consciously. The detached model is likely to make children fear guilt and blame if they take on decisions. The attached one may encourage them to feel supported and respected.

Children's Consent to Surgery

During 1989 to 1991, my colleague Jill Siddle and I interviewed 120 people aged 8 to 15 years, who were in hospital for orthopaedic surgery (Alderson, 1993). We also interviewed their parents and seventy health professionals. Interviews took place in three London hospitals and one in Liverpool. We asked children about their views and experiences of their chronic illness or disability, and their extensive treatment. We selected experienced young patients in order to discover how well, given time, they could understand their condition and treatment. We asked them and the adults caring for them, when they thought they were able to understand medical details in a fairly adult way, and when they were able to make a wise decision about proposed surgery. We also asked whether they wanted to be the 'main decider' or to share in making decisions or to leave the adults to decide, and what they thought had happened before their latest operation.

Although the 1969 *Family Law Reform Act* stated that young people over 16 could give valid consent to treatment, the Act did not say that those under 16 years could not do so. In the mid 1980s the Law lords in the *Gillick* case finally ruled that people under 16 could give legally effective consent if they had sufficient understanding and discretion or wisdom. Our study was designed to investigate when understanding and wisdom develop. We did not set out our own standards of 'sufficient understanding' and test children to see who passed or failed. Instead, we asked the children and adults concerned for their views. Understanding and wisdom are concepts which repeatedly recur in legal and philosophical discussion about maturity, competence or personal integrity. Children are frequently assumed to lack these qualities.

Orthopaedics, apart from the treatment of bone cancer, generally has two major differences from most cancer treatment: it seldom involves life-threatening conditions but is concerned with life-improving and cosmetic treatment; it tends to involve pain and visible deformity and disability, whereas cancer is often invisible, asymptomatic and felt to be alien and mysterious. Children considering orthopaedic surgery are more likely to have clear knowledge and less fear of their problem and its effects than children with cancer. They are therefore more likely to be willing to contribute their views and to share in making decisions. We also selected young people with chronic problems and long experience of hospital treatment and of talking with doctors. However, some of these young people were unwilling to share in giving consent to surgery.

In our research, those children and adults who gave an age of ability to consent as 16 years or higher tended to believe, 'That the law says you're not allowed to before then'. They identified having the maturity and integrity to cope with making serious, complex decisions with 'being grown-up'; 'you can decide an operation when you're old enough to go out to work, or leave home'. Replies were affected by experience. For example, Kevin (aged 11) may have been influenced by guilt and bad luck. His leg was injured in a traffic accident when he was seven. After three operations, including a skin graft when his leg became severely infected, he was critical of staff at his local hospital. They eventually referred him to a specialist centre. 'They knew they done it all wrong, so they sent me here to the professionals.' His operation date was brought forward because his leg was so painful. Kevin was asked:

Int: Who do you think the doctors should talk to, your parents, or you or all of you?

Kevin: They should talk to my Mum, 'cos she understands more and she'll tell me.

Int: Who decided that your operation should be done now? Doctors, or parents, or you, or all of you together?

Kevin: Me.

Int: Who do you think should decide?

Kevin: Me, 'cos the pain in my leg might be getting worse all the time, and if they leave it, it might get really bad. But, well, maybe it should be decided all together. I don't know. It's up to me, but if my Mum and Dad wanted it left until later, then I'd have to go with them, 'cos they have to sign 'cos

I'm their son. And if I decide and then it goes wrong, then I'd get the blame.

Int: How old do you think you'd be when you were or will be old enough to decide?

Kevin: 18, 16. At 7, the parents can decide without the child, and after 8, they start talking with him.

Mother: I think Kevin is right. About 8 you can start, and he could understand as well as I could at about 8 or 9, and decide for himself when he's 17.

Kevin and his mother implied a detached model of people deciding in lonely autonomy, and risking a burden of guilt and blame.

In contrast, Tina (aged 12) can be seen as speaking within an attachment model. Although she disagreed with her mother, she argued that she should be accepted as herself. She was willing to risk blame and to take personal responsibility, yet she also conveyed a sense of being a 'whole person' with integrity, physically and mentally. She was convinced that she should decide to refuse growth treatment for her very short stature, against her mother's wishes. They debated many pros and cons of having treatment and Tina insisted that people would have to 'accept me as I am, why should I go through all that just to make other people feel better about me?' She was also sceptical of new growth hormone treatments being developed to lengthen bone.

Tina: I'd rather stay like me. I don't want false bones and all that stuff.

Mother: It's not false. I have to be guided by the doctors, and if they think it's fair enough, it might help.

Tina: Yes, but they're not sure. My bones are different, they're soft. If anything happens to me it's going to be your fault.

Tina identified responsibility with the potential for blame. Earlier she had said, 'If I make the wrong decision it's my fault not my Mum's'. Their whole discussion (Alderson, 1993, pp. 36–40) centred on debates about the child's integrity, how much deformed and disabled people should be accepted 'for who they are' and how to balance children's present wishes against their putative future adult interests. Four years later, Tina wrote:

I felt I was responsible enough to make my own decisions and also my own mistakes if necessary. Children with any type of health problem to overcome grow up very quickly and more credit should be given to them. Society should accept people of all types, and respect everyone's right to make their own decisions once they have all the facts, be they adults or children. If parents and professionals listen to children they will know when they are ready to make decisions for themselves, whether they are 7 or 17. (*Bulletin of Medical Ethics*, 92, p. 36)

In our research, it was rare for a child to decide against adults' advice. Tina's doctors had suggested the treatment with reservations, and her mother repeated that she only wanted whatever was best for Tina. Yet there was no question of her mother rejecting or abandoning Tina herself. Despite the disagreement, Tina was able to feel respected and supported by the adults. Most children in the study came to agree with their parents' and doctors' decisions. Alison fainted when she first heard about her proposed spine surgery but after a few months felt ready to accept it. Her comments suggest that her father's respect for her integrity helped her to agree with his views on her best interests. Alison and her father were interviewed separately. Her father said:

I have always trusted my children. I have never forced either of them to do anything, I have never hit them, and they make all their own decisions. From the time that they can walk, they can make wise choices. If you wait until they are 18, you have failed them as a parent. I can't see any decision, unless it was life-threatening, that I would have to override.

Alison said:

My Dad and I are the same. We're not father and daughter, we're friends. He stands up for me if I want something, within reason. I ask him what he thinks, though I might not take it, but then he wouldn't really mind. But I would always decide about something like an operation with him, because he is a doctor.

Our interviewees illustrated how parents' perceptions of a child's competence affected the child's confidence. It could be argued that children become competent by first being treated as if they are competent; a baby learns to talk partly through being treated as if she already can talk. Intense disputes, besides splitting families apart, united some, when they realized that, by definition, a dilemma had no perfect solution; each solution offered advantages, but also the loss of advantages offered by other solutions. If there is an obvious solution, then you are dealing with a problem but not a dilemma (MacIntyre, 1981). Some parents accepted compromise, like the mother who said,

I cried buckets over my daughter's decision, but in the end, your children have to live their own lives, and you have to let them make their mistakes and help them to make the best of it.

Many interviewees identified maturity with more equal, detailed discussion, rather than with decisions made in lonely autonomy. Mothers would say, 'If I needed an operation, I'd always want to talk it over with my family first, and we'd come to some kind of decision. I wouldn't just decide on my own'. Children are more willing to express and assert their views if they feel confident that they will be loved and accepted whatever they say. As a hospital chaplain and former headmaster said:

> But are you going to lay on children the weight of their future? Perhaps let them make a decision that could lead to their death? These are impossible questions, but hospital staff have to find the answers. Am I big enough to say, 'Whatever you choose will be valued, even if you decide against the tide; okay, you've made that decision, I'll do all I can to support you, and we'll go forward together'? It's such a big step for the adult to surrender power to the child.

'Am I big enough?' suggests that those adults who have their own integrity, recognize and respect children's integrity: integrity in the sense of courage, honest admission of uncertainty and of difficulty in knowing what is best, as Tina's mother admitted, also uninterest in coercion and power games. These adults tend not to think in sharp dichotomies of wise adult/immature child, infallible doctor/ignorant patient, but to see wisdom and uncertainty shared among people of varying ages and experience. So the reply to the question whether children can or do have integrity very much depends on the respondents' beliefs about childhood, integrity, professional and adult power and decision-making.

Pressures and Beliefs which Encourage or Restrict Respect for Children's Rights to Integrity

Some changes have taken place in notions about childhood. At a theoretical level, findings about children's egocentrism have been challenged. Psychologists find that 3-year-olds can solve the abstract mountain puzzle and harder puzzles too, when they are expressed in more personal terms: naughty boys hiding from policemen (Donaldson, 1978). Experiments with babies have shown that they appear to reason and to link cause and effect in ways which were once thought to be impossible in small children. Siegal (1991) reviews numerous experiments and observations which disagree with Piaget's findings. His thesis is that Piaget's questioning broke quantity and quality conventions expected in adult conversations, but which Piaget did not think that children would expect. However, the children's sophisticated response to the broken rules confounded his simplistic analyses. Detailed observations of

1- and 2-year-old children have found that they show intense empathy with other people, and moral appreciation of others' approval or distress (Dunn and Kendrick, 1982). It seems that, in designing dull, repetitive tests, Piaget could not appreciate the child's viewpoint. He then projected his own egocentrism onto his research subjects. Piaget was so convinced of the young child's egocentricity 'shut up in his own ego [and] following his own fantasy' (Piaget, 1932) that he interpreted all his data in order to support his theories.

Kohlberg's scheme of moral development culminates in the impersonal, abstract sixth stage, when decisions are made in lonely autonomy. However, new psychological theories enable us to see children as more integrated beings. Kohlberg's work has been reassessed by his colleague, the psychologist Carol Gilligan (1982). She reconsidered Kohlberg's third stage (which few women progress beyond) — helping and pleasing others and proposes it as a personal ethic of care, which complements the impersonal ethic of justice. Gilligan's research into women's tendency to fear isolation and men's tendency to fear intimacy (1982, p39f) relates to the two models of integrity as threatened and violated by close relationships or as enriched by them. Gilligan's insights have been welcomed for recognizing the mature morality of many women, thus granting them a new moral status. In so doing, her work also implicitly recognizes the mature moral understanding of many children. Terri Apter's interviews with mothers and adolescent daughters question the notion that integrity matures through a process of growing away from one's parents. Many women said, 'We must be very unusual but we are not growing apart, we're becoming closer' (Apter, 1990). She envisages children as maturing in integrity through growing independence and also through deepening relationships.

Our research with young people having orthopaedic surgery found examples of understanding and maturity in young children gained through their personal experiences. The examples included children making life-extending decisions, as related by one sister in a heart-lung transplant unit. She described children with the severe, chronic illness of cystic fibrosis having extensive discussion of the 'pretty horrendous' details of the purpose and nature of organ transplants, and mentioned:

> One 10-year-old who said, 'I don't want it'. These children are given that right of choice. It's not a question: are they capable of making a decision? If a child truly understands what is involved and the alternative outcome, then they are not forced into agreeing to a transplant. That causes a lot of problems for nursing staff when the age of consent is now what — 16? Certainly that is an age we are comfortable with. Because transplantation is a limited resource, it is important to select the children most likely to benefit from it, and we have time to do this. I would say that often as young as four or five they can understand a lot about a transplant. Of course, it varies very much, and you can't generalize. I believe the child *always* has to be

involved. We know that they literally have their life in their hands afterwards. If they stop taking their medications, for example, they will die. Children may find a way of keeping control. One, previously very active, little seven-year-old girl with cystic fibrosis became desperately ill. The family had been denying how ill she was. Our assessment indicated that she only had a few months to live. She cried desperately when she was told she needed a transplant. She died two weeks later. She had developed an infection, but medically there was no reason for her to deteriorate quite so dramatically. I think that if children don't want something, then they can give up, and I believe she gave up.

The sister discussed whether young children can evaluate risk and benefit, and her comments show how psychological and bioethics theories about children's immaturity (Buchanan and Brock, 1989) do not fit all children. One 7-year-old 'ended up by summing up what I had said beautifully' — all the risks of the transplant failing, the suffering from unpleasant symptoms of her treatment and illness, and that she might die before or during the treatment. The girl finally said, 'But there is a chance that I could feel really good and I could come first in a race on my pony. All those other things are going to happen to me anyway, so please ask them to give me some new lungs'. The sister commented:

I think for someone of seven or eight to say that illustrates how she had totally taken on board as well as I could, the consequences of transplantation. She had managed to set it all out and look at it very clearly. She had understood the uncertainties. Okay, on a child's level, but who could better it? I couldn't . . . They are the most sure, mature children. They're physically immature, but their understanding of life and death knocks spots off us. I think they're immature in some of their attitudes, but their understanding of their own well-being and what life is all about is mature.

What do children's rights to integrity mean and entail?

Advantages and Problems when Respecting Children's Competence

The autonomy of adult patients is justified as a prima facie good in itself, and also as a source of further good, in that patients who are informed about and committed to their treatment are more likely to benefit from it (Beauchamp and Childress, 1983). Laws which assume that treatment can be enforced, if necessary, on uncomprehending and unconsenting children raise several problems. They sanction, in highly influential ways, the belief that adult might is right, though this can violate the child's integrity and has been identified as a major incitement to endemic child abuse (Violence against Children Study Group 1990). These laws ignore the growing evidence of very young children's ability to reason, to understand and misunderstand, to fantasise and to suffer mentally. Denying children's right to physical and mental integrity, through dismissing their rational competence, means that what would be assault to an adult is legitimate discipline to a child, as already mentioned.

If young children experience unexplained treatment as assault, this opens a credibility gap between the child's perception of harm, and the adults' intention to benefit. Severe or prolonged treatment can induce terror and despair in the child. Children who perceive treatment as worse than the disease risk having similar reactions to those of torture victims. Torture has been defined as 'breaking down a person's sense of identity'. It is exacerbated when people are in a strange culture (such as a hospital ward). It arouses feelings of utter helplessness, being out of control of events and one's own body (inability to sleep, or concentrate, irritability), confusion between feeling bad and being bad, the disintegration of mind and body (Melzac, 1992). Stress and depression have been found in children as young as two years (Yule, 1992). If such feelings become habitual, children can be emotionally crippled. The higher the risks of treatment, the higher the chance that the child has severe, long-term sickness or disability which has already affected their confidence and self-esteem. This type of research with very young children suggests that integrity develops, and can be nurtured or damaged in early childhood.

It can be argued that treatment decisions are either reasoned with patients or forced on them, and that reason and force are at opposite ends of a spectrum, with persuasion in the centre. Impartial, rational discussion is inevitably qualified by medical uncertainty, choice of words, pressures intrinsic to the illness or disability being treated, and attempts to respect children, but also to protect them from frightening news. So persuasion overlaps broadly with reason at one end and force at the other. Yet at some point persuasion moves from informed optimism to deliberate distortion. In our study, adults who argued for high ages for consent tended to dismiss coercion as necessary firmness: 'Kids only play up'; 'They're only frightened', as if fear is irrational and therefore unimportant; 'They've got to learn to put up with it for their own good'; 'There isn't time to hang about until they're ready'. The most powerful way to justify coercion is to deny that children can be competent, and to align adult reason with force; children's resistance is then seen as mindless 'self-destruction', to be overridden by rational adults. Adults who respected competence and integrity at younger ages worried about the reason-force divide. A sister said, 'I would always try to get a compromise'. A surgeon said, 'I don't try and persuade people. If someone isn't happy with the idea of surgery, we'll talk again in a few months time, or a few years, and very often they've changed their mind'. Another surgeon commented,

I regard the issue of consent as a partnership between parents, the patient and the doctor — none of these can work independently. The success of this depends on a lot of things, including the age and understanding of the child. Because of the risk that children will refuse necessary treatment, it is so important that the atmosphere is right, so that the child can voice their fears.

Forcing information onto patients who would rather not know can be a form of coercion, but was usually seen as the lesser evil, compared with forcing treatment onto unprepared, resisting children.

Some interviewees in this study believed that it was unwise and unkind to expect children to share in making major decisions; they were concerned about the neglect or abuse (through under- or over-treatment) which young people could be exposed to if they took responsibility for their life. Others thought that children should be involved and that, given information, support, and time, they would usually arrive at an enlightened decision. These adults were concerned about the neglect or abuse which young people are exposed to if they are prevented from taking some responsibility for their life, and have to continue in enforced vulnerability and dependence (Kitzinger, 1990). In these cases adults and children were working on the attachment model discussed earlier: of shared decision-making within a supportive ethic of care.

In English law, no one has the unqualified right to decide. The adults have responsibilities but not rights; the child does not have unrestricted choice, but has to choose 'wisely'. In our study, children and parents usually agreed. In cases of disagreement a middle way could often be found, through reasoning and compromise, until informed and willing consent was agreed. Such an approach depends on everyone taking the child's competence seriously. Our study investigated an unusual group of experienced children and we are cautious about over-generalizing. However, the understanding and maturity of this small group, mainly during adversity, raise many questions about the potential and actual capacity of all children. This chapter has dealt briefly with a few of the complexities of the vast topic of children's competence, and raises more questions than it answers.

Gerison Lansdown drew a comparison, in the previous chapter, between women's and children's rights. In the past, in effect women had no rights; they depended on men's whim and on precarious privileges. The turning point for women's rights to resources, such as equal pay, and rights to protection, such as from rape within marriage, began with recognition that their reasoned assessments of their own interests could be valid: that women can be as rational as men. The turning point for rights to protection and resources for many children is linked to recognition that some children can be as rational as some adults, that young and old share a partial rationality. Only with this recognition, will children's own assessment of their interests be taken seriously. Adults are not perfectly wise, but fallible, so that their rights to control children are questionable. Children do not have to be perfect to qualify as competent, that is, reasonably informed and wise.

Acknowledgments

I thank all the children and adults who took part in interviews for the Children's Consent to Surgery project, Jill Siddle my co-researcher, many people who helped with the consent project, and the Leverhulme Trust and the Calouste Gulbenkian Foundation for sponsorship.

4 The Family — A Refuge from Demands or an Arena for the Exercise of Power and Control — Children's Fictions on Their Future Families[1]

Gunilla Halldén

What do we mean by family? What are its distinguishing features and functions? In sociological contexts 'coreness' is a predominant feature of the family — a quality whose nature varies depending on the period in history and the cultural setting we choose for the study of the family. Must we always include children if we wish to speak about the family? And what is the role of children in the family?

My interest here is in how children and adolescents conceive of the family and how they imagine future family constellations. Looking at the family from the child's point of view is a special field of study in its own right. It can give us insight into children's thoughts about family relationships and about how power is distributed among adults and between adults and children. Often the family is studied as a sociological arena in which the child is the family member upon whom influence is exerted. It is adults who are the subject of sociological inquiry, it is their actions that are studied in relation to the child. Even when children are included in the research, they are seldom studied in their own right. This conclusion is quite apparent if we look at the statistics on children. Children are accounted for in the statistics as members of a family and are thereby less accessible for study (Qvortrup, 1990).

In research on childhood as a field of study that has relevance even outside the domain of developmental psychology, support has been won in recent years for the view that children are research subjects in their own right and not merely as 'adults in the making' (my quotation marks) (Prout and James, 1990). Children should be studied as children and not only as small individuals who are in the process of taking their first steps towards development. Thus, the perspective on children has shifted from that of the school and educators to that of the children themselves. And here a problem immediately arises. How does one apply a child perspective? Isn't it in the nature of research to objectify the child and to acknowledge, by virture of their greater power, the adults' right of interpretation? The ethnographic method may be a way out of the dilemma. An interesting study was conducted by Kelly-Byrne (1989) in which she acted as participating observer of a child's play activity. While baby-sitting for a little girl over a period of several years, Byrne was able to document the child's play activity in which Byrne herself took an active part. Thus she was able to study play activity 'from the inside' and could then analyze it from a child perspective.

The child perspective is also evident in Carolyn Steedman's book, *The Tidy House* (Steedman, 1982), which is based on a narrative written by three 8-year-old girls in the course of their schoolwork. The girls wrote about two couples, their love life, their longing for children, but also about the bothersomeness of having children and the fact that children tend to restrict women's lives. The narrative is Steedman's point of departure for her thesis on the early socialization of women. The narrative of the three young girls gives insight into what they imagine to be the life of mothers and the kind of life that lies before them. The girls were only instructed to write a narrative on a topic of their own choosing. It is therefore quite likely that the topic they chose lies close to their hearts. It would also be reasonable to conclude that the manner in which they depict adult relationships and relationships between adults and children expresses how they conceive of 'life as it really is'. In their tidy house, the children made room for romance, for fussing children and for dissatisfied women. Their narrative can be understood as role-play in which relationships are examined and ideas on power and subjection are expressed symbolically.

I use an approach similar to Steedman's in my research project in which children wrote about their future family. My idea was to inspire the children to engage themselves in a particular writing task over an extended period of time and to concretize their family portrayals in such a way that the exercise would seem like play to them. Thus I hoped to obtain a child perspective on family life and on conceivable scenarios of the future.

Researching the Child Perspective on Family

The material discussed here comes from a writing project undertaken in a Swedish school class of 8- and 9-year-olds.[2] The drawings and narratives produced by the children provide us with a picture that can be described, but whose meaning cannot be ascertained with any great certainty. For some of the children, the family theme seems to have sparked a process of intense creativity bearing some of the characteristics of role play, and this may very well have had an emancipatory effect on the young writers. For others, the process of narration was a difficult one, and the resulting text is often scanty and almost inaccessible to interpretation. However, all the children were absorbed in completing the task and appeared to take it seriously. It was as if they were actually in the process of creating a family for themselves.

The material that accumulated in the form of drawings and narratives does not in itself tell us how children experience family life nor how they view the role of the family. The narratives are works of fiction created in a particular context using one or another style in accordance with a particular genre. The context is that of the school, of doing what the teacher expects one to do ('What may I write about?'). And even if one decides not to let the other pupils read what one has written, their eyes are always on one. The genres that may have had an influence on how the narratives developed are family serials on television, books written for children, comic books, etc. The children's drawings and narratives must be understood as children's fiction, pictures shaped by dreams, fantasies, role models and cautionary examples. They can be analyzed in order to see what comes into focus when the subject of family is introduced, what are the central themes and which of the family members are involved in key events. Thus the data consist of children's fiction mediated through a language and written in a particular tradition. What are we able to say about the family, to whom and in what contexts? How do children depict family scenes taking place in a fictive future family of their own? What is being presented to us are the children's perspective, fictions and stereotypes.

I am not interested in how the material relates to the children's real families. When writing, children build in one way or another upon their own experiences. At times, the narratives seem to be concerned with the children's own families, at other times they seem to reflect wishful thinking in direct contrast to existing family relationships. The children draw and write from their own experience and fantasy. They use a style that is influenced by different genres such as the film medium, comic books and children's books. The figures that appear in their fictive families seem at times to bear the features of comic strip characters, at times characters taken from popular children's literature. In several cases the figures that occupy a central position are household pets and the narrative takes on the quality of a fable.

The narratives can be analyzed from the point of view of how children treat the theme of reproduction (Halldén, 1993). It is also interesting to note in the girls' narratives the similarities and differences as to narrative style and choice and treatment of themes (Halldén, 1994). The theme of this chapter concerns power relations in the family as depicted by boys and girls. How do they handle the question of power when depicting family life? Who is the main character and who has power over what? The interesting thing to note here is the respective roles assigned to the adults and children in the family. Family dramas are played out where power and powerlessness are on exhibit and where there is, on the one hand, an identification with one's future role as an adult and, on the other, reflections of the dependency of childhood.

Relationships, Caring and Control

What constitutes a family is not a simple question, and the children in the study appear to have considered themselves free to create their own family constellations. Three of the fourteen boys and one of the eighteen girls in the study portray the life of a single adult living together with his or her pets. And there are no children in the families of another of the girls and two other boys. The remaining narratives describe family life consisting of both parents living together with their children (i.e. sixteen of the eighteen narratives written by girls and nine of the fourteen written by boys). If we look at how the 'I's' of the narratives relate to their families, we find that all the girls depict relationships. Even the one girl who lives alone describes relationships with relatives and friends. In the narratives of the boys, the relationship theme is much more diffuse. Seven of the boys do depict family life where interaction occurs among family members. But in the case of the narratives of four other boys, there is no interaction whatever among family members. Of the three boys who live alone with their pet or pets, two of them depict interaction between the main character and the pets in such manner as to resemble family life. The third boy is more completely alone, with the exception of a short episode depicting an outing with a friend.

In other words, the relationship theme is more clearly in evidence in the girls' writings than in the writings of the boys. The question remains how these relationships are depicted. The scenes that are played out in the narratives concern both everyday situations as well as more dramatic incidents and festive occasions. One way to depict family relationships is to describe the care members give one another and how daily routines such as preparing meals are carried out. If we look for caring rituals in the narratives, we find that they occur more frequently and are described in more detail in the girls' writings than in the boys'. The girls' narratives are longer and are often concerned with the inner life of the family. If we limit the account of caring rituals in the narratives to the simple mentioning of the fact that the family members eat, shop for food, sleep or otherwise carry out the functions necessary to daily survival, we find that such rituals occur in sixteen of the eighteen narratives written by girls, but in only eight of the fourteen narratives written by boys.

Decision-making in the Girls' Narratives

Conflicts occur more frequently in the girls' writings than they do in the boys'. Thirteen of the girls describe conflicts, usually in situations involving children. Only six of the boys do so, but even here children are usually involved. We can try to grasp how relationships develop by looking at who solves conflicts and who decides in situations where opinions differ. Of the eighteen girls, thirteen describe themselves, in their role of protagonist, as being the ones who make the decisions and resolve situations of conflicting interests. In four other cases it is unclear who makes the decisions, either because all parties seem to be in agreement or because a situation of disagreement is depicted without its resolution being clarified. In only one instance does a child make a decision, in this case the family's elder son.

Often there is disagreement about how to spend one's time on Sunday.

> *What should we do on Sunday?* — Let's go over to grandma's, says Erika — I don't want to do that, says daddy — But I want to, said mommy — Me me (babytalk) said Camilla (baby). OK, said daddy, then we'll go. So all of us (the whole family) went to see grandma.

In this episode it is 2-year-old Erika who comes up with a suggestion. It is daddy who has to give in, but the question remains: who finally decided? I see the decision has having come from the mother, although she is not the author of the suggestion. Her position in the family is such that it is reasonable to consider her point of view as being the guiding one. In this narrative it is the mother who creates order while the child is the mother's fellow-player and confidante.

> One morning I told Erika that I was going to have a baby and that she couldn't fool around with me so much any more. Now nine months have gone and so one night it was time, so we called up our neighbours and they came over to baby-sit so that she would know where she was when she woke up.

Here the main character is the caring mother who not only confides in her daughter, but also at the time of birth sees to it that her daughter is well cared for.

Conflicts involving children are depicted by another girl in the following way:

> *I had a big argument.* Emil was supposed to go to school and Emilia was supposed to go to nursery school and Janne and me were supposed to go to work. But Emil didn't want to go to school and Emilia didn't want to go to nursery school, and that made me angry so I scolded them, and then Emilia began to cry so I lowered my voice and did what I could to make her feel better, then I said don't be sorry about going to nursery school. And then Emil and Emilia went off to school like they were supposed to.

Even in this case the main character is the caring mother who, although she argues with her children and scolds them, also comforts them and gets them to do what must be done.

Gunilla Halldén

Decision-making in the Boys' Narratives

The boys' narratives are much less clear about who in the family makes the decisions. Four of the fourteen boys let the main character decide (observe however, that two of the four live alone and thus do not exercise their right of decision over any other person). In three other narratives, it is not at all apparent who makes the decisions. On the other hand, in four of the narratives written by boys, it is the children who decide and it is the children who have the crucial influence in situations of conflict. As we have seen, this is the case in only one of the narratives written by girls. In still another narrative, it is the partner who decides, and in two other cases the decision-maker is the grandmother and the boy's pet, respectively.

> *What should we do on Sunday?* Let's go swimming, says Karl (child). I want to go, too, says Fredrik (child). We all want to go, says Kim (child). They all go swimming, Karl jumps in first, then Fredrik, then Kim, then Andreas (the husband/father), then Susan (wife/mother).

The narrative continues with the portrayal of how the two elder boys, Karl and Fredrik, swim and play in the water. The central theme of the episode is playing and having a good time. There are passages in the narrative where care is provided, but at the same time the boy's identification with children is quite clear and he ascribes considerable influence to them. Giving care occurs in the form of preparing the breakfast meal.

> One morning I got up and made breakfast, and then Karl came in the kitchen and said I want breakfast. Yes, you'll get your breakfast, but go and wake up Fredrik and Susan and Kim first.

Later in the narrative, the person giving care in the above scene becomes dependent instead on the decision of others.

> *That's when I felt disappointed.* Once we were supposed to go and buy a dog, but I wasn't allowed to go along and that made me feel disappointed.
> *One day we went shopping.* Once we were supposed to go shopping and the kids could have as many sweets as they wanted. And then we drive home again and make some food. And then they have sweets after dinner. Then they watch some video. Then they're supposed to go to bed. One day Karl started to make a fuss about wanting another pet and he said he wanted a mouse. So we drove off to buy a mouse. Jippi, jippi, I got a mouse.

The main character is depicted on the one hand as a dependent person, and on the other as someone who is able to gratify the children's every whim. In the last sentence in the passage above, the narrative shifts from third to first person and the 'I' expresses happiness at getting a pet. This can be interpreted as indicating that a shift to an alter ego has taken place; the boy who is writing the narrative suddenly lets the child become the main character and begins to speak in the voice of the first person singular.

Even if it is the main character who seems to make all the decisions in the family, this does not mean that the child does not exert his own will, as the next passage will illustrate:

> One morning. The kids are noisy and running up and down the hall. Cissi (the wife) gets up and makes breakfast. Sometimes they take it easy and sit and watch video or play computer games. Toben goes to kindergarten and Susan goes to nursery school and Niklas goes to school and the pets are fed.
> What are we doing on Sunday? — I want to go to the movies.
> — No, I want to go swimming. — Stop fighting, we can go swimming for part of the day and then go to the movies for the rest of the day.

The illustration accompanying the narrative shows a wild fistfight, drawn in comic strip style with a big cloud out of which stick arms and legs. The father stands off to the side looking at the fight with a smile on his lips. Family life is depicted in a charming but chaotic manner. The main character suggests a solution but there is no dénouement and we do not see how order is restored.

In one of the narratives in which a boy lives alone with his pets, in this case a parrot and two snakes, a conflict arises between the main character and his parrot about what they are going to do together on Sunday. The conflict is resolved when grandmother comes for a visit.

> *What should we do on Sunday?* — I want to go to the market, says Bertil (the parrot). — I don't want to do that, says Jan (the main character). — I want to go to the zoo, Jan says. Then grandma came in and said we're going to the zoo.

This could be one way of playing with the genre. This is not the traditional family that is being depicted — the central position in the family is occupied by pets. But the joking around is also a way of relating to the family theme. It is possible to interpret this boy's narrative as showing a way of solving a personally experienced lack of power. His household pets can be seen as symbolic representations of himself — the parrot stands for the mischief-maker and rule-breaker while the snakes represent a powerful and dangerous force that can scare the living daylights out of visitors.

> How my family works. My parrot Bertil gets into a lot of trouble. He makes messes all the time, that's what he's like. Peyman and Greta were a couple of snakes, both of them were cobras. When my

grandmother and grandfather came to visit me, the snakes got loose and scared grandmother. Most of the time Peyman and Greta stayed wrapped around my neck.

Who is the Central Figure?

We can summarize by saying that the girls depict in their narratives a family life where interaction takes place among the members of the family. Conflicts occur in their families more often than they do in the boys' families. The chief decision-maker and resolver of conflict situations is the main character, that is, the adult woman in the family. In the boys' narratives, interaction does not occur in all the families, nor do conflict situations occur as frequently as they do in the girls' narratives. The boys do not assign themselves the role of the decision-making adult as often as the girls do. The fact that decisions are made by someone other than the main character can be seen as indicating that the boys do not give themselves a central role, that is, of an individual possessed of extensive powers. It can also be seen as indicating that their alter egos tend to shift. Decisions made by the children of the family give an indication of where the narrator's solidarity lies. Letting one's partner, grandmother or household pet have the power of decision-making may be a way of putting oneself in a subordinate position. Thus the girls depict their main characters as adults who possess power and in whose hands the responsibility for the care of the family rests, whereas the boys often as not fail to identify with the adult in their narratives. Nor does the adult in the boys' narratives always have the power to make decisions.

Breaking Rules and Rule-breakers

Another way of getting at the distribution of power in the family is to see who is assigned the role of rule-breaker and how the breaking of rules is depicted. First of all, we can see that the theme of rule-breaking occurs in nine of the girls' narratives and in eleven of the boys'. Here the pattern is the opposite of what we found to be the case with respect to conflicts. Family members may be in disagreement about how to spend their time together, who is to do the shopping or who gets to eat the biggest piece of cake. Conflicts of this kind concern control and the right of decision-making, and we can see that they occur more frequently in the girls' narratives than in the boys'. Rule-breaking as a theme is about doing what is forbidden or inappropriate. We can see it as a way of highlighting what is correct and appropriate by showing deviant behaviour instead. We can also see it as being at the same time a challenge to authority. Thus breaking the rules may lead to a conflict, but not all conflicts arise through breaking rules. In the girls' narratives rule-breaking occurs in half of the cases (nine of eighteen), and in six of them the culprits are the children in the family, acting in collusion. In three cases it is the male partner who breaks the rules. In three other cases, the rules are broken respectively by the son acting alone, by the daughter acting alone and finally by the main character herself. (Note that different instances of rule-breaking may occur in one and the same narrative.)

So in the girls' narratives it is the children, acting in collusion, who answer for most of the instances of rule-breaking. The following episode is a good illustration:

> I got mad at my kids! When I woke up one morning I heard the dogs bark. Then I saw that the kids were pulling them around by their leash. That made me mad because it hurts the dogs' neck. So I said that if they do that again, they can't have any sweets for two weeks.

The same girl makes an unusual comment about the man in the family. It concerns an instance of poaching on her preserve, and in that sense is an infraction of the rules.

> *That's when I felt disappointed.* One evening after dinner I had a stomach ache so I went to take a rest, and when I felt better I went out to the kitchen and there was daddy doing the dishes. That made me feel disappointed.

When I later interviewed the girl about this episode, she explained that in this case the man (called daddy in the narrative) was taking over her place. The kitchen was her territory and he was welcome to help her when she was sick. But in this case she had recovered, and so his helping her had made her feel disappointed instead. This episode gives a good illustration of the importance of having a preserve and a child perspective on how to guard it. The woman in the family is the one who runs the home and she wants to do it in her own way.

On the same theme of disappointment, another girl complains about the man in the family.

> *That's when I felt disappointed.* One day Jan (the man) was fixing the car and he was going to get some water, and he left footmarks on the floor. That made me feel disappointed.

In describing how the men in these two cases break the rules, the girls do not imply that authority is being challenged. The texts serve rather to highlight the woman as the one who makes the rules and the man as the one who fails to live up to them. Depicting an infraction of the rules serves to point out the role of the woman as the upholder of order.

The boys' narratives show a quite different pattern. The children, as a collective, are depicted as rule-breakers in only two instances. The son in the family is the culprit in three other instances, the daughter in one instance and in another three instances it is the household pets who break the rules. The main character breaks the rules in two of the boys' narratives, whereas there are no instances in which the female partner is the culprit.

One of the boys lets the youngest child, a boy, play a comic role.

> At Easter we colour Easter eggs, we eat eggs and dress up like Easter witches. When we were going to hang up the Easter things, Toben brought out a Santa Claus and started pestering us about hanging it up, and so we had to do it! Then some visitors came and then they asked us if it was Christmas? Oh boy, were we ashamed!

Toben jokes with the Easter ritual and succeeds in getting the others to hang up a Christmas decoration. This is a different kind of rule infraction than being too rough with dogs or making footmarks on the floor. Here Toben is going against an established pattern. Who does Toben represent? And who is the 'we' of the narrative? Is Toben an aspect of the narrator, just as the parrot and the dangerous snakes are in the narrative described earlier? The use of the first person plural in describing activities that children usually do, such as colouring Easter eggs and dressing up as witches, indicates that here we have another case of a shift in the alter ego. The boy allies himself with the group of adults and children who know what Easter decorations are, but at the same time he introduces an element of play. Toben disrupts the seriousness of the moment and succeeds in doing the 'impossible', something perhaps that many children would like to do. When the family later receives visitors, they feel ashamed of what Toben had got them to do.

A parrot as the rule-breaker occurs in two narratives. I have already mentioned one of them above. In the other, the parrot is both rule-breaker and decision-maker.

> One morning when I woke up my parrot was gone. I looked all over but couldn't find him. So I went outside to look for him. Then I saw him up on the roof. He jumped down to me.
> *What should we do on Sunday?* On Sunday my parrot was 6 years old. I asked, what do you want to do? The parrot said, I want to go to the movies. OK, then we'll do it, I said. —
> *That's when I felt disappointed.* When I came home Sune (the parrot) wanted to go out, but I didn't want to go out. So Sune said I'm going out by myself. So he went out. I felt disappointed when he went out.

This boy drew a picture of a family consisting of himself, his wife (?) Anna and a parrot named Sune. But Anna is never mentioned in the narrative, and despite the drawing, family interaction takes place solely between the boy and his parrot. The parrot occupies a central position in the family with the result that the main character is at times made powerless. At the same time, it is the main character who is the owner of the pet which symbolizes human nature in caricature.

What is the import of allowing someone to break the rules? For the girls, it is most commonly the children acting in collusion who are the culprits. The mother is the one who exercises control and restores order. The infraction of the rules throws authority in relief. For the boys, the rule-breakers most often act alone. They are more often depicted as comic figures who, through their mischief-making, indicate a deviation from the norm without order being restored. It is more often a case of challenging authority.

When is the 'We'-form Used?

Earlier I touched upon the question of how pronouns are used and I pointed out that there may be a significance behind the choice between 'I' or 'we'. A simple way of reviewing the material from this aspect can be to note on how many pages the we-form occurs in the narratives. In the boy's narratives the we-form occurs on the average on four pages while the length of the narratives averages ten pages. The girls' narratives average eighteen pages and the average occurrance of the we-form is on six-and-a-half pages. Quantitatively speaking, there is little difference in the way the boys and girls use the we-form in their writings. Both use the form on about one-third of their text pages.

Another way of studying the occurrence of the we-form is to note in what contexts it is used. Because the length of the narratives varies considerably, a comparison between boys and girls may be misleading. In a lengthy narrative, many more different episodes occur and thus there is a greater number of contexts in which the we-form may occur. However, by basing the comparison on the themes in which the we-form occurs in the boys' and girls' narratives respectively, we can avoid the source of error connected with the disproportionate lengths of the narratives.

The themes in which the we-form occurs are the following: decision-making, daily routines, outings/family get-togethers/festive occasions, Easter celebrations, and 'We have' situations — for example, when describing the home. The first three categories are the most interesting. Celebrating Easter in the narratives usually means colouring eggs and getting candy, while the 'we have' theme usually relates to describing rooms and listing objects. If we go through the use of the we-form in connection with the themes in which it occurs, we arrive at an overview of the themes in which the we-form is most prominant, for the girls and boys respectively.

The most frequent use of the we-form among the girls is in connection with decision-making situations and daily routines, whereas among the boys it is in connection with outings/family get-togethers/festive occasions. It would be a mistake to make too much of these distinctions. It can be interesting to note, however, that the girls use the we-form most often when writing about decision-making situations, despite the fact that they have also assigned themselves the role of decision-maker. This would seem to indicate that the word 'we' means different things in different contexts. In the girls' narratives, the actions of the 'we' are directed by an organizing main character. In the boys' narratives, 'we' most often refers to a group in which the main character is a participant but less often the organizer.

Here we are beginning to arrive at an important difference between the narratives of the girls and the boys. The girls depict themselves as being an important main character, often as the one who organizes family life. Even the girl who assigns her main character the more traditional role of homemaker, empowers her with control over vital areas of family life — she is a central figure. The boys often describe themselves as living in a family where they have no control over situations that arise and where comic incidents and the infraction of rules bring to light the chaotic aspects of family life. The boys commonly depict family life in connection with outings, trips, and in somewhat escapist contexts. On these occasions, 'we' consists of the whole family, children and adults, out having a good time.

The Presence of the Strong Mother Among the Girls, her Absence Among the Boys

In the girls' narratives, we find a strong mother figure embodied in the main character. A central theme is reproduction, and in several of the narratives the woman gives birth, as does the household pet. Birth among household pets also takes place in the boys' narratives, but not the birth of children. In the boys' narratives there is no strong and authoritative adult. What are we to make of this? Can we justifiably say that what is absent in the boys' narratives is exactly that which is so central to the girls' narratives, namely a strong and powerful mother figure? Is this figure so potent that the boys are unable to describe her in words? Several of the boys go so far as to imagine a family without a woman, or they include her in their drawings but omit all reference to her in their writing. Most of them, however, depict a family consisting of a mother, a father and the children, where daily life consists of carrying out various routines, fighting with the children, going on outings or to parties, but where neither of the adults has an organizing role. Life is either free from conflicts or it is so chaotic that organization is impossible.

The diffuse adult identification apparent in the narratives of some of the boys may be caused by their undeveloped writing skills, which would make it more difficult for them to adopt a consistent perspective. It may also be a case of their being reluctant to write about traditional family life and to involve themselves in the game of mummy-daddy-baby. A far more interesting interpretation, however, is to see it as being influenced by the different genres that are used by the media to depict family life. The joyful and the

Brown and Gilligan, 1993) notes that girls tend to take relationships into account. We have seen the same phenomenon in the girls' narratives analyzed here. We can read the narratives as signifying identification with a nurturing figure. A good deal of attention is given in the girls' narratives to making decisions, carrying out daily routines, and negotiating with unruly or wilful children. In the boys' narratives, more attention is given to going on family outings and buying capital goods like cars and computers or acquiring household pets. There are instances of providing care and attending to the routines of daily life in the boys' narratives as well, but it is not nearly as dominating a theme as it is among the girls. What I have brought into focus here is the question of power and authority. The girls write about relationships, but they also write about power and control. The boys' narratives are not primarily narratives in which personal relationships are missing. They are stories about being part of a group, and about using the device of rule-breaking to make jokes about power and authority.

What Gilligan has noted is that the girls' dilemma is one of growing up in a world where becoming a woman entails denying one's thirst for knowledge and one's right of self-assertion out of consideration for others. One view on this dilemma links it to the process by which the identity of girls develops (Chodorow, 1978 and 1989). Walkerdine's approach puts the focus on power relationships in the society as it is reflected in the pedagogic discourse, rather than on the psychological development of girls. For both of these researchers, a prime question is how girls relate to a culture where individuation and development are linked to autonomy and the male world. What are we able to say, and what are we unable to express? How much of one's own thirst for knowledge and curiosity about life is one allowed to gratify? Such questions are often brought to the foreground in the light of the school setting (Brown and Gilligan, 1993; Luttrell, 1993; Walkerdine, 1988). The material obtained in this study has been collected in a school setting and is influenced by what takes place in such a context. At the same time, the theme is the family. What message is conveyed to young girls about the possibilities of acquiring power and of having access to a whimsical free space? The girls in Steedman's study depict children as being a hindrance for women (Steedman, 1987). In the narratives discussed here, the girls assign themselves a potent role and describe an expansive life for themselves. At the same time, we can ask ourselves if this is not a case of simply having come upon a new way to define the relative subordinate position of women. The boys depict family life as a game and turn the family sphere over to someone else. And the girls step in and assume control over that sphere, at the same time showing how they exercise control over the children. In the girls' narratives, the children are not treated differently according to gender; they are shown to be creatures that are subject to control. The boys' show in their narratives that they will not allow themselves to be controlled. The complementarity of the boys' and girls' narratives becomes clearly visible. Power, which the girls desire, is something the boys simply turn a blind eye to, while their infraction of the rules is something the girls look upon with indulgence. The narratives analyzed here show how, by treating the woman as caretaker and the person with authority within the family sphere, the relative subordinancy of her position and her role as the fosterer of 'the child'/boy are maintained (Walkerdine, 1988).

The aim of this chapter has been to throw light on children's conceptions of family relationships as revealed through written narratives. Through the analysis of the family scenarios, we can begin to understand how children relate to the family and to the power relationships and conditions of dependency that are a part of family life. The narratives can be read as fictions in which the children test their own position. What I have described here are various family scenarios created by girls and boys. An underlying theme in the writings of both girls and boys is the powerful mother figure which each group treats in different ways through their choice of narrative style and genre. Furthermore, how the powerful mother figure is treated is also an effect of whether the woman's/mother's relationship develops in relation to a child whose future is one of autonomy — in other words a boy, or a child whose future is one of nurturing — in other words a girl.

Notes

1 The research reported here was financed by the Swedish Council for Social Research. I wish to express my thanks to Carina Fast who, as the classroom teacher in the study, was an important partner in collecting data from the children and in discussing and analyzing the material. I am also greatly indebted to Noella Bickham for linguistic assistance.
2 Over a period of two months, the thirty-two children in the class — eighteen girls and fourteen boys — wrote and illustrated a running narrative on the theme 'My future family'. In an initial stage of the project, the teacher discussed the theme of family and different kinds of family constellations with the children. She encouraged them to imagine a life lived at some time in the future and to consider the different forms that life might take. The children were then asked to draw a picture of the house in which their fictive families lived, and to depict the family members in both words and drawings. The children's narratives on the family developed largely through topics suggested by the teacher, for example, 'One day', 'What should we do on Sunday?' and 'That's when I felt disappointed'. But the children were also free to write on other topics of their own choosing within the family theme. The narratives were collected in individual booklets where each cover was made up of the child's plasticized drawing of his/her fictive family's house. Creating such a framework for the telling of a story served the interest of establishing continuity in the children's writing.
3 In the original the children's writings contain errors of spelling, sentence construction and punctuation; readability suffers as a result. For the sake of clarity, sentence construction and punctuation have been modified and spelling errors corrected in the English translation. In all other respects, I have sought to reproduce the children's writing style. Text fragments are italicized where the children have done so. The annotations in parentheses are my own. The dash mark in cited text indicates that passages have been omitted.

5 Television and the Definition of Childhood

David Buckingham

Early in 1993, the British public was gripped by reports of the murder of a 2-year-old child. Jamie Bulger had been abducted from a shopping mall near Liverpool and then horrifically killed by two 10-year-old boys. For weeks afterwards the press and TV featured analyses of the incident, made all the more gruesome as the actual moment of his abduction had been captured by video surveillance cameras. Yet attempts to explain the killing in terms of poverty and economic recession, or the erosion of leisure provision for young people, soon gave way to another, depressingly familiar, set of arguments. For it was the media that were responsible for the murder of Jamie Bulger. The simultaneous publication of Michael Medved's bizarre attack on Hollywood morals (Medved, 1993), and the appearance of a number of films that were seen to have reached new peaks in screen violence (notably Quentin Tarantino's *Reservoir Dogs*), contributed to the development of a full-scale moral panic. Television executives were called to account, and new guidelines on TV violence were promised. TV talk shows featured teenage criminals only too ready to blame their misdemeanours on the media. And the British Board of Film Classification (the industry censorship body) hastily commissioned research into the viewing habits of young offenders.

In the debates that followed the trial and conviction of Jamie Bulger's murderers, the issue of media violence again came to the fore. Pursuing remarks made by the judge in his summing-up, the press seized on the fact that a horror video, *Child's Play 3*, had been found in the home of one of the boys — although, at least according to his father, the boy himself had not actually seen it. The story of the murder was rewritten as a gruesome re-enactment of the film, as video shops all over the country hastily removed it from sale. As Rupert Murdoch's *Sun* urged its readers to burn their copies of the tape, MPs from all political parties urged the government to exert even tighter controls on the censorship of video films.[1]

Popular pleasures, and in particular the pleasures of the screen, have been the focus of anxieties and repressive campaigns of this kind throughout history (see, for example, Barker, 1984a; Lusted, 1985). In recent years, video and computer games have begun to take the place of television in this popular demonology, just as television took the place of comics, and comics took the place of the cinema in earlier decades. Indeed, such concerns about the effects of popular media on young people can be traced back as far as the Greek philosopher Plato, who proposed to ban the dramatic poets from his ideal republic, for fear of their negative influence on impressionable young minds. Yet if the focus of attention has changed, the concerns and the rhetoric in which they are expressed remain very familiar. Television, video and computer games, like other media before them, are seen to be responsible, not merely for murder and delinquency, but also for undermining children's social, moral and intellectual development.

These arguments seem to possess a powerful appeal right across the political spectrum. The dominant voice here remains that of 'moral majority' campaigners such as Britain's Mary Whitehouse, whose long-running crusade against television's promotion of moral depravity and violence still wields considerable influence on broadcasters themselves. Yet there are remarkable similarities between this position and that of many on the Left, who regard the media as the primary source of racism, sexism, consumerism, militarism, and any other objectionable ideology one might care to name. In both cases, the media are seen as an extremely powerful, and almost wholly negative, influence which children are effectively powerless to resist. As in the Jamie Bulger case, blaming the media often seems to provide a simplistic, reassuring explanation of events that may be too painful or difficult to face — yet it also deflects attention away from more complex underlying causes that may be much harder to remedy.

Significantly, however, it is children who are seen to be most at risk — and in this respect, debates about children and television almost inevitably invoke broader ideological constructions of childhood, of the kind discussed by other contributors to this book. Children are defined here as vulnerable and innocent, and thus in need of adult 'protection'. Yet as Martin Barker (1989) has noted, there is also a sense in which they are regarded as inadequately socialized: the media, by virtue of their direct appeal to the emotions, are seen to have the power to penetrate the thin veneer of civilization, and to release the darker forces that lie beneath. Ultimately, it is these fears of disorder and social unrest that provide the justification for adults' attempts at regulation and control.

Perhaps the clearest example of this concern is Neil Postman's influential book *The Disappearance of Childhood* (Postman, 1983). Postman asserts that the electronic media, and particularly television, have blurred or indeed abolished the traditional distinction between children and adults. While print literacy serves to exclude the child from aspects of the adult world, Postman argues, this is impossible in purely oral cultures or in those based on what he calls 'total disclosure' media such as television. Television removes barriers and exposes adult 'secrets', and thereby undermines children's respect for their elders and betters. It is no mere coincidence, Postman suggests, that the generation that rebelled so spectacularly against their parents in the 1960s was the first to be brought up on television.

There are clearly several major weaknesses in this argument (see Hoikkala *et al.*, 1987). The evidence that these distinctions are in fact being eroded, and that television is the primary cause, remains quite limited. Nevertheless, Postman's thesis is also symptomatic of much more fundamental fears about the decline in respect for adult authority. Perhaps surprisingly for one of the great educational radicals of the 1960s,[2] Postman explicitly seeks to promote a return to the traditional nuclear family, and to hierarchical power-relationships between generations. In describing parental authority as essentially 'humane', Postman effectively ignores the ways in which it is abused, and has been abused throughout history. And in asserting the need to keep children ignorant, he effectively denies them the right to develop their own critical perspectives.

Research: Changing Paradigms

Research on young people and the media has inevitably been framed and informed by these kinds of concerns. A great deal of energy has been expended on the search for evidence of negative 'effects', much of it based on simplistic forms of behaviourism, and on functionalist theories of socialization. The major preoccupation here — and the most spectacularly unproductive — has been with the influence of television violence. In measuring children's imitative responses to violent 'stimuli', researchers have effectively avoided fundamental questions about the *meanings* of 'violence', and the ways in which they are established by viewers themselves. Children are perceived here as mere blank slates, on which television scrawls its harmful and indelible messages.

More recent research has challenged many of these assumptions, as cognitive and developmental approaches have increasingly (although in many ways only partially) supplanted behaviourism (see Dorr, 1986). Nevertheless, the relationship between children and television continues to be seen as a primarily *psychological* phenomenon. It is a matter of what television 'does' to children's minds — or, more recently, what their minds 'do' with television. In the process, children have been defined as somehow a-social, or perhaps pre-social — as 'cognitive processors' in isolated communion with the screen. Almost inevitably, such approaches are based on normative assumptions about 'rational', adult behaviour, against which children are judged as more or less inadequate (Anderson, 1981).

My own research is located within a rather different tradition, that of cultural studies. Emerging initially from the encounter between literary studies and sociology, cultural studies has increasingly drawn on theoretical approaches derived from semiotics, post-structuralism, Marxism and psychoanalytic theory. Within this tradition, there has been a broad shift of emphasis in the past decade, which has led to a greater recognition of the role played by audiences within mass communication. There has been a growing acknowledgement that texts can be read in a variety of ways, which do not necessarily correspond to the intentions of their producers. According to this approach, meaning is not simply contained within the text, but actively produced by readers — and readers themselves are not simply 'positions' inscribed within texts, but real social beings, living in specific social and historical contexts. This theoretical shift has led to a growing body of audience research, much of it using qualitative and ethnographic methods of investigation.

The emphasis here, therefore, is on the diverse ways in which children use and appropriate television, and the role this plays within specific subcultures of gender, ethnicity and social class. At the same time, the research has sought to develop new approaches, particularly in relation to the social role of language. Audience researchers in cultural studies have tended to adopt an uncritical approach to language: language is often seen as transparent, a straightforward means of access to what people 'really think'. By contrast, I have drawn on recent work in 'critical linguistics' (for example, Fairclough, 1989), in paying much closer attention to the ways in which children's judgments and observations about television, and the concepts and criteria they use in talking about it, are established in language itself. This leads in turn to a rather different notion of the relationship between viewers' talk about television and their social position. Cultural studies researchers have often taken a rather inflexible, and indeed deterministic, view of the role of social categories such as class and gender. Individuals are often seen to make sense of television in particular ways 'because' they are middle class, or female, or black. By drawing on some of the methods and insights of 'discursive psychology' (for example Potter and Wetherell, 1987; Edwards and Potter, 1992), I have argued for a more dynamic view of individuals, which regards them as more active and creative in defining the meaning of their own social positions, and in assuming social power. These approaches derive in turn from broader social theories of language and cognition, for example in the work of Vygotsky, Volosinov and Bakhtin.

In researching children's social lives, we inevitably construct definitions of childhood — definitions which in turn play a part in ongoing debates and dialogues of the kind I have described. In fact, there is now a growing body of research that challenges popular notions of children as 'television zombies', or as victims of some irresistible process of conditioning by the media.[3] Yet ultimately, a great deal of the research in this field appears to have been framed by a series of either/or choices — according to which television has to be seen as either 'good' or 'bad' for children, and children themselves as either 'active' or 'passive' viewers. Given the level of public anxiety about these issues, it remains necessary to insist that children are in many respects much more active, sophisticated and critical viewers than is often assumed. Yet in making such arguments, there is a significant risk that one will end up merely seeking to replace a conventional view of children as innocent and vulnerable with an equally sentimental view of them as 'street-wise' and knowledgeable. If our understanding of this central aspect of children's lives is to progress, we need to be asking rather different questions.

In this chapter, I want to suggest that what it means to be a 'child viewer' — and thus, by implication, an 'adult viewer' — is subject to a considerable degree of negotiation. The subject position 'child' is not, in this sense, simply fixed or given: on the contrary, it is constantly redefined, reasserted and resisted in children's (and adults') talk about television. In the following sections, I want to use evidence from my own research to explore the different ways in which the 'child viewer' is defined in two particular contexts. I will begin by considering the domestic uses of television, and the ways in which children respond to their parents' attempts to regulate their viewing. I will then go on to examine how these shifting definitions of 'child' and 'adult' are established and negotiated in peer group discussions of the medium.

The data here are taken from an extensive research project, which covered a number of dimensions of children's use and understanding of television.[4] The research took place in schools, although the children were taken out of the classroom into a room elsewhere in the school, and interviewed in pairs or groups. Broadly speaking, the aim of the interviews was to encourage the children to set their own agendas and to nominate their own topics of discussion within the broad focus established by the interviewer. Our role as interviewers was generally to 'chair' the discussions — although this is not to imply that it was merely neutral. On the contrary, as I shall argue, the social relationships between adult researchers and their child 'subjects' significantly determine what we can 'know' about children as viewers.

Family Viewing

Television is sometimes praised for its ability to 'bring the family together' — although it is more often blamed for destroying the harmony of traditional family life. Television is frequently seen as an 'intruder' in the home, an uninvited — and mostly unwelcome — 'guest' in the family living room. Yet to ask questions about the 'effects' of television on the family is to assume that its meaning is somehow given, and that it simply impinges on the family from without.

Recent research has begun to move away from this approach, however. Ethnographic studies of 'family viewing' (for example, Morley, 1986; Lull, 1988; Morley and Silverstone, 1990) have shown that television viewing needs to be understood in the context of existing social relationships between family members — relationships which are inevitably characterized by struggles for power and control. Thus, Morley (1986) and Gray (1992), for example, have drawn attention to the very different viewing practices of men and women — not simply in terms of their tastes and preferences, but also in terms of how television is related to their other domestic activities. This research has often painted a picture of absolute male power, symbolized by the father's possession of the remote control device, and his guarding of the video recorder as a uniquely male preserve.

Of course, in many households, television may be used as a bargaining counter in quite unrelated struggles — as indeed it was in my own childhood. Among the children in our sample, the threat of withdrawing viewing privileges appeared to have been used to encourage them to eat food they disliked, to tidy their bedrooms or to stop quarrelling with their brothers or sisters. Yet in many ways, struggles over television are qualitatively different. The television is not simply an appliance like a dishwasher or a vacuum cleaner. On the contrary, in considering 'family viewing' we are inevitably considering relations of power and knowledge, both within and beyond the family itself.

The rationales which parents use in regulating their children's viewing often invoke broader moral and psychological discourses: they reflect normative definitions of child development and of cultural value which effectively prescribe subject positions for both parents and children. On one level, of course, these discourses are merely part of a much broader range of discourses which are used to normalize and regulate parenting itself (Urwin, 1985; Grieshaber, 1989). In this context, regulating and intervening in your child's viewing — or at least claiming that you do — is as much an indicator of being a 'good parent' as ensuring that your child has good table manners, eats and dresses appropriately, and behaves well on trips to the supermarket. As Lull (1982) observes, successfully regulating children's viewing behaviour 'confirms proper performance of a particular family role', and may thereby confirm the individual as a 'good parent' — whereas the failure to do so can presumably generate feelings of guilt and inadequacy. To use television as an 'electronic baby-sitter' — or to admit to doing so — is clearly to invite social disapproval, albeit particularly among middle-class parents.

Nevertheless, past research has pointed to significant discrepancies between parents' and children's accounts of regulation (Rossiter and Robertson, 1975; McLeod and Brown, 1976) — and there were certainly some glaring instances of this in my own research. Parents would typically present themselves as responsible viewers, carefully regulating the amount of television their children watched. Limiting television, they argued, was ultimately in the child's best interests: it was simply a form of 'good discipline'. Their own preferences, they said, were for news and documentaries, rather than 'childish' entertainment. Yet their children would often tell a rather different story. One father, for example, dominated one of our discussion groups with lengthy perorations about the negative effects of television, and the need to resist its evil influences upon children. Yet his 10-year-old son offered quite a different account:[5]

> I go in the front room when I come home from school, I look at the television for a little while, I just got, when I just got interested in something that I really really like, in / colour, my dad comes home

from work and he turns it over to a western and when I ask him 'why do you do that?' he says 'well, it's good, it's better to read a book than look at the television.' So he says 'read a book!' and then I say 'don't want to' [laughing]. So he sends me into the back room to look at black and white television.

Many of the children were keen to present themselves as successfully evading such attempts at regulation. There was a formidable battery of techniques here. In some cases, it was simply a matter of pestering your parents until they broke down: many of the children adopted a whining, 'child-like' voice in recounting these incidents, suggesting that this was a particularly effective way of persuading parents to give in to your demands. In other cases, it came down to sneaking around the house to watch another TV set — for example, in a lodger or au pair's room — or alternatively creeping downstairs after everyone else had gone to bed. In other situations, children sought to exploit the differences between their parents — in many cases, using the father's imposition of his own tastes to counter the mother's attempts at regulation. More deviously, one 9-year-old boy described how his mother would hide the remote control to prevent him watching TV after bedtime, and how he had bought his own without her knowledge.

Of course, this kind of struggle for control characterizes many areas of children's lives. Throughout our discussions, the children exchanged anecdotes about how they managed to stay up past bedtime, how they avoided domestic duties, and how they traded one parent off against the other. Getting to watch TV when your parents have said you can't is, in this respect, merely one aspect of the ongoing guerrilla war of family life. And obviously, there can be an element of bravado here. If parents have a great deal invested in presenting themselves as responsible controllers of their children's viewing (especially in the company of other parents, and of an academic interviewer), children may have an equal investment in presenting themselves for the benefit of their peers as the one who calls the shots in their household. In general, it was boys who were more likely to boast about the degree of licence they were given — for example, that they could watch whatever they liked or go to bed at any time they liked. And as I shall indicate, a number of children claimed to have watched 'adult' material which they clearly had not.

The key point here, then, is that the regulation and control of television in the home is not accomplished without a considerable struggle. Children (or indeed mothers) do not blindly consent to adult or male power — despite the arguments of some previous research. Yet if such regulation is not always effective, it does seem to have a considerable discursive force. The children in our sample were well aware of popular discourses about the negative 'effects' of television. Yet even where they were inclined to parody or reject them, these discourses seemed to set the terms for what would be defined as 'appropriate' for children of different ages — and, more broadly, for what it meant to be a 'child' or an 'adult' viewer in the first place.

Inevitably, these definitions were often ambiguous. Some children, for example, offered powerful moral condemnations of programmes like *Neighbours* and *Home and Away*, which were accused of being 'bad for children', primarily on the grounds of portraying violence and drug-taking. Yet these criticisms were often mingled with fascination and humour. There was clearly considerable interest in 'adult' material — and no little social status to be gained from claiming to watch it — even if this was difficult for some of the children to talk about in the presence of an adult. The younger girls occasionally talked about 'kissing' and sex in the soap operas, amid considerable amounts of embarrassed laughter, but the boys would rarely talk about this kind of material at all. While some of the youngest children claimed that their parents had banned 'rude' or 'sexy' programmes, there was occasionally some uncertainty about precisely what this meant.

This question of what is 'suitable' becomes more complicated in larger families. Anne (aged 9) was the middle of three children, and came from a white middle-class family where parental regulation was much more of a constraint than for many of the working-class children. Her parents' rationale for regulation was partly concerned with cultural value, and partly with morality. Negotiating with this, and with the different tastes of other members of the family, proved a difficult balancing act:

Anne: Well in my family we haven't got Sky Television because my parents don't approve of it. They say 'you'll only be watching more TV — you watch enough as it is. You shouldn't be watching those soap operas.' // And // when / they don't like *Neighbours* and *Home and Away* but we've — we've convinced my brother that he understands Neighbours. He doesn't by=

Interviewer: =[laughs] How have you convinced him he understands it then?

Anne: Hm, we've said 'Look, you know what's going on here, don't you? Henry's making plaster gnomes' and he says 'Yes', and so we say 'Well, [laughs] why don't you watch *Neighbours* with us?' and so we get our way. [laughs]. But if we can't do that and mum doesn't want it, like the news then we can't watch it and (. . .) it's tough luck! Cause if it's on a Saturday, my dad'll be watching football results upstairs, which means we've got to all agree on what's on downstairs but since my brother's younger, he would, he would get his way. I mean if it was — my brother was away for some reason then my sister's older so she would get the — her way. But it never seems to come to me that I would get my way, because mum doesn't like what I watch. (. . .) she's very against Australian soap operas.

Int:	Why is she against them then?
Anne:	She says the — she says they're too grown up for us and so we shouldn't be watching them and she says that we are too young to understand what happens (. . .) and that she just doesn't approve of them. Like when Gary fell off the cliff she said (mimics mother's 'nagging' voice:) 'This is not suitable for young minds'. (. . .) My parents say my — my imagination is deteriorating.
Int:	Is that what they say?
Anne:	Yeah. 'You shouldn't watch these, it'll make your imagination deteriorate'. 'But mum it will make my imagination grow!' 'No it won't, it'll make it deteriorate dear'.
Int:	So — have they got quite strong views about what you're watching? Are there programmes you're not supposed to watch?
Anne:	Mm. But we watch them all the same.

Anne directly parodies and contradicts her mother's arguments, and claims to be able to evade regulation. However, getting to watch what she wants also depends on gaining the consent of others — which accounts for her attempts to delude her younger brother in relation to *Neighbours*. Here again, the central focus of debate is the extent to which particular programmes are 'too grown up', both in terms of morality and in terms of whether children are seen to be able to 'understand' them — although her mother's argument about Sky TV would suggest that class-based assumptions about cultural value are at stake here, too.

In this family, the parents monitored the first episodes of new series — particularly the popular Australian soap operas, which appeared to have distinct 'bad object' status — in order to check that they were 'suitable'. Anne also reported that she was occasionally recruited to monitor programmes on behalf of her younger brother and sister, for similar reasons. Nevertheless, as these extracts show, Anne displayed considerable independence from her parents' arguments, presenting herself as able to make her own autonomous judgments. Significantly, her parents' view of her as more 'sensible' than her siblings seemed to be based on the assumption that she was somehow less vulnerable to the 'effects' of television, and less likely to repeat the 'swear words' she heard. Yet like many of the children here, Anne sees herself as caught, too young to take control, but too old to get preferential treatment. While she claims that her younger brother has precedence when it comes to choosing programmes, she is also recruited by her parents to monitor his viewing. In this case, what is seen as 'suitable' is subject to a process of negotiation, in which a certain amount of power has been 'delegated' to the children. Particularly in the case of larger families such as this, 'child' and 'adult' have clearly become relative, rather than exclusive, terms.

As these accounts suggest, therefore, definitions of 'child' and 'adult' are often flexible and subject to considerable negotiation. They are notions which are often used as bargaining counters or rhetorical devices in the ongoing struggle for control. Thus, parents can use the notion of 'being adult' as a means to gain children's compliance: saying 'grow up!' or 'be a big boy!' implies that if you obey my wishes now, other privileges may be granted to you. Yet these weapons are undoubtedly double-edged: while parents may exclude their children from certain experiences on the grounds that they are 'too young', children may also use the same rationale to get out of responsibilities they wish to avoid. What it means to be a child, or a child of a certain age, is not a given fact. On the contrary, it is socially and culturally relative, and can be defined and redefined in the constant process of negotiation between parents and children.

Age and Power in the Peer Group

These processes of negotiation are also apparent in discussions among children themselves. Here again, discourse needs to be read, not as a transparent reflection of what individuals really think or believe, but as a form of social action that is designed to achieve specific social purposes. In talking about television, children are claiming particular subject positions, and thereby defining and constructing their social relationships. Differences of age, class and gender serve here as significant markers of social power, albeit ones whose meaning is often fluid and unstable.

In this case, for example, the definition of which programmes are seen as 'adult' or 'childish' is crucial — and for this reason, is often contested. Putting down other people's preferences as 'childish' implicitly represents a claim to be more 'adult' oneself. Professing a preference for 'adult' texts — preferably those, such as horror, which are legally proscribed for children — can serve a similar function. Nevertheless, both strategies are open to challenge from others; and a variety of alternative options are possible.

In this research, these strategies took different forms in different age groups, and according to gender. For example, it seemed to be safe for older children, particularly girls, to express a preference for more anarchic cartoons like *Fantastic Max*, and even a kind of nostalgia for cartoons aimed at a pre-school audience. By contrast, while boys were much more likely to express a preference for action-adventure cartoons than girls, the girls often claimed that this was further evidence of their 'immaturity' (this accusation was routinely levelled by girls against boys, but never the other way round). Yet there was often some ambivalence here. While cartoons were often condemned for their predictable narratives, there were also some extended retellings, even among the 9-year-olds.

Furthermore, there was a considerable amount of negotiation in a number of groups about which programmes were to be defined as 'childish', and which were not. One group of middle-class 7-year-olds, for example, spent a great deal of time discussing the puppet show *Sooty* — a programme which appeared to enjoy a strange cult status in their school as a whole. Attempts to launch alternative topics, such as the Australian soaps, repeatedly failed, as they returned time and again to 'magic moments' from the programme — moments which frequently seemed to involve the adult puppeteer being duped or humiliated by the anarchic child puppets, often through the agency of Sooty's magic wand. Their account of the programme was also highly 'situated' in the viewing context, in that they seemed to have to struggle to watch it against the very different preferences of adults and older siblings. At the same time, the 'childish' nature of the programme did become problematic, as the following extract illustrates. Here, Michelle has been talking about how she has to look after her younger sister, and often gets into fights about what they are going to watch.

Michelle:	My sister watches baby ones. (laughs)
Int:	She watches?
Michelle:	She watches baby ones. (laughs)
Int:	What — what — what do you call baby ones?
Michelle:	Oh! Phew! Sooty, things like that.
Christina:	Yeah, I used to like them // I used to like *Rainbow*. (laughter) I agree with Richard, because if you're bored and there's something like *Playbus* on you er can — you can just sit down and watch it. (. . .)
Int:	Charlotte?
Charlotte:	I've got the video tape of Sooty as well.
Michelle:	(laughs)
Int:	Did you get that for a present or?
Charlotte:	Yeah.
Int:	You bought it — [it was bought for you?
Charlotte:	[um my broth — my brother bought it for me.
Int:	'Cause he knew you were a fan.
Charlotte:	Yes.
Int:	Do you think Sooty's a baby programme / too? // or
Charlotte:	[// Sort of.
Boy:	(Urgh!
Int:	Sort of / you're not sure about that.
Charlotte:	I'm only half watching it because it's boring me sometimes.

Despite the considerable pleasure all the children take in describing the programme, Michelle clearly defines it as 'babyish'. This places Charlotte in particular in a rather difficult position: while the others have been quick to disavow their preference, she seems more reluctant to do so, hence her hesitation. Charlotte is in fact the youngest child in a family with four older brothers, and this struggle over what is 'childish' is probably a depressingly familiar one for her. The interviewer's return to the topic towards the end of this extract effectively shut her up completely — although it did not seem to prevent the others returning compulsively to yet more retellings of the antics of Sooty.

On the other hand, there were instances where individuals claimed distinctly 'adult' tastes in an attempt to gain status with others in the group, or to outrage the interviewer. Violent videos seemed to serve this function in a number of groups, as the following extract, featuring a group of 9-year-olds, illustrates. Here, the boys seem intent on disrupting the dynamic established at the start of the interview, in which the female interviewer had engaged the girls in an extended discussion of the soaps. Malcolm begins by whispering 'Bruce Lee', eventually saying he likes it 'because there's loads of blood in it' — a debatable observation, perhaps. Steven responds by offering *The Karate Kid*, prompting Malcolm to raise the stakes with *Robocop*.

Malcolm:	*Robocop* [laughs]
Int:	Have you, have you got *Robocop*? Have you watched *Robocop*?
Amarjit:	Oh! That's good.
John:	Loads of blood
Int:	Certainly bloodthirsty, my god!
Amarjit:	Yeah.
Malcolm:	There's this man with this acid and it's eating him up and he's going around [like that
John:	. (yeah and a car chucks him up
Malcolm:	Yeah, blood squirts everywhere. (. . .)
Malcolm:	*Nightmare on Elm Street.*
Int:	Oh, yes.
Amarjit:	That's good.
Int:	Everybody seems to have and?
	(Freddy (choking sounds)
Int:	(&) seen that. You haven't seen that Donna?

(Various confirmations and exclamations.)

John:	It's not scary.
Malcolm:	It is.
John:	I've seen one at night time.
Malcolm:	Yes it is. You must be joking. How would you like it if a [man with claws
Amarjit:	(Freddy and he comes out (of this (. . . .)
Malcolm:	(scratches you (. . .) Yeah, he's got these great big claws coming out (&)
Amarjit:	(yeah, coming out.)
Malcolm:	(&) and scratching everyone.

Amarjit:	Yeah. They're like spears, instead of nails.
Int:	Sounds horrific. (choking sounds) I'm afraid I'm not very good at watching scary films.
Donna:	Oh, my sister's scared at all the scary films.
Int:	But you're not?
Donna:	Nah.
Malcolm:	They're lovely.

These children are talking about material they are legally forbidden to watch, and they know this. Their account offers nothing in the way of narrative context, but goes straight to the 'good bits', the parts that have the greatest power to offend. The interviewer's response here more than confirms Malcolm's success in outraging her — although his subversive intention is perhaps signalled by the laugh with which he introduces *Robocop*.

This parading of violence may possess a gendered dynamic — as I have noted, it effectively disrupts the girls' discussion of the soaps — although it is something to which the girls contribute with enthusiasm. In fact, Malcolm's position is rather ambiguous in this respect: interestingly, he later confesses to watching *Blind Date* specifically 'to see everyone kiss'. Note that it is he who is keen to argue that *Nightmare on Elm Street* is scary — perhaps partly because to argue otherwise would be to undermine its subversive potential — while the others (including the girls) assert that they can handle it, a much more common response.

This focus on 'adult' material occurred in a number of other younger groups. In fact, many children were keen to retell incidents from 'adult' films which they had not seen, either on the basis of hearsay or occasionally the trailers. (This may be the case, for example, with the account of *Nightmare on Elm Street* above.) On the other hand, the News, which was clearly defined as 'adult', was routinely reviled by the large majority: while some children did admit to watching it, there was very little status attached to this. Again, their account of the News was often situated in terms of the viewing context: as one 9-year-old girl said, 'all we gotta do is go in our room and play till the News is finished, and it lasts for half an hour!'

As I have noted, perceptions of what was 'adult' often appeared to be determined by parental regulation — although in general this would appear to be more of a middle-class concern. For example, the 11-year-olds in one group described the ways in which their parents prevented them from watching horror or 'violent' films. Perhaps, partly for this reason, there was a considerable degree of status attached to this material — leading one girl to resort to retelling a horror film she had half-watched at a friend's house.

While the working-class children were less likely to describe this kind of regulation, they were occasionally more frank about their perceptions of 'adult' material. In the following extract, featuring a mixed group of 11-year-olds in an inner-city school, it is Julia, the middle-class girl, who 'owns up' to a humiliating experience of regulation:

Obinna: Um, I hear sometimes that people say that television changes the way that children act, I don't think that's true//

Int: //You don't//

Obinna: //Hasn't changed the way I act or anything

Julia: My mum, my mum wouldn't let me, 'cause it was my friend's birthday and Bonnie's brother, Daniel (oh yeah), she wouldn't let me watch a film, *Eraserhead*, 'cause she said she didn't want me

Tracy: (Yeah, it's scary

Obinna: (There was this / (&)

Julia: 'Cause he's a lot older

Obinna: (&) little baby and he watched the Last Dragon a lot, it does affect little children quite a lot but if you're a bit older you should be allowed to watch it, when you're

Int: Do you think you should be able to watch anything?

Obinna: Yeah, it wouldn't change the way you act at my age, it wouldn't change (yeah) but um, this little baby watching last *Dragon's Nest*, *Kung Fu* film there's *Kung Fu* in it and he, he watches it a lot and he learns the moves, and then when some, someone tells him off, he goes, 'YOU WANNA FIGHT ME? WAH, WAH,' and starts fighting them and starts doing um things that they do on the programme. (. . .)

Dawood: It will affect little kids, that fighting (. .) and karate films and things, they learn (all the moves, that's dirty

Obinna: (Yeah, I can remember when I used to play the *A Team*, [laughs, others join in) I used to play the *A Team* and pretend that we'd got guns and go (makes the sound of machine gunfire) (. . .)

Simon: I hate it when you got, when there's a film like some 18-year-olds aren't really scary, just a bit hard to understand and they say 'OH YOU CAN'T watch that' just because it says eighteen. Sometimes they're not scary DAMN!

Tracy: And like even the fifteen ones are not scary

Simon: And they just put, they just say NO, like that. ERRR!

Obinna: I like horrors, sometimes, (talking over Tracy and Dawood) I like horrors (and I like music (laughs)

Simon: [I don't, they scare me (. . .)

Obinna: Yeah, there's sometimes if you think that you're going to get nightmares, I wouldn't watch them but um, er

Simon: No, I watch them (. .)

Obinna: (I don't usually dream, um, it might, I don't usually get, if I get a nightmare, I don't usually get a very, bad one,

	like it seems all that real, sometimes I do get ones, but, I'm sometimes the hero and I beat up the monster (laughs)
Int:	Oh well, that's alright then
Simon:	I hate, I, once when I was with my friends we watched *Werewolf of London*
Obinna:	*American Werewolf*?
Simon:	Yeah or whatever and um, I never been able to watch a horror film with werewolves or anything in it cause it scares, it doesn't scare me, but it stays with me for ages (and, and, cause it was really gruesome (&)
Obinna:	(yeah, that's true (yeah)
Simon:	(&) it was an 18-year-old. I didn't want to watch it, I was saying 'let's not watch it, let's not watch it', and my friend was saying 'Come on, let's watch it, are you chicken or something?' and I was saying, 'No, no,' so I watch it, keeping my eyes closed when a gruesome bit comes up, and you see a werewolf slashing up people and everything, werrrrr!

This group displays a much greater ambivalence towards horror films than the previous one: while they admit (unusually, in the context of these interviews) that they are frightened, and that the films give them nightmares, they watch them nevertheless. Part of the explanation for this may lie in Simon's final comment: watching horror may be a test of strength, in which you have to train yourself not to display your fear. Again, this may be more common among boys, although this is by no means the only example in this research of boys admitting to being frightened. There is certainly a good deal of hesitation and contradiction in the boys' accounts: Obinna gets a nightmare, but he doesn't usually, Simon is scared, but he isn't scared, and so on. But for whatever reason, they do not feel compelled to offer a display of bravado here.

These children are certainly familiar with popular discourses about the 'effects' of television, yet they attempt to distance themselves from them in various ways. Indeed, these discourses may well be 'cued' by the interview context: Obinna's spontaneous introduction of the topic at the start of this extract suggests an implicit recognition of the agenda which he suspects may be framing the research — although he explicitly seeks to contest this. As repeatedly happens in discussions of television effects, the process is displaced onto 'other people': and just as adults typically displace effects onto children, children are often keen to displace them onto those younger than themselves (cf. Buckingham, 1987; Cullingford, 1984). This is apparent here, for example, in the way in which Obinna defines the karate fanatic as a 'little baby', and the irony with which he describes his own childhood games. By implication, Obinna defines himself as much more 'adult' than this, and as possessing the critical maturity these others are seen to lack. While these children are very much aware of censorship 'ratings', they also dispute the system on which these are decided. Simon in particular stands out against what he perceives as an arbitrary form of adult authority. Nevertheless, their own 'confessions' later in the extract partly contradict this argument: while horror films may not have influenced their behaviour, they certainly appear to have had unpleasant 'effects'. In these respects, then, the children in this group are attempting to negotiate an intermediate position between 'childhood' and 'adulthood'.

Implications and Conclusions

As these children acknowledge, public debates about the 'effects' of television are often based on behaviourist notions of stimulus and response. Children are constructed here as passive consumers, and as helpless victims of ideological or behavioural influences. By contrast, I have implicitly assumed that children cannot be seen merely as 'dupes' of television, who are narcotized into mental inertia by the power of the box. As these extracts show, television is actively used by children in their attempts to make sense of their own social lives.

At the same time, I have sought to move beyond the limitations of these debates about the positive or negative 'effects' of television. Rather than taking what children say at face value, I have sought to illustrate some of the social functions that may be served by talk about television. In particular, I have suggested that such talk, both in the home and in the peer group, provides an arena in which relationships between adults and children are established and defined. In talking about their tastes and preferences, and in asserting their right to have access to them, children are actively negotiating with, and often resisting, the constructions of childhood that are made available to them.

This argument has wider methodological — and indeed political — implications for research into 'children's culture'. Discussing television with children in the context of the school (as was the case here) crosses several boundaries — not merely between education and recreation, but also, crucially, between adults and children. In this case, the children were told that we were interested in 'finding out what they thought' about television — and significantly, few of them challenged our right to do this, or sought to probe our motivations further. Nevertheless, it is hard to identify quite what children think we are 'up to' in asking questions about pleasures which they may be keen to preserve in their own, separate domain. Displaying our own knowledge of the programmes they discuss — which might seem at first sight to be a useful means of establishing complicity with them — is, in this respect, fraught with ambiguity.

This is perhaps true of researching any aspect of 'children's culture', although it is particularly acute in an area such as television, where each encounter is so heavily framed by the kinds of debates identified above. Children know that most teachers disapprove of them watching 'too much' television — and unless proven otherwise, most researchers are likely to be grouped in this category. As I have suggested, many children are familiar with at least some of the arguments about the harmful 'effects' television is supposed to exert upon them. In seeking to refute these arguments, they may have a range of options, some of which are exemplified in the extracts I have quoted here. They can directly reject such views, as Anne and Simon do, albeit in different ways; or they can attempt to displace the 'effects' on to younger children, as in Obinna's case. Alternatively, and in many respects most beguilingly, they can attempt to use the discussion as an opportunity to display their critical acumen — their ability to 'see through' the false claims of advertising, for example, or the illusions of television realism. Like a great deal of popular discourse about television, all three strategies clearly depend upon distinguishing the speaker from 'other people', who are typically absent and unable to speak on their own behalf.

Yet even this is to oversimplify the complex dynamic between the re-searcher and the child 'subject'. Clearly, children can choose to play what they perceive to be the researcher's game: they can try to tell us what they think we want to hear. But they can equally well choose to subvert it — an option which in this context is perhaps only marginally more risky. Talk about horror or other 'forbidden' texts of the kind identified in my third extract above is only one among many potential strategies here. Such talk may outrage the interviewer, but it clearly holds out the promise of approval from peers — and of course in itself entails a powerful claim for 'adult' status.

Children in industrialized societies — and indeed in many developing countries — spend more time watching television than they do on any other pursuit, apart from sleeping. For this reason alone, research into children's uses of television should form a significant element in studies of their social understandings and relationships. Yet what and how we can learn about 'children's culture' crucially depends upon the power relationships that ob-tain between ourselves as adult researchers and the children whom we study — relationships whose inequalities cannot simply be abolished or wished away. As I hope to have shown, the study of children's talk about television can offer some productive insights into the complexities and contradictions of those relationships.

Notes

1 There is a significant parallel here with the case of Michael Ryan, who in 1987 shot sixteen people in the small town of Hungerford in Southern England. See Webster (1989).
2 Postman was co-author of that seminal post-69 educational text, *Teaching as a Subversive Activity* (Postman and Weingartner, 1971).

3　This broad assertion would probably be accepted by most cognitive psychologists (for example, Noble, 1975; Bryant and Anderson, 1983; Dorr, 1986), social psychologists (for example, Durkin, 1985; Gunter and MacAleer, 1990), 'uses and gratifications' researchers (for example, Brown, 1976), as well as others working in cultural studies (for example, Hodge and Tripp, 1986).

4　This research was part of a project on 'The Development of Television Literacy in Middle Childhood and Adolescence', funded by the Economic and Social Research Council, UK (grant no: R000231959). Thanks to fellow members of the research team, Valerie Hey and Gemma Moss, with whom the fieldwork, transcription and initial analysis of the data were shared: responsibility for the arguments presented here remains my own! A fuller account of this research is contained in Buckingham (1993a). For further and related work in this field, see Buckingham (1993b).

5　The transcription conventions used here are a simplified version of those used by Potter and Wetherell (1987). Vertical slash (/) denotes a pause; dots in brackets denotes material has been omitted; single brackets denote interruptions; ampersand (&) denotes speaker continuing over an interruption.

6 Creating the Capable Body: Discourses about Ability and Effort in Primary and Secondary School Studies

Lise Bird

> Clever, intelligent people do not need to try very hard to do well at things. People who aren't so bright really have to put in a lot of effort to achieve the same results. Ability is something you are born with, but you can make up for a lack of ability if you really try. (Anon., *Facts of Life*)

The ideas above are a rather bold expression of a constellation of ideas about ability and effort that I hear every day. Glimpses of these ideas appear in routine conversations amongst educators and students around the world. The basic tenet of such a discourse[1] appears to be that an individual's ability and effort are inversely related in producing personal achievements, within certain limits. There may be a number of contradictory discourses about ability, effort and intelligence. These ideas have interesting contradictions with concepts such as development and human potential. In this chapter I consider my encounters with these contradictions in the sphere of the primary school and in the world of a secondary school.

There is now a huge literature on the concept of 'ability' if we include the thousands of research studies which have examined mental abilities and skills of all kinds. Sociologists and historians have for decades built a convincing critique of psychology's accounts of intelligence and its psychometric counterpart, the IQ, (Lewontin, Rose and Kamin, 1984; Rose, 1990).[2] I pay homage to this important critique, which is well known in educational circles. Much has been written about cultural biases in the creation of IQ tests and about the importance of recognizing talent in its diversity of expression. Despite the wide dissemination of these ideas, educators often refer to the 'abilities' of students as though making factual observations. Even educational critics seem to find terms such as 'able' or 'not very bright' indispensable in talking about students, friends or the children of their acquaintances. Such phrases appear to have some consensual meaning. A Western discourse about personal capacity may be so important in our world-views that it is almost impervious to critique. It is the intractable presence of certain words in everyday speech which gives me courage to step onto ground already well trodden by herds of determined scholars. Language about ability is ostensibly transparent, purporting to represent an unproblematic truth about inherent capacities of persons. It is the assumed certainties and silences about this topic that have fascinated me during my fieldwork in primary and secondary schools in Aotearoa/New Zealand.

While the study of ability is a well-established field, the supposed links between intelligence and effort have received less attention. When Michael Young first coined the word 'meritocracy' in the 1950s, he did so by considering the linking of intelligence and effort. As the blurb on the back of the Penguin edition put it, it would appear that the formula I.Q. + effort = MERIT may well constitute the basic belief of the ruling class of the next century (Young, 1968).

Young was marking a change in Western societies, notably Britain, from an oligarchy of hereditary privilege to a supposedly more democratic society. Education was seen as a key factor in the move to a meritocracy. In the above equation attributed to Young, ability and effort are treated as additive factors in performance. This seems too simple. It is the perceived balance between ability and effort that is usually crucial in judging the merit of a person's accomplishment. Ability and effort are not equal partners in this balance. A success attributed to ability usually counts for more kudos than one attributed to effort. There are exceptions to this: in considering the achievements of a lifetime, merit may be more likely to be conferred if a person's success is deemed to have been due to a life of effort rather than to 'natural ability' (Brown and Weiner, 1984).

Several lines of research have proposed that there is a change from childhood to adolescence in people's beliefs about ability. This research, some of which is reviewed briefly below, has not considered the place of signifiers such as ability and effort in Western discourses about individual achievement. A discourse about ability and effort as a balance has a number of contradictions with discourses about child development as a process of unfolding potential. 'Development' implies that each child is improving, enhancing personal capability along a path of increasing differentiation and complexity over age. Questions about plasticity in ontogeny have inconsistencies with the view that each organism has a unique fixed capacity which limits its ultimate form. There are longstanding historical debates about these views (Gould, 1977).

Following Foucault, I am interested in an analysis of discourses which offer a taxonomy of subject-positions which includes the 'bright', 'dull' and 'hard working'. Foucault's (1977) analysis pointed to historical changes in the expression of power and knowledge in bodies, with changes from external domination over movements of bodies through direct force of sovereign rule to processes of regulation and control as though within bodies themselves. The rise of disciplines such as penal systems and education was linked with 'an increase of the mastery of each individual over his own body' (Foucault, 1977, p. 137). Foucault explicitly mentioned ranking procedures, such as those within schools, as a means of ordering personal capacities to control and hence to maximize the efficiency of bodies for use in a society. A Foucauldian analysis of discourses about ability and effort would consider ways that the effortful body is created through timetabling and assessment practices of discipline and control. While I find Foucault's ideas insightful, I am not prepared to assume that there is a basic bodily capacity to be augmented or controlled through discursive operations, since I consider the idea of bodily capacity to be itself enmeshed within certain of these discourses.[3]

My analysis has also been shaped by the work of Valerie Walkerdine (e.g., 1988). More than anyone else, Walkerdine has formulated a comprehensive critique of the way our ideas about mastery, rationality and effortful diligence are discursively produced. She has also considered the construction of the child as a subject within discourses of the 'child-centred' movement, linking practices within a pedagogy/childrearing couple. My analysis is also informed by another feminist post-structural theorist who has studied discursive formations, Bronwyn Davies (e.g., 1989). Davies has been innovative in research which takes multiple readings of classroom conversations which are analysed as complex texts in which children and teachers take a variety of positions in gendered discourses.

While cognizant of previous studies of classroom and playground interactions, in this chapter I take a somewhat different tack. First I look at a controversy in U.S. research on children's views of the ability/effort relationship. My reading of the controversy is then implicitly contrasted with an analysis of excerpts from my fieldwork with primary and secondary school students in Aotearoa/New Zealand. Rather than assuming that there is a central discourse that is learned by students through their years of schooling, I consider ways that issues surrounding notions of ability and hard work may be differently articulated in primary and secondary schooling. My analysis is influenced by a new reading of Harkness and Super's (1983) concept of the environmental niche as a spatial and temporal location within culture in all its expressions, including language and physical environment. I am not positing that an individual child is a biological organism prior to culture (Burkitt, 1991; Riley, 1983), or an organism located within an external niche. The concept of niche provides a vessel for navigating between possible discourses about ability and effort in a primary school class and a different expression of such discourses in a secondary school class. I am interested in the ways that certain discourses seem to overdetermine possibilities for the performance of talent at particular ages in life.

Empirical Studies of Children's Beliefs about the Ability/Effort Balance

Psychological research on children's conceptions of ability and effort centres on the child whose cognitive advances allow a greater understanding of a physical and social world. From the late 1970s a series of psychology experiments in the U.S. pointed out that beliefs about ability and effort change as children get older. In a series of studies, John Nicholls (see 1989 for a summary; cf. Kun, 1977) proposed that the concepts of effort and ability become differentiated as the child develops. In such studies, the child's conceptions of ability and effort are usually assessed using hypothetical examples. For example, a story may be told of two children in the same classroom who are working separately on the same task. The task is usually one with a clearly quantifiable outcome (for example, completing a set of ten puzzles). The child interviewed is asked why the depicted children completed the same number of puzzles correctly when they differed in their efforts (for example, if one child 'worked hard' and the other did not), or why they differed in numbers of puzzles completed correctly if both children worked with the same intensity. Older students interviewed have said that 'smart' people do not have to try as hard, or that people can compensate for a lack of ability by putting in extra effort. Younger children interviewed have said that people who try hardest are also the most able, and that trying hard can make you clever. From these findings researchers have concluded that young children make little distinction between effort and ability, seeing them as interchangeable factors in performance, while older children see them in an inverse, compensatory relationship. Piagetian theory forms a crucial backdrop for the consideration of age-changes in conceptual understanding in these psychological studies. Older children are purported to be better than younger children in understanding reciprocal functions, in separating appearances from underlying principles and in grasping other formal concepts such as the concept of a statistical distribution.

A different explanation has been put forward from a sociological perspective on ability formation counter to the dominant views in developmental psychology. Rosenholtz and Simpson (1984) argued that the change in children's professed views of ability could be a reflection of their changing experiences in the education system, especially age-changes in assessment practices. They proposed that the 'multidimensional' nature of early schooling changes to a more restricted 'unidimensional' assessment process in later schooling. The focus of early schooling on good behaviour and moral conduct would also encourage the child to consider that a 'good' performance is both effortful and capable. According to their argument, feedback converges in later school years as academic subjects become more clearly delineated and performance on exams or standardized tests is scaled so that all individuals can be ranked in a linear fashion. Not only is a single standard of competent performance the standard in many secondary classes, there may also be public knowledge of each person's marks, giving each student a typical rank in the class distribution. Such rankings may then become part of a student's 'self concept'. Rosenholtz and Simpson focussed on the power of the school to create hierarchies of ability in a finesse which hides an overdetermined status distribution for ability in the classroom.

Rosenholtz and Simpson (1984) took a radical reproductionist view of ability formation in focussing (not always consistently) on the way children's beliefs in their own abilities may be produced through school practices. This contrasts with the proposal by British theorist Burkitt (1991) that capitalist societies actually produce selves differing in abilities. He proposed that '(c)apacities are only developed in people if they are needed for the accumulation of capital, not for the benefit of the development of human potential' (p. 195). This assertion implies that some people have deficient capabilities. I prefer to leave open the question of the expressive forms of capacities in material terms. Any analysis of concepts such as ability and motivation is difficult to carry out without some reflexivity on the part of researchers, given that these issues are presumably loaded concerns for academics who succeeded in getting through their own systems of education.

Changes across age in ideas about effort and ability in the U.S. research reviewed above have tended to assume a binary split between individual and society in locating causal factors for developmental change. I will attempt to step away from this dichotomizing gaze as I move to rereadings of my fieldnotes from work in two schools. A brief description of the scope and settings for the two studies may be helpful.

School Life in Two Settings

For the primary school study I was an observer who attended two different classes, for four hours (morning classes and lunchtime) one day each week over a term (Bird, 1992). I also spent several whole-day sessions with the classes before this, in the middle term, and during the next year. Moana School was small and classes covered the first six years of schooling. The fieldwork described below is based on my time in a class of 7–8-year-olds. I was a quasi-participant in the classes, attempting to minimize my authority as an adult and to interact more with children than the teacher. I took fieldnotes in the classroom when the children were also working with pencil and paper, and on other occasions in more private spaces around the school grounds. Some interviews with children were audio-taped.

In the secondary school research, Deborah Willis and I have been studying modularized science lessons which are assessed internally within schools while being monitored with scaling from a nationally-normed moderating test. I was one of three adult researchers[4] who acted as participant-observers in several fifth form science classes (further details in Willis and Bird, 1993). Researchers sat in on all the sessions of a particular module, attempted to do the work of the modules as students while participating in lab-work in class, took fieldnotes during class when this seemed appropriate, audio-taped the class session, interviewed students and teachers in a semi-structured format, and gathered quantitative information on the assessment practices of each module.

In looking for examples of the discursive practices surrounding issues of ability and effort in each school setting, I have been struck, each time I read my fieldnotes, by the incommensurable contrast of my experiences in these two settings. It is as though the differences are beyond age, particular enactments of a curriculum, or pedagogical processes. The reasons for some of the differences seem obvious. Though most of the classes I observed were similar in size (about twenty students, unusually small for New Zealand schools), the school organizations were quite different. The primary school had a small number of teachers who knew each other well and worked as a cohesive team. They also had regular interactions with parents each day. Strong links were made between different parts of the curriculum. In contrast, the secondary school was a large campus with over fifty teachers. The secondary school emphasized divisions in curriculum content for different subjects which had differing statuses as important teaching areas. There were some similarities between the schools. Both had girl and boy students drawn from communities that were mixed 'working' and 'middle' class, with proportions of Maori and Pacific immigrant students somewhat greater than in the general population.

In looking through extensive fieldnotes from both projects, I tend to lose my way in the developmental narrative of the emergence of the secondary student from origins in a younger self. My samples of the older and younger students are not matched, which makes the task of talking about change over age particularly difficult. My description below is not so much a summary record of fieldwork as a reflection upon two kinds of field experiences.

A High School Story: Enhancing Natural Ability with a Bit of Effort

I will first tell a story about ability and effort as some kind of compensation balance from a reading of my fieldnotes from the science project. This seems the most obvious story to me, the one that seems to need little effort in the telling. In my conversations with several teachers during the fifth form science project, I thought there was a belief at the school that the nationally normed moderating test had some final authority as an arbiter of students' 'natural intelligence'. In the following excerpt[5] from an interview between one of our research team and a male science teacher, Bill, there was a clear link between examination performance and 'intelligence'.

> *Bill:* I think this sort of assessment is really tough on people like Peter in particular. (. . .) Peter is, will do well in tests and will not do well in things that require some effort and input.
>
> *AS:* Mm mm.
>
> *Bill:* So I, I think modular science discriminates against people like Peter.

AS: Yes yes.

Bill: So at some time in his life he's going to, at some level of education he's going to come up against the fact that, he can't rely on his own intelligence. So perhaps learning that now may be a good thing for him.

AS: Yes, yeah right.

Bill: But it's tough on him, and *people like him.*

Bill described a male student as having 'intelligence' which helps him to do well. He did not think that Peter did as well with 'things that require some effort and input'. Bill expressed a clear dichotomy between intelligence and effort. He also mentioned in several conversations with researchers that students have to increase their effort when they reach university studies. It is as though he believed 'natural intelligence' could be enough to get people like Peter through secondary school exams, but that an augmenting effect of effort on ability would be needed for more advanced study. Certainly the compensating effect of effort on ability is evident in these comments.

There was a tone of censure in these and other of Bill's comments about Peter's lack of effort, as well as some admiration for his presumed natural talent. Some interesting psychological research has suggested that students would like to see themselves as having ability, while believing that their teachers would prefer students who put effort into their studies (cf. Nicholls, Patashnick and Mettetal, 1986). The importance of effortful study has complex links with practices of adult control over children in schools. In secondary classes, young people who are nearing their maximum height and adult strength must be kept within the confining structures of compulsory schooling. This means that students must adhere to institutional codes for observable characteristics such as clothing and the physical placings of bodies at any particular time during the set hours of the school day. Though teachers may reward students perceived to have ability, schooling practices are focussed on maximizing effort from students as an important means of classroom control. For teachers, it may be rewarding to have 'able' students, but more important to have students who do their schoolwork without disrupting the classroom.

Bill's comments also alluded to stable properties of a certain group of people, presumably 'intelligent' people. Some of Bill's ideas about intelligence appeared to be mirrored in the remarks of the student in his class, Peter, to whom he had referred.

AS: And do you study a lot?

Peter: Not that much.

AS: Right.

Peter: I find that I can, I can do tests quite easily without studying.

AS: Mm.

Peter: But if I study I get like 75 per cent or something or over but if I don't it's sort of like about 60 per cent.

> *AS:* Right. Right.
> *Peter:* Which is, which is fair enough.

Peter's description is behavioural, yet clearly he seems to think that most of his performance (60 per cent) is already set. He does not attribute his performance to factors such as his skills in sussing out tests, his concentration or technique. He seems to generalize his experiences past and future to tests in general, not distinguishing between tests differing in content or format. One way to believe in such stability of performance is to rely on a stable feature of the self which will ensure good test results: intelligence. I make an inference about Peter's beliefs about himself, though intelligence is an area of silence here. In an interview such as this one, the mention of intelligence would perhaps have been in bad taste, an uncool sign of bragging. His final comment, 'fair enough', seemed to concede that he cannot expect to do extremely well without studying, as such behaviour is not that of the good student. This possibly showed his deference to school discourses about the importance of hard work.

Peter went on to say that another boy in his class, Brian, would 'get high marks'. When the interviewer questioned Peter about this, he did not refer to ability as a characteristic of Brian. Instead, he focussed on Brian's rather unsociable tendencies to do a lot of homework.

> *Peter:* Um well basically he goes home every day and does two hours homework. And that, I don't know, he doesn't have much of a social life but he just goes home and does homework.

Here Peter made a negative comment about a boy who gets high marks because he works hard. Peter's comment that Brian 'doesn't have much of a social life' positions Brian as a 'swat' or a 'nerd' rather than a socially popular person in their peer group. Brian was thus created by Peter's comments as an other to Peter himself, which allowed Peter to be positioned as the student who can have more fun because he does not really need to study.

During the science fieldwork, we seldom had conversations with teachers about 'natural intelligence' in girls. One girl who did well in science, Hannah, was referred to as a 'high achiever' by two teachers. In our first days at the school one of her teachers, Angela, commented to me on the discrepancy between Hannah's score on the national moderating test and her much higher marks for in-class work in science. Angela also expressed concern that Hannah might be under pressure from her family which 'pushes' her to do well. I questioned Angela specifically about whether perhaps Hannah just had an unusual interest and excitement about science. Angela disagreed and suggested that Hannah's tendency to do extra work on every project at school was rather excessive, and that such work did not necessarily indicate that Hannah had a deep understanding. Angela's comments led me to hypothesize that Hannah was being stereotyped as a girl who tries hard but is not able (cf. Walkerdine, 1988). When, several days later, I saw Hannah's first assignment for this module I was surprised by its length and detail. Much of the prose was irrelevant to the task of learning to make a biological drawing and appeared to have been taken uncritically from encyclopedias. I started to question my assumption that Angela was simply not appreciating Hannah's work because she was a girl. I wondered if Hannah had really enjoyed or learned much from the assignment, and whether she had other interests common in 15-year-old girls.

Despite these qualms, I found that Hannah, more than any other student I interviewed for that module, showed a keen, almost zealous interest in science.

> *Hannah:* Yeah, I um found it kind of interesting to find out you know how they (i.e., plants) interact with people and um and how they're just so vital for our survival on the planet. I thought it was quite interesting. I enjoyed all the experiments we did and to prove photosynthesis occurring.
>
> *LB:* Is science something that you find interesting, in, just, everyday life?
>
> *Hannah:* Yes. (. . .) It all depends if you're interested in, into it, you know make a career that you do and love. That's what I do so, so I enjoyed it (laughs).

When I saw Hannah at lunchtimes with her friends or in class, she did not appear to me to be stressed or unsociable. Like her teacher Angela, I was convinced that something was not right with Hannah; I determinedly looked for stress-marks in her appearance and behaviour. Both teachers and students expressed concerns about Hannah and Brian, about the balance between their academic study and social life. A healthy teenager is presumably someone who studies, but not too hard, and who has an active social network of friends. It is interesting that the male teacher, Bill, referred spontaneously to a boy who appeared to be doing well without studying, while the woman teacher, Angela, focussed on a girl who had done well, seemed to study a lot, and may not have had much social life. Walkerdine (for example, 1988) has considered discourses crossed by gender and class which would seem to be well represented in these excerpts. For girls, there are pressures about being a good student academically, looking attractive and being sociable, which can be seen as contradictory discursive possibilities for subject-positioning. This issue emerges again in my last example from the primary school study (below), though I do not have space here to do these issues justice. It is also interesting that in the excerpts above Peter was the only student who was, in ethnic terms, pakeha (an anglo/white person). He was the student to whom natural intelligence was attributed (by his male teacher) and implied in his own comments.

The teachers at Farflung school seemed to be well versed in a discourse about ability and effort as an inverse. I realise that I may be determined to read the comments above as exemplars of this discourse, for my own reasons, not reflected upon here. There are other discourses that could be considered here, but not the space in which to let them germinate. In this chapter I will have to leave the secondary school setting in order to move to a contrast with a primary school context without giving a full picture of issues at Farflung. As I move on to a consideration of these issues in a primary school, I am over-whelmed by the culture shock of changing from writing about events in a secondary to those of a primary school.

A Primary School Story: Fighting for a Good Name

The subtle, competitive statements of students vying for positions in their fifth-form classes appears to me highly 'civilized' compared to the movement, the shouting, the physical aggression of the 7- to 11-year-olds I came to know in the years preceding the high school study. Yet I find myself believing that there was some primitive 'potential', some honesty, energy and unaffected-ness 'lost' between the younger children and older students.[6] In my readings I will emphasize the flavour of contestation, often violent, in several events which seem to centre on ability issues. I will try to interrupt my own readings of these fieldnotes as 'early signs' of a later discourse about ability and effort, to open up spaces for some new readings about these concerns in the lives of some children in New Zealand.

According to my fieldnotes, the term ability was rarely mentioned by teachers at Moana School, and there were few examples of children's spon-taneous use of the word. The longest discussion about the issue took place when I was speaking with the teacher of the younger class, Anne, during a morning 'developmental' time.[7] In describing to me the reading groups in the class, she mentioned that a particular cluster of children (five girls and two boys) formed a cohesive reading group who were 'the most advanced readers', and that, because of their 'ability', they had 'the most advanced comprehen-sion so they can go to a deeper level'. Anne's comments were specific to the ability of reading. Within compulsory schooling, reading is a skill that every child is supposed to achieve. Anne's comments could be read as suggesting that these readers might continue to work with more challenging material as they grow older, thus remaining more advanced than other children in class.

Practices at this school did not seem to have an underlying assumption that children's school performance was limited by their intelligence as a fixed capacity. As is common in reading practices in schools of various countries, the class was structured into reading groups, each identified by the teacher as having a different level of skill and each given a distinctive name. Though the teacher explicitly avoided making hierarchical references to these groups, I found myself immediately ranking them in my fieldnotes. I now question the extent to which practices at Moana School were successful in leaving open judgments about individual student's intelligence or abilities. The attempt to downplay the linear ordering of reading groups along a level of skill and density of printed text could be read as a strategy for keeping silent about ability issues. Such silence might be part of larger social practices which keep dangerous information away from young children's tender ears (Kitzinger, 1990). Silence does not imply, however, that children in this primary school confronted a vacuum regarding discourses about ability.

Positions of Ability or Incompetence

Despite exposure to the hierarchising awareness of adults such as myself, the children seemed more concerned with a binary status, i.e., whether or not a child was seen to be 'a reader'. I never heard the teacher refer to a child with this label. The term 'reader' was the only way that academic competence was used to identify a category of person. Children who could read fluently already were noticeable in their performances in front of other children, as there were many occasions during which children would simply read aloud from their printed stories to others at their tables, as well as times when students would be asked by the teacher to read something aloud to a group of others. On one occasion during reading time in this class, 7-year-old Debbie went with her friend Carrie to the front of the room where three girls were seated on the floor in the mat area reading silently and occasionally chatting. Debbie, standing near the girls, said, 'Me and Carrie are both readers'. She and Carrie then stood together in front of the other girls and read from a book in unison, demonstrating their skills. In my notes I remarked that 'they were indeed good readers'. Clearly the students were using an identity category ('reader') that I found unremarkable at the time.

A violent incident related to the labelling of a 'reader' identity occurred one day before school began, in the play area just outside the classroom. The teacher had not yet come across from the assembly room. In the excerpt below a taunt referring to reading had explosive consequences. The events unfolded after a 7-year-old girl, Sylvia, had pushed a younger boy off a swing. The boy had been surrounded by several other boys who spoke comforting words to him as he cried in the middle of the playground. I could not hear all the words in the excerpt below, though shortly afterwards I made detailed notes on the positions of children and the emotional tone of the interactions.

Ben and another boy go up to Sylvia, who is now sitting on the swing. They start speaking to her in a 'taunting' way. Then Sylvia stands up, and Ben and Sylvia get into a mock fight, using arm gestures without making physical contact, and with angry facial expressions. Ben does a karate kick in the air in front of Sylvia. Sylvia then says to Ben, in a strong, clear voice, 'You can't even read.' Ben then stands still, his whole body 'stiffens'; he looks angry with his reddened face. He then turns away from Sylvia towards the classroom. I am standing just inside the door of the classroom looking at them. While looking at the ground, Ben says, 'She's being stupid. She's a liar'. Ben then turns to another boy behind him some distance away and calls out something to him. Immediately afterwards Sylvia runs inside the classroom, past me, crying. As she runs inside she calls out, 'I'll tell' and 'Ben hurt my feelings!' She pauses briefly right beside me, looks back and yells out, 'Stupid Ben!'.

The adjectives 'stupid' and 'dumb' were often used as negative descriptors by the children at Moana, and were used with greater frequency for some children than others. They acted powerfully in the excerpt above to stigmatize the child so described as an outcast because of a perceived lack. Ben upped the ante of insults with his remark (directed away from me, and hence unheard by me). The taunt of 'can't even read' suggests that reading was considered important, yet basic. To fail to show a skill in this area is for these children possibly a sign of a serious lack, an inferiority. It was to me and/or the other boys that Ben directed comments about Sylvia's intelligence and moral standards (by using the third person rather than addressing Sylvia directly). I was the adult observer, the audience for Ben's attempt to humiliate Sylvia in return for her insult.[8] Sylvia parried with the same insults directed back at Ben, but she then threatened to bring in the teacher's authority ('I'll tell!') which was more powerful than mine. The teacher, of course, would have known who 'the readers' in the class were. Given the silence surrounding such information at the school (seen to be unhelpful for children's self esteem) the teacher would probably not have voiced her views to the students.

The schoolyard tauntings of my tales here are not 'new' data. I would guess that most readers have witnessed (and experienced) such taunting in their own lives. What I would like to focus upon here is the violence with which such taunts, clearly connected with issues of ability, are used. In the altercation between Sylvia and Ben, Ben seemed to be aware of the humiliating impact of a public charge of stupidity, since he appeared to be strategic in directing a remark to Sylvia and other children which was inaudible to me, yet upsetting for Sylvia. Sylvia also appeared to be making a public statement by announcing in a loud voice that Ben 'can't even read', to the boys nearby as well as to me.

There are interesting connections between the status of the 'readers' at Moana School and the group of people that the secondary teacher, Bill, referred to as similar to one of his 'bright' students ('people like him'). What seems to me to connect such disparate events and casts of characters is a discourse about ability as some internal form of truth within bodies. There may be contradictory discourses about the fixity of such capacities in children. One set of ideas about childhood centres on talent as either precocious or 'late blooming', which implies that children differ in general intelligence or ability but that for various reasons (for example, that children are 'whimsical' and more difficult to test) these individual differences are not as clearly seen until children are older. Another set of ideas might posit that childhood is a more liminal time in which there is change in the real abilities of children, so that there can be some repositioning of children in terms of some ranking of their abilities. Children, families and teachers make predictions about children's potential or problems which may reflect both sets of discourses. How children then negotiate a subject-positioning regarding their abled body, at any moment, becomes a complex task indeed.

Putting Ability in Doubt? Inflating Achievement

There were a number of occasions on which I noticed that positive feedback from an adult could be followed by negative reactions within a group of children. In the following excerpt several of the children changed their response to one girl's work after a comment from the teacher.

10:20	Children are working on their stories. At a table with several girls and boys, Janet explains the plot of a Mac-Gyver episode while Sherry listens. Janet shows the people around her how much she has written in her book by flipping through the pages.
Janet:	Look how many pages I've done. I started there and went there.
Debbie to Carrie:	She's done a story. She's done a whole long thing.

The teacher, Anne, stands by Janet to look at her work.

Anne:	You don't have to double space your story, Janet.
Sherry to Janet:	This is the best thing I've ever done. This is the best thing I've ever done.
Debbie to Janet:	You haven't done much, Janet.

Janet raises her shirt to show that underneath it she is wearing a t-shirt with a koala printed on it.

At the time of this discussion I was at the side of the table, nearby. As Anne made her comment to Janet, I thought that she had been very subtle in pointing out that Janet was being a bit fussy with her double spacing. I assumed that Anne's concern might have been partly a resource problem. At this school it was sometimes difficult getting quantities of paper for students' work. Often recycled computer paper was used for art and some printing work. Most children were careful about their use of paper. I was surprised at Debbie's negative response to Janet after the teacher's comment. Debbie picked up the teacher's remark as a criticism of Janet, with which she concurred with a more extreme put-down. Debbie could have pointed out that Janet had wasted paper, but instead Debbie commented negatively about the amount of work that Janet had done, casting doubt on Janet's efforts as a good girl and a good student. The sin of wasting paper was perhaps compounded by the implication that Janet was deceitful in attempting to make her story appear longer than it was.

Sherry's comment to Janet was perhaps a more subtle and competitive slight, in pointing out Sherry's own achievement that day. This seemed quite possible given that Sherry's repetition of her comment was rather theatrical and directed at Janet rather than to the table at large. Janet's response, which appeared to me to be a 'so there!' response, was to lift her shirt to show that she had on an interesting t-shirt underneath. The koala bear on the t-shirt also brought in the class issue of travel to Australia. On another day, a different girl had lifted her shirt during morning news time to show the class a koala t-shirt her aunt had brought back for her from Australia. Janet's gesture of revelation, showing a valuable item of clothing that had been hidden before, was possibly a strategic and non-violent competitive move. For girls, it is possible to focus on one's accomplishments in the area of glamour, appearance and the sexualization of the body when one's mental ability is called into question. This may be one way for girls to recapture some position of power in the discourses about achievement when intellectual ability appears to be in doubt.

In describing girls as bringing to others' attention their feminine appearance or possessions, I position such girls as having agency to choose to present themselves as having one kind of capable body or another. In my earlier stories about Hannah and Brian of Farflung College I suggested that these students were positioned by others as though they were people of good academic ability but poorer social abilities. For girls, there are contradictions in discourses about beauty and ability as having some inverse compensation scheme of their own, as well as perhaps more recent discourses about the importance of 'having it all'.[9] My mention of gendered issues brings up the contradictory positionings of girls as student, rational thinker, feminine nurturer (cf. Walkerdine, 1988). The ways that these contradictions are negotiated at different ages needs much further conceptual elaboration.

Endnotes

It is difficult to make conclusions about discourses surrounding ability and effort in childhood. I am going to leave more threads dangling than any capable quilter should. My field experiences have helped me to form an analysis of some issues which I can outline only briefly here. In contrasting events in the primary and secondary school, I consider problems involved in avoiding terms usually found in developmental theorizing.

Physical Contestation

One major contrast between the primary school and secondary school students was in the use of physical force by younger children in their altercations about people positioned as capable or stupid. For some children at Moana School, there seemed to be a hierarchy of domination and power based on verbal assertion and, sometimes, physical force. The words and gestures of Sylvia, Ben and Janet were assertive in refusing self-definitions of stupidity or incompetence. Such refusals by children were also, on many occasions, violent. It does not seem that these children were being slotted into some national, class-based meritocracy without a fight. It should be noted that these primary students were not vocal or aggressive towards their teacher. She in turn never referred to students with words such as 'stupid'. The contestation of labels was done amongst peers. Secondary students who made verbal rebuttals of negative ascriptions from others were seldom as vocal or violent in class discussion as the primary children. My guess would be that the subtly directed insults vocalized with such amazingly accurate skills in voice-projection by the 7-year-olds were finely honed in the repertoires of the secondary students. There may be less need for physical contest when a cutting word could do the same job, and avoid the wrath of the teacher attempting to keep control in the classroom. It is also possible that there was less contestation about subject-positionings for the 'bright spark' and the 'slogger' that individuals in the secondary school had come to occupy as a result of their individual assessment histories. Perhaps by secondary school students have accepted their 'allotted' places in the school hierarchy, and turn their defiance to other issues such as the gaining of adult privileges.

The Place for 'Development'

Foucault's (for example, 1977) comments about disciplinary self-control by modern citizens seem harder to believe when I am with children in a primary school, where brute force still seems the most important factor in practices of power between children.[10] To find an explanation for the age-differences I am drawn to extrapolate from the historical changes outlined by Baumeister (1986) in his work on the development of ideas about the 'self'. Baumeister thought that the peoples of medieval Europe identified characteristics of persons with reference only to observable, physical features. He argued that in more recent times there has become more emphasis on the idea of an inner self, having intentions and qualities that might be discrepant with exterior appearance.

Baumeister's description of historical changes would seem to have confluence with some ideas in developmental psychology about changes across age in perception of other person, from a focus on external appearance to greater understanding of internal motives (see Flavell, 1977, for an overview).

If children, like the people of medieval Europe, focus on external features in making judgments of other people's abilities they might focus on stereotypical bodily features such as gait, speech or facial features. Older children, like people of modern times, would make judgments based on an assessment of the person's inner qualities, their true internal abilities. I must confess that my tendency to consider age-changes using this recapitulationist logic is partly a function of my training in child development (cf. Morss, 1990, for views of biological recapitulation in theories of development). Like Baumeister, I tend to take the view that a self which has binary, inner/outer properties is the more developed and therefore better and more progressive self. Issues of interiority are probably culturally as well as historically specific.

For children there may be a focus on the personal possession of capability which may not be seen as fixed so incontrovertibly within a particular body. The altercation described between Sylvia and Ben in the excerpt above seemed to include an audacious element, with both Sylvia and Ben surprised at how far the other would go in using insults. Comments about reading appeared often to be 'loaded', despite the low-key approach to issues of reading achievement by their teachers. In Aotearoa there is a great concern with early literacy, which is probably the most valued skill in primary school. The children's concern about their capability in this valued area is not surprising, given this context. It is interesting to me that I think few adults would consider children who are early readers to be showing signs of later greatness. I suspect this is partly because reading is something girls tend to do better than boys. Perhaps children at this primary school were participating in a discourse about ability as a fixed quantity within an individual body, in which some people are seen as having 'more' of the quantity than others. This might be so even if the content of the children's concerns (reading) were not seen as such an important sign of 'ability' for older students. Children may use signs important within their culture in a functional way in their social interactions before they are used in the sense of shared meanings amongst adults of that culture.

It is difficult to describe changes between the events in the primary and secondary school classes without using concepts which refer to a clear linear trajectory of development. The demographic, topographical and temporal dimensions of the primary and secondary school days were entirely different. In thinking about differences between events in the two schools, I seem to 'discover' developmental trends easily. For example, I have mentioned the rather obvious difference between the shouted labels (such as 'stupid!') used to describe a person's ability at Moana School and the more subtle and complex discussions of the secondary students about issues of test performance and personal work habits. While the older students appeared to me to spend time pondering their allotted quota of the inner quantity of ability or intelligence, the younger children appeared to be looking for obvious indicators of the 'stupid'. The discursive production of notions about ability may operate quite differently in the two settings, yet widely-held views that younger people hold within them the seeds of the future create inevitable links between these contexts. Discourses about developmental processes are likely themselves to create continuities between practices in one social age-group and another. Ability may be seen as something with which each person is born, but there is much debate about the limits and possibilities for the unfolding of a child's capabilities over the years of schooling.

The complexities of our ideas about development and about education are part of the assumed fabric of our lives, difficult to interrupt in order to see the outlines of our own cultural constructions. In the west there is a long transition from the world of the primary school to the very different structures of secondary schooling. What happens along the way may be a blossoming of natural potential, programmed in the truth of individual bodies, which is then either enhanced or distorted by environmental forces such as poverty or experiences of support. Or there may be other possibilities hidden within our usual stories about development that we have yet to hear. Our capabilities for understanding childhood may some day extend far beyond our concerns about natural talents and dutiful efforts.

Notes

1 I use the word 'discourse' loosely throughout the paper, without adhering to a particular theoretical viewpoint. I like Sarup's (1989, p. 70) description of Foucauldian discourses as 'practices that systematically form the objects of which they speak'.
2 The signifiers for 'ability' and 'intelligence' are intertwined, and I will not try to separate them here.
3 I do not have the space here to consider a critique of Foucault's ideas on aptitude.
4 Two other researchers have been involved during the project at different phases, Andrea Scott and Anne-Marie Tupuola.
5 Notation for fieldwork excerpts includes elipses (...) for material omitted.
6 I recognize that in saying this I am positioning myself in rather romantic discourses about childhood in which I am enmeshed as a 'developmental researcher'.
7 'Developmental' time is a period set aside for children to choose their own activities in class.
8 Judging from the way these children positioned themselves when they spoke and the way their words were addressed to a wider audience than the two themselves also makes me wonder if the presence of the university researcher might have made a taunt about competence in the classroom more salient.
9 English comedian Dawn French might list the accoutrements of having-it-all as 'beauty, education, great job, wonderful husband'.
10 I feel the same incredulity when I am in a huge megopolis such as New York City. Perhaps it is a middle class, western fantasy that the world is ruled by a meritocracy of intelligence, qualifications and jobs. There may be more effective 'pecking orders' of physical strength and weaponry in and outside the rule of law.

7 Children in Action at Home and School

Berry Mayall

Introduction

This chapter is concerned with children's experiences of their daily lives as they are lived in two social settings, the home and the school. The argument of the chapter is that whilst children undoubtedly view themselves and may be viewed as actors in both settings, their ability to negotiate an acceptable daily experience is heavily dependent on the adults' understandings of childhood and of appropriate activities by and for children in the two settings. Broadly, parents and teachers present different sets of understandings of childhood and of programmes of activities for children. The lived experience for children is that life at home is more negotiable than life at school. What children learn and the value they put on their knowledge and that of adults is interrelated with the character of children's interactions with the adults.

The long and continuing tradition whereby adult behaviours towards children are conditioned by the understanding that they are best regarded as beings in process rather than as members of the category people has been linked into adult considerations of how best to educate children. Durkheim drew on psychological theory to enunciate a theoretical formulation which still carries currency today. Influenced by Rousseau's writings in *Emile*, he was clear that childhood, a period of growth, was characterized by both weakness and mobility; childhood is unstable:

> In everything the child is characterized by the very instability of his nature which is the law of growth. The educationalist is presented not with a person fully formed — not a complete work or a finished product — but with a becoming, an incipient being, a person in the process of formation. Everything in child psychology and in educational theory derives from the essential characteristic of this age, which is sometimes manifest in the negative form — as the weakness and imperfection of the young person — and at other times in the positive form as strength and need for movement. (Durkheim and Buisson, 1911, in Pickering, 1979)

Durkheim ties these psychological insights together with a sociological definition of the functions and goals of education.

> Education is the influence exercised by adult generations on those that are not yet ready for social life. Its object is to arouse and develop in the child a certain number of physical, intellectual and moral stages, which are demanded of him by both political society as a whole and the social milieu for which he is specifically destined. (Durkheim 'Education and society', 1922, in Giddens, 1972)

This complex of knowledge — psychological and sociological — presented the teacher, and continues to do so, with a clear underpinning for the exercise of authority. In this chapter, I want to suggest how school and teachers are experienced by children in the light of, as it seems to me, the continued force of the analysis developed in the first quarter of this century.

The home, the other main social setting where children spend their days, is conditioned by somewhat different understandings of childhood, of the proper activities of children and of how adults should behave towards and with children. It should be noted, though, that there has been little work on these topics, as regards parental knowledge about and behaviours towards school-age children. The Newsons' data (collected in the late 1960s on 4-year-olds and in the early 1970s on 7-year-olds) are unique here, but are inevitably conditioned by their particular interests — in mothers' views on discipline and training. Indeed these interests, together with the data they consequently collected, allowed them to state that 'The whole process of socialization — the integration of the child into the social world — is the cornerstone of the parental role.' The parents' task in the early years was 'to mediate cultural expectations and beliefs and to ease him out of the total egocentricity of babyhood into modes of behaviour which will be acceptable in a wider world' (Newson and Newson, 1978, p. 441). This vision would probably be judged by many parents as offering only a partial account of how they define what they do and should do. Some more recent work has suggested that whilst parents, or to be precise mothers, accept socialization tasks, both on the common-sense understanding that they are integral to parenting, and because the Psy experts (Donzelot, 1980) tell them to do these tasks, they also, and centrally, operate on experiential knowledge acquired by living with their children. This experience teaches them a complementary set of understandings. Thus mothers indicate that from the earliest days they regard their baby as a person with individual character and wishes. They recognize their child's right and wish to make her own way, to establish her own space and to construct a social life within the family and beyond (Halldén, 1991). It is also obvious to parents who spend their days with small children that they wish to participate in the social and household activities they observe taking place. As Liedloff (1986) describes (though for a society less hedged about with dangers and complexities than ours) parents recognize these wishes and enable children to take part in cooking, cleaning, self-care, social occasions. Her analysis is intended to draw attention to Western parental deficiencies as regards respect for children as social beings; but it seems to me to draw attention to an essential understanding that parents develop in daily life with their children. The understanding that this individual child has rights and wishes, abilities that will be used and built on, and an innately social nature — underlie these parental understandings, based on experience (Mayall and Foster, 1989; Mayall, 1990).

This brief sketch of teacher and parent understandings of children and of appropriate adult behaviours draws attention to the differing social frameworks within which children, according to their own accounts, attempt to live out a reasonably acceptable daily life. Whilst we may be becoming accustomed to recognizing in theory as well as in practice that children can appropriately be viewed as actors, it is also important to recognize the varying limitations on their actions imposed in different social settings.

Are Children Different?

As the above paragraphs suggest, this chapter uses as a starting point consideration of the interplay of agency and structure, in order to consider where children stand as actors, negotiators and acted-upon. Thus this chapter is concerned with the activities of children in relation to and in interaction with adults and the ways in which and the extent to which they act to modify the social settings where they live their daily lives. As commentators note, it is critical to take account in these transactions of power relationships (for example, Giddens, 1979; Craib, 1993). These relationships can be characterized through the proposition that adults have organizational control over children's activities (see Oldman in this volume). In this chapter, I wish to pursue the point that whilst children may be regarded as part of the group people (rather than outside the category people, or subsumed as part of the family or as parental offspring) the critical and distinctive characteristics of the subgroup children's interactions with both other people and with daily settings depend not so much on their absolute powerlessness vis-à-vis adults, but on the precise nature of the power-relationship between the children and the adults in any given setting. Thus I want to suggest that the level of their powerlessness varies according to how the adults in specific social settings conceptualize children and childhood. Childhood, it is argued here, is not experienced as one consistent set of relationships; rather its character in time and place is modified by adult understandings in those times and places of what children are, and what adult relationships with children are proper.

In particular, I wish to indicate some characteristics of two settings, the home and the school, in order to highlight how and why children's social positioning with regard to adults differs in the two settings. In carrying out this analysis, I aim to show how an adult outsider's/theoretician's view of children's social positioning can be counter-balanced with that of children themselves, to indicate their own understanding of how their position differs at school as compared to home.

In contemplating people in a social context, one may examine how agency and structure co-exist, interact, engage with each other to perpetuate, deconstruct and re-construct institutional and individual behaviours and norms. It is critical to bear in mind that people's impact on other people and on social conventions or requirements will vary across settings; and that this point is dramatically important as regards children's success in affecting their social environments. Thus the proposition exemplified below that children have ability to influence and modify their social environments itself requires modification: by taking account of the impact of adult constructions of childhood and adult assumptions of authority in any given setting.

> The unfolding of childhood is not time elapsing just for the child: it is time elapsing for its parental figures, and for all other members of society; the socialisation involved is not simply that of the child, but of the parents and others with whom the child is in contact, and whose conduct is influenced by the child just as the latter's is by theirs in the continuity of interaction. (Giddens, 1979, chapter 3, p. 139)

Giddens' summary suggests that children's experience of and interaction with adults is unitary, of a piece. Yet I think it is not only children themselves but the onlooker who is struck by the relatively high ability children have to influence adults and social conventions at home, compared to their relatively low ability to do so at school. The rigid social norms and goals of the school represent, as Craib (1993) puts it, 'congealed action', and are relatively impervious to individual challenge, in particular to children's challenges.

Study of people in their interactions within social settings raises issues about identification and identity. Thus each person will feel more or less a part of any given social arena, and may have different degrees of identification in relation to different arenas. These points are commonly recognized in considering, for instance, the case of children who spend time in hospital, but they are less seriously considered or recognized as regards their days in school. Though adjustment to school entry is a topic for study, thereafter the character of children's identification with school and of their identity as schoolchildren has been relatively neglected. Still less is known about children's identification with home. What does school mean to children, and do they belong to school? Children's own accounts suggest that not only as individuals, but also as a social group, their sense of belonging has widely different intensity and complexity in relation to the home, as compared to their relation with the school. The interactive dynamics of individuals within social settings will also play an important part in constructing specific identities for people and in shaping what they may and may not do. In their first five years children may be observed to acquire an identity at home, which continues to be developed in succeeding years. But on entering the social world of the school, children have to acquire, work on and develop another identity — that of schoolchild (cf James, 1993). Since the interplay of the child at school with the adults and with the social norms of the school will have a different character from these interplays at home, and since the adults construct the child differently in the two settings, a child may well construct a separate identity for herself as schoolchild. I am suggesting, therefore, that whilst issues of identification and identity concern people in general, including children, children differ from other people in their experience, for adult constructions of them available and brought into play vary radically as between adult social groups; mothers at home and teachers at school provide strikingly different accounts of children and childhood.

These ideas about the variability of people's sense of who they are may be well recognized by adults in thinking about their own lives and those of others. We feel different at home and at the workplace. But these ideas have had less currency and salience as regards children. Indeed they fly in the face of the essential propositions of developmentalism. The supremacy of developmentalists' ideas of children and childhood has allowed us to bask in the comfortable view that children are the same children wherever they are. Their emotional, relational and cognitive competences and incompetences, relate to their age and their stage. In this vision, children can be observed and described as having attained a certain level of development and competence whatever the social context, rather than perceived as people whose competence, confidence, knowledge and interactions vary according to the social context. The goal of much developmental psychology, to find universal truths about 'the child', blinds us to the personhood of children, viewed both as individuals and as groups, and their exposure to the same social forces as anyone else.

Thus far, then, the argument goes, children are similar to adults, in that they similarly are agents in interactive encounters. It is argued, though, that their identity varies widely in response to adults' constructions of them. Where they also differ from adults, crucially, is as regards intergenerational issues. The crucial distinction that makes children children is that they are not adults; as individuals and as a social group, they lack adulthood. This lack can be defined variously as deficiency, disadvantage, and/or oppression. The components may vary according to individual and societal standpoint. What is common to the intergenerational relationships of children to adults, is that children are inferior to adults. This inferiority is demonstrated in many ways: children are not allowed to make decisions affecting them; must defer to adult knowledge and authority; have little economic power (see Oldman in this volume). More generally, one may say that, in any given society, the relationships between the generations are governed by generational contracts (Alanen and Bardy, 1991), which set out adults' understandings of the division of labour in that society, and the permitted and required activities of children.

The inferiority of children is demonstrated, if we need further demonstration, by the fact that they have little negotiating power as regards the intergenerational contract. They must work within it.

However, I am arguing here that within this intergenerational contract, children's identities, knowledge, permitted behaviours, their negotiating power and their interactions vary according to social context. A wide range of factors play into the character of adult-child relations and interactions and serve to determine decisions, and children's independence and choice. These factors and how they are brought into action, weighed and modified will be discussed below. They include: adult understandings of what children can, may and should do; children's confidence in relationships and in their rights to choose and determine their daily lives; and the social norms of the setting. The essential argument proposed here is that the home and the school present children with widely differing social environments as regards the workings of the intergenerational contract and the workings out of tensions between the child as actor, or agent, and the impact of the social structure itself.

Children at Home and School: An Empirical Research Study

This chapter draws briefly on some data I collected in a study at an inner-city primary school, which had a reception class for 5 and 6-year-olds and age-grouped years above that. The school was popular with local parents and the teachers themselves rated it highly. I spent two terms in 1991 in the school, two days a week, mainly as a helper in the reception class (5–6-year-olds), and in class 5 (9–10-year-olds). I collected data as fieldnotes from observation, through informal and more focussed conversations with children (in twos and threes), through whole class discussions and, with the older children, through some writing. I kept running notes on conversations with teachers, and interviewed them more formally. I also talked with and interviewed the headteacher, the secretary, the four helpers/supervisors and some mothers of the reception class and older children.

The study had a specific focus: on the health care of the children, including their own participation in health care, at home and at school, and how they learned about health-related behaviours. However, these topics were approached, not so much through direct questioning or discussion, as through the elicitation of accounts of daily life, from both children and adults. Mothers' accounts of daily life with children, and, as it turned out, children's own accounts, tend to raise issues of the division of labour in care (childcare and health care), including children's part in decision-making. These are framed by discussion about or assumption about some key concepts: independence, consent, negotiation, authority, social norms, social habits. The data collected are therefore useful for considering how children make their way as agents in relation to adults: how far they interact and negotiate, how far the social norms of the setting are fixed or mutable in response to child and adult action and how far the actors — child and adult — work within and in tension with intergenerational relations and contracts.

It should be noted that presented here is an outline of some complex data, which are considered in more detail elsewhere (Mayall, 1993; Mayall, 1994). The aim here is to highlight the main points for discussion.

Children at Home

Both the home and the school are commonly regarded as sites of socialization, and the evidence is overwhelming that mothers at home and teachers at school recognize and accept their socialization tasks. However, whilst health, education and welfare professionals and policy-makers unite in giving primacy to the home in the first five years, the ascribed division of labour is much less clear once children start school. Certainly mothers in my study regarded their work as continuing in respect of their 5 and 9-year-olds; and the teachers regarded socialization as a central task through the years of primary schooling. The characteristics of the implementation of socialization in the two settings are very different.

At home socialization takes place in a social context governed by personal relationships within which negotiation is a legitimate and normal activity, which structures knowledge, activity and experience. For the youngest children, these relationships will be the most important in their social worlds. My data suggest that they are for the top juniors too.

Further to these essential points, a range of factors complicates and modifies the socialization agenda. Children teach their mothers to characterize them as people. Both mothers and children value children's independence. Children at 5 assert their confidence as members of the family; and their competence and knowledge in day-to-day health maintenance, within their mothers' protection and provision. Mothers value children's independent activity both as evidence that they are becoming capable, and to relieve the burden on themselves. For mothers have other agendas: paid work, unpaid household and family work, personal relationships and social lives. As has also been noted, mothers value the home as the place where their children can be themselves, can behave in ways that public social worlds may not approve of (Halldén, 1991). There is therefore emerging from both children's and mothers' accounts a definition of 5-year-old children as health-care actors in their own right. In sum, although some of mothers' goals and behaviours may be subsumed under the broad heading socialization, the character of mother-child interactions may perhaps more accurately be defined as mutual social learning and teaching.

Thus, both children and their mothers promote the view that children play an important part as agents in structuring and restructuring the home as a social institution. Children do not just belong to the family; they, to an extent, together with other family members, continuously create the family.

They construct and refine relationships and social customs, and negotiate the division of labour within the home, settling conditionally for duties and freedoms, and re-negotiating these over time.

Yet children perceive that the norms of their home and their daily life at home are structured by adult authority, though families will vary according to how far parental directiveness is the driving force and how far children operate on a long lead (du Bois-Reymond *et al.*, 1993). Adult control as a structuring force is something not commonly stressed in mothers' accounts of their daily lives with children. Whilst mothers stress personal relationships, how to enable children to develop well and how to manage children in their best interests (for mothers are continuously under instruction from health staff), children themselves give greater prominence to power issues. At both 5 and 9, children in the Children at Home and School Study, when talking about family life, noted their subordinate position and adult control over their activities, though there was more emphasis at nine than at five that they found it more restrictive and irksome.

For the 5-year-olds, that parents demanded certain behaviours was both recognized and accepted, and the protectiveness and provider-function of mothers was a modifying, softening and enabling factor. Nevertheless, at 5, children understood there were unresolved issues at stake. For instance, if your room is your room, why should you bow to parental demands that it meet their standards of tidiness? For the 9-year-olds, parental authority was more of a constraint, in the face of their growing competence and the development of their own individual patterns of daily life both within and beyond the home. However, the affective relationship provided a context which both made parental authority essentially acceptable and provided the context for negotiation. Furthermore, parental authority did not reach into every corner of their lives; but impinged in respect of some norms, tasks and activities. And, a further positive point, it was evident that children felt they did contribute to the maintenance of the home as an ongoing social environment and experienced their contributions as satisfying.

Both sets of children in my study noted the consensus prevailing between adults and children at home: that children's duties, responsibilities and actions as regards health maintenance were a proper topic for negotiation between adults and children. This was the case as regards both self-maintenance and home maintenance. I am referring to such matters within self-care as dressing appropriately, washing, dental care, consuming a socially approved diet; as well as to the activities that determine the home's character as a healthy place to live: shopping, preparing food, setting tables, clearing up, washing up, social relationships. What children should do and what should be done to them was a matter for interactive negotiation, within the understanding that children were people rather than projects.

In sum, therefore, I am suggesting that children's evidence on the home is that intergenerational authority was mediated by recognition of their status as people with the ability and right to take responsibility for health-related decision-making. The adult goal of socialization was crossed with the adult and child goals of encouraging independence, and of making space for individuals in the home to pursue their own agendas. Consent to do and to be done to was negotiable, and was indeed negotiated within a framework of critical personal relationships.

Children at School

The social institution of the primary school presents children with a different weighting to various agendas. For a start, the school differs from the home in its character as an institution with accepted social goals and norms formalized within and implemented through the regime; or as has been neatly put: standardized modes of behaviour (Radcliffe-Brown, quoted in Giddens, 1979, p. 96). The goals of delivering a curriculum and of socializing the children are realized in, notably, the grouping of children, the organizing of the children's day, and in the monitoring of performance and behaviour. As one observer puts it, activities are bureaucratized (Hartley, 1987). The school as a social institution is a setting where (obviously but) crucially, adult authority is more salient and less challengeable than at home.

Many schoolteachers (including those studied) think of their schools as child-centred, as model environments, as havens of ideals and good practices in an imperfect world. The school's goals, delivery of the curriculum, social norms and practices are founded on knowledge of the 'facts' of child development. This set of understandings amongst schoolteachers is critical as far as children are concerned, because they find they are not taken seriously. If children challenge school norms, teachers find it irrelevant to attend to the points underlying the challenge. Since the school is a model environment, the fault must lie with the children — or their homes — if they dislike it.

Furthermore, it is intrinsic to the developmental view that the socialization of children is an ongoing task throughout childhood, until they reach the goal of mature adulthood. With each year-group, therefore, the teacher's task is to socialize the children, since (according to the teachers I interviewed) she faces poorly socialized children at the start of the school year and ends it having moved them further along the road. This vision compounds with adult knowledge of the school as ideal environment to ensure that children have no legitimated voice. They never reach maturity or independence at school. The independence that teachers say they aim for in children turns out to be conformity with school norms, both academic and social.

These adult understandings and the rigid structures framing and maintaining them leave children little scope for negotiation. Adult knowledge and moral codes are not regarded by the adults at school as negotiable by children. Furthermore, the social patterning of relationships ensures that children are mostly dealt with as a group, and that individual relationships between child and teacher are not thought appropriate. Thus the interactive, negotiated processes whereby for children at home knowledge grounded in valued individual relationships is developed are not available to children at school.

And whilst parents at home have many agendas, and may value leaving the children to manage aspects of their daily lives themselves, as well as welcoming their wish to spend time developing their own activities, teachers have no other interests during the day than those of socializing and teaching the children within the frameworks of their understandings of the good child.

It is also of considerable interest that the emphasis by schools on the psychological dimensions of childhood runs alongside (and perhaps determines) the low-grade recognition of children's physical health as an appropriate concern for the teachers. The low status of the physical care of the children can be seen in, for instance, the fact that schools are not required to include trained health care workers as staff. It is common for the treatment (of illness and accident) to be delegated to low paid helpers, dinner ladies or supervisors (rather than, say, to a health professional). Indeed, the data suggest, teachers prefer inculcating moral precepts within a health education framework to recognizing children's wish to negotiate a health-maintaining environment at school. At a more general level, it may be observed that in their discourse and their practice, teachers emphasize the relevance of the psychological over the physical in considering children's well-being and behaviour, and tend to relate school academic performance to psychological rather than to physical factors. The school and the education system downplays the whole child in favour of the psychological child.

Within this complex social setting, children find that the competence and self-reliance they have acquired before they start school is devalued once they get there. The ordinary daily self-care they carry out at home, as regards pacing the day with activity and rest, eating, drinking, going to the toilet, is all subjected at school to the demands of the school day, mediated through the teacher. At the age of 5, according to my informants, learning school norms, and establishing an acceptable social life is both challenging and stressful, as well as fun. Being refused permission to go to the toilet, or get a drink, can be distressing. So can sitting in a noisy hall eating food you have had no part in choosing.

By the age of 9, the children indicated that they have learned how to manage self-care within school limits. Whilst they recognize the value of school-based education as a good they also understand the implications of compulsory all-day schooling as regards health maintenance: some are acutely aware of the health-damaging aspects of school routines, boredom and tedium, noise, stressful social relations with adults and children, from which and from whom they cannot escape.

Children provide a useful corrective commentary on the adult commentator's view that as schoolchildren they act as agents, both since they work themselves, and turn themselves into employable citizens, and since they provide work for others — that is, teachers. Undoubtedly, children's accounts indicate their recognition that they regard themselves as engaged, essentially, in a useful and productive enterprise. But they also indicate their understanding that they are the objects of the school enterprise, persons to whom actions are done; and, further, that they are powerless to reconstruct the school as a social institution to meet their own ideas about what would constitute a child-friendly educational setting. For them, the school is indeed an impervious, congealed construction of social norms.

In sum, from the children's point of view, the intergenerational relationships of the school are founded on adult direction, within laid-down social norms. Compared to life at home, life at school offers little scope for negotiation with the adults in authority, though children do learn to work the system or to skive off; or for independent activity. Children find themselves treated as group members rather than as individuals, and as objects of socialization rather than as participating people.

From the children's point of view, the principal site of health care activity is at home, and during their daily life at school, they are conducting a holding operation, health-wise. Their psychological health (as defined by teachers) takes precedence over their physical. Or to put it another way, the school is less holistic than the home in its understandings of children and its dealings with children.

Discussion

It may be useful, though inevitably it is a crude representation, to summarize schematically the main points made above about children's experience at home and school.

CONTEXTUAL FACTORS INFLUENCING LEARNING AND BEHAVIOUR

HOME	SCHOOL
socialization as negotiation	socialization as prescription
adult authority in context of relationships	adult authority in context of institutional norms
adult construction of child as actor	adult construction of child as project
child construction of self as subject	child construction of self as object

---

The above schema summarizes the main points made earlier about children's positioning at home and school, and their opportunities for participating in decision-making, in learning and activities.

Common observation and research data on children at home and at school, indicate that children's social positioning is very different in the two settings. Crucially, intergenerational relationships differ not only because the social construction of the child differs as between mothers and teachers, but because the social setting of the home presents a different frame from the school.

For at home children are identified not merely as socialization objects but as participants in and negotiators of their social worlds, and thus as important family members. At school, they are essentially projects for adult work. In complement to these differing understandings of agency, the two settings differ as frameworks for daily life. Whilst both may be coherent social systems, as regards relations and interactions between underlying beliefs and overt behaviours, the social system of the home is less formally defined and operated and more open to negotiation; the school's social system is both more fixed and overt as regards the linkages in place between goals and practices, and less open to negotiation.

Indeed, the two settings have different kinds of cohesion. The home is holistic, in that its functions as socialization setting are coherent: the social norms of the home are constructed and implemented by the adults. Yet because the interests of the participants are individual, varied and are played out in both the home and in arenas beyond the home (at work, at school, other social settings, the wider family), adult control has to be flexible to take account through interactive processes of these other and varied agendas. School, on the other hand, is coherent in other senses: it is a closed, complete system, where goals and practices cohere, and where the activities of the teachers (during the school day) are limited to a focus on the teaching and training of the children. It is thus less flexible and open to negotiation. Thus it comes about that we can see the home as place of negotiation within relationships and the school as prescriber within social norms.

This chapter is arguing, therefore, that children's experience in social settings compared to that of adults is the same but different. It is critical to recognize the power of adult constructions of the child to shape children's experience in different settings. Because adult experiential knowledge about children differs so widely from theoretical psychological understandings — at least as commonly and crudely represented to and by adults in the 'caring' professions, children live along with and interact with two contrasting adult constructions of the child: as person and as project. Whilst parental understandings may have been somewhat affected by the Psy-complex: the intervention and supervision of representatives of the welfare stage (Donzelot, 1980): children are constantly active at home to provide experiential correctives to these outsiders' views. At school, however, teachers are shielded by social conventions and shield themselves from direct interaction with individual children; and thereby from the lessons such interaction would provide. In an earlier study, my colleague and I observed a similar insulation: health visitors who had children of their own did not use their experiential knowledge in their paid work, but, like their childless colleagues, relied on book learning about the management of children (Mayall and Foster, 1989).

It seems to me that these contrasting constructions of children are more extreme than any available as regards adults; and they are crucial for children's experience. For in complement to how they are regarded, children's own construction of identity will vary between settings. Though at school they may adopt an alienated response, that is may resist being downgraded from personhood to projecthood, in order to survive they will have to accept some of the conventions of the game. These can include not only conformity, but calculated measures to work the system, and tactical balancing of the advantages of deviance against those of conformity. At home, it seems that adult constructions of children in general match more closely those of the children — broadly, children are regarded and regard themselves as valued people. However, we need to know much more about children's experiences at home. In particular, for instance, research is needed to investigate the importance of siblings; to study whether they in some circumstances act as a form of childhood group defence against power (cf Dunn, 1984). We also need further investigations of friendships and of activities in children's own domains — where they construct social worlds outside, or alongside, adult-controlled settings (for example, Moore, 1986; and see Ward in this volume).

The argument proposed here has implications for the kinds of work that are necessary to increase understanding of children's social relations. It is necessary to break down discussion of intergenerational relationships to take account of social context and of adult and child constructions within them. And it is necessary to study the processes whereby these factors operate, and whereby social norms are constructed and implemented. Study of process requires detailed investigation of adult-child interactions within social settings. It is perhaps at this point in debate about these complex issues that the long-established conflict between sociology and psychology can be if not resolved then tackled, through using the strengths of both to carry out these investigations. What is required is work which tracks the construction, modification and development of social norms and behaviours in a range of settings over time; critical factors to be taken into account will be children's and adult contributions, the flexibility of the social setting, the impacts of larger social forces (societal expectations of, for example, the family, the school). Very little work (as far as I know) has been done using this approach, on the home — which in any case is notoriously difficult to study in depth and over time. As regards the school, study of process has been mainly to do with the early adjustment of children to primary school.

In this chapter, I have reported only briefly on a detailed study which attempted to explore the complex interactions outlined. This chapter, and the study on which it is based, are limited mainly to consideration of children as a social group in their daily interactions with adults. The study took some account of age and of gender, but has not to any important extent tackled some important dimensions of difference within categories: children (individual difference as well as ethnicity and class); homes (the character of parental authority, socioeconomic and cultural considerations); schools (strength of authority structures, class size). At this stage in studying children and childhood it has seemed to me important to focus primarily on childhood status and experience at general levels, as a basis for taking account of difference (Qvortrup, 1991).

Nevertheless, I hope this chapter has contributed to the task of breaking away from the idea of 'the child', by at least considering children as construed and in interaction in two settings. The chapter has focussed on how characteristics of specific social environments (the home and the school) are critical in determining children's experiences and activities. This has involved as a necessary enterprise taking account of children's perspectives, and indeed putting them at the centre of the analysis.

8 Responsible Children? Aspects of Children's Work and Employment Outside School in Contemporary UK

Virginia Morrow

Introduction

This chapter discusses aspects of children's work outside school in contemporary UK, drawing on a data from empirical research carried out in 1990 and 1991 with children aged between 11 and 16 years in secondary schools in the city of Birmingham and the county of Cambridgeshire (Morrow, 1992a). It explores the notion of 'responsibility' as it relates to children's roles and the way in which childhood (in the industrialized west, at least) is constructed as a period of dependency, thus signifying children's lack of 'responsibility'. It argues that this social construction of children and childhood effectively renders children's labour outside school 'invisible', and challenges traditional conceptualizations of childhood within sociology.

The starting point for this research is the attempt to see childhood as socially constructed (see James and Prout, 1990). Within sociology, the tendency has been to neglect children's activities, and to assume that children 'develop' within the two institutions of 'the family' and 'the school' (Qvortrup, 1991). Adult-child dichotomies have dominated sociology and the assumption is often made that children are an undifferentiated category, with the effect that disparities within the broad category, whether along the lines of gender, ethnicity, class and age, are obscured. Even defining the taken-for-granted concepts of 'child' and childhood, and 'work' as it relates to children, is problematic (see Morrow, 1994). The research presented here is about older children, aged between 11 and 16 years. The work activities of children in this age group has been underresearched and undertheorized within sociology, although at a common-sense level, there is a general awareness that school children do undertake paid work, because we see them working on market stalls, delivering newspapers, working in shops and so on. We may speculate that some children help at home, because often teachers will comment that girls are kept off school if there is a new baby in the house, or a parent is ill and so on. However, no official statistics are kept on these kinds of activities, and the questions are simply not asked. There have been a few small, empirical policy-oriented studies of children's employment in the UK, carried out mainly by pressure groups such as the Low Pay Unit and the Anti-Slavery Society, but these are mostly quantitative, a-theoretical and not set in socioeconomic or historical context (Lavelette *et al.*, 1991; MacLennan, 1980 and 1982; MacLennan *et al.*, 1985; Moorehead, 1987; Pond and Searle, 1991).

The chapter is organized in three sections. Firstly, it describes the research methodology used in collecting data from children, and gives an outline of the main general findings. Secondly, it discusses the notion of 'responsibility' as it relates to children's roles, drawing from examples of children's responsibilities at work both in the labour market as well as within their families. The final section explores in some detail why children want to work, and concludes that we need to reconstruct the way we think about children both sociologically and in social policy terms.

Research Methods

Given that there have been remarkably few purely sociological studies of children's everyday lives, it is not surprising that very little has been written on 'doing research' with children. There is literature on qualitative research in educational settings, but this has more to say about dealing with other adults in the research process, that is to say teachers, than with children themselves (for example, Burgess, 1984). Children occasionally merit a mention in handbooks on sociological methodology, though discussion often relates to fairly young children and is rather patronizing in tone. Spradley (1979), for example, suggests that 'children usually make good informants and they have adequate free time' (p. 51). The aim of my research was to assess the prevalence of children's involvement in work, as well as the implications of children's work and I wanted a fairly large sample. The main source of data was a collection of written accounts of everyday life outside school, from 730 children in secondary schools (children between 11 and 16 years of age) in Birmingham and Cambridgeshire. To set the socioeconomic context, I carried out background studies by collecting demographic and economic data from the relevant local authorities. I interviewed the Head or Deputy Head of the schools in my sample at some length; these interviews were largely unstructured, and were conducted around a series of general topics, such as the children's home environments, the local labour market, the ethnic minority composition of the school, attendance rates and so on. By focusing on particular schools and relating the children's accounts to information gathered about the school and its environment, it was possible to build up a picture of children's involvement in work and set it in context.

This technique provided a large amount of data in a shorter time than would have been possible with questionnaires. It also revealed aspects of children's lives which a questionnaire might not have included, or might indeed have excluded because of the form of the questionnaire. For example, in the case of direct questions about 'working', the children might not relate their informal activity to the question because the concept 'work' tends to be constructed as formal wage labour (see Ennew, 1982 and 1985; Ennew and Morrow, 1994). Indeed, other 'adult categories' imposed on children's experiences may preclude children from describing them. The children were asked to describe all the things they do, not just work, outside school hours, and they were 'prompted' by being told that by writing the essay they would be helping with some research into the work that children do, such as a part-time or holiday job, and also helping at home, doing the shopping, baby-sitting, and so on. The essays were anonymous but prefaced by the child's age, and gender. I deliberately did not ask the children directly about their social class background, ethnic origin or family composition, although sometimes children did make interesting comments, particularly about their families. 'Ethnicity', 'class' and 'family composition' are adult categories that children may have difficulty 'fitting' themselves into. For example, there may be no such thing as a 'single parent' from a child's point of view. Many Asian children do not consider themselves to be 'black', for many Muslim children their primary identity may be their religion, and many 'Afro-Caribbean' and 'Asian' children may consider themselves to be primarily British. These variables and contexts were elicited in a general way in the socioeconomic descriptions in the informal interviews I carried out with teachers at the schools I visited.

As a follow-up, I interviewed a very small (n=5) number of Cambridge-shire children who worked, and I carried out classroom discussions with two groups of children (12–13-year-olds and 14–15-year-olds) at an inner-city school in Birmingham. I analyzed data from a subsample of Birmingham children who had part-time jobs during term-time from a survey of 1800 children carried out jointly by the Low Pay Unit/Birmingham City Education Department (Pond and Searle, 1991). This allowed me to analyze for a range of statistical variables which affect children's employment (ethnicity, age, gender, type of work, rates of pay, and location within the city). I interviewed local authority professionals responsible for enforcing the legislation relating to children's employment, and interviewed one employer, the Direct Sales Manager of a local evening newspaper, which employed about 100 school children through its branch offices to deliver newspapers.

Although I was trying to see children as 'nothing special but simply as actors in the social world' (Waksler, 1991, p. 62), I am frequently asked whether I can really 'believe' these children's accounts. There seems to be a reluctance to take children's ideas seriously, and this is not surprising, given that, at the macro level at any rate, adults tend to trivialize and devalue children's acts. As Waksler suggests, 'Adults routinely set themselves up as the understanders, interpreters and translators of children's behaviour' (*ibid.*, p. 62). I took what the children wrote very much at face value and have, I hope, avoided imposing my own interpretation upon their words.

Main Research Findings

The work that children described fell roughly into four categories (cf. Rodgers and Standing, 1981): wage labour, marginal economic activity, non-domestic family labour, and domestic labour. 38 per cent of the children described work that corresponded to the first three categories, and roughly 40 per cent described carrying out some kind of domestic labour. Some children mentioned work which fitted only into one category, some that which fitted into two or more categories. There were interesting differences across a range of variables, including gender, age variations within the broad category of childhood, ethnicity and geographical location.

Wage labour (in other words, a regular part-time job, employed by others) — The most common form of wage labour for younger children was (not surprisingly) working in newspaper delivery (13 per cent of the children in the sample, and proportionally more boys than girls). Indeed, this has become a 'traditional' form of employment for children and children are clearly an important source of labour in this type of work. Older children in the sample, 14–16-year-olds, however, appear to be venturing into youth or adult labour markets, mainly in service sectors of the economy, the retail trade, hotel and catering and personal services such as hairdressing. Very small numbers of children were found working in the primary sector (agriculture) or the secondary sector (manufacturing and construction) and this is not surprising given the restrictions on types of work that children may do and the localities in which the research was carried out. Children are ideally suited to take on part-time employment, particularly Saturday work, because it fits in with their school commitments. Further, the service sector notoriously relies upon a supply of flexible, cheap labour to work the unsocial hours that are a feature of this sector of the economy. Women and young people appear to make up a sizeable proportion of the labour force, and to a small extent, older children also appear to be part of this labour force. There were some interesting gender differences in the type of work children actually perform within these broad categories. For example, in hotel and catering, girls seemed to be more likely to work as waitresses while boys were more likely to describe work out of sight in kitchens.

Marginal economic activities/'self-employment' — Children described a wide range of activities which do not fit clearly into other categories of work: activities which were typified by their irregularity and short-term nature, though some of the children described undertaking these activities on a regular, long-term basis. These included baby-sitting for non-family, car-washing, and other odd jobs that are performed on a kind of self-employed basis. Baby-sitting was the most common form of this type of work, particularly for girls. Twenty-three per cent of the total number of girls in the sample contrasted to 3 per cent of the boys mentioned baby-sitting, and I discuss this in more detail below.

Non-domestic family labour (in other words, helping in family businesses) — 10 per cent of the children who worked described doing so for their family businesses. The assumption is often made that the involvement of children in family firms is characteristic of some ethnic minorities, and ethnicity did appear to be related to children's involvement in this type of work. However, it would be wrong to assume that only ethnic minority families use children's labour because several children in the rural sample (which had a very low proportion of respondents from ethnic minorities) mentioned working in their family businesses.

Domestic labour Domestic labour has been divided into three inter-related categories in the sociological literature: routine daily tasks, childcare and other caring activities, and household work such as self-provisioning, house maintenance and repair, car maintenance and so on (see, for example, Pahl, 1984). About 30 per cent of the boys in the sample and 50 per cent of the girls described undertaking some form of domestic labour. There was clear gender stereotyping in the forms of work girls and boys described, though it seemed likely that a range of factors, such as maternal employment, age, birth order, and family form, interacted with gender to increase the likelihood of children's contributing to domestic labour (see Morrow, 1992b).

Children as Responsible Actors

I want to explore the notion of 'responsibility' as it relates to children's work activities, drawing examples from each of the forms of work that children described. Responsibility is a rather nebulous concept and has different meanings in different contexts. Being responsible involves being accountable, answerable, capable, competent, dependent, reliable, trustworthy and so on. These are not qualities which are usually associated with older children or teenagers, because childhood is defined and constructed in social policy terms (at least in the industrialized West), as a period of incompetence, of a lack of responsibilities. Indeed, the lack of responsibility attributed to adolescence/youth is regarded as particularly dangerous and threatening to the (adult) social order (see, for example, Warwick and Aggleton, 1990). However, some adults do appear to acknowledge that late childhood is a time when some responsibilities may be passed on to or negotiated with young people (see below). Children described taking on a range of tasks and duties they undertook and as such they were effectively being given responsibility for things and people, whether the work they were doing was paid or unpaid. For example, a 15-year-old boy who was working at weekends and during the summer holidays in an ice factory, wrote:

The work I do is a cross between a storeman and a factory worker. On (a typical morning) I would work from 8–12 in the factory packing ice, then in the afternoon I would go into the cool store at −14°C, where I would work using a pump truck and a forklift truck (which I am allowed to do). In the store I would arrange the store, where I have full control of about 100 pallet spaces and I basically make the best of the space and try to leave plenty of room, for the next day, by shifting about pallets, stacking them on top of others. I also load and unload lorries with the forklift . . .

A 15-year-old girl described how she had worked on the cash desk of a fast food restaurant:

To start with here I was a waitress and after some experience and they had gained trust in me I went on to do a variety of jobs, I worked on the cash desk, in the kitchen . . .

Several children described working at riding stables in return for free rides. Usually this involved taking responsibility for animals, but one 12-year-old girl described teaching younger children to ride:

. . . then at 1.00 pm we lead the younger ones round the paddock and teach them. This is for two half-an-hour rides, for beginners . . .

Other children mentioned working for their family's businesses, like this 15-year-old boy, who was probably an important source of labour for his parents:

Evenings and weekends I help my parents run their company. They run a towing service. I help my dad out in the motor, so I can end up anywhere in the country, doing a job . . . If we are towing a toilet block or office block, I will help, hook the trailer on, the lighting board to the unit. Or I can be loading or unloading anything off our own trailer. I . . . also rope down and sheet the load or unsheeting and unrope the load . . .

and another 15-year-old boy described how

After my dinner I go out with my dad to where I work at my brother's butchers shop. I usually help my brother and dad for about two hours most evenings . . . In the mornings before school I get up quite early and bike to a nearby village to a field which my dad owns. I have to go there to check that the sheep which are in there are OK . . .

I should say that it is I, the researcher, who is defining these tasks as 'responsible', and that it seems likely that responsibility is not necessarily an important issue for the children concerned but, rather, a preoccupation that adults have about children. Indeed, Holland (1992) in a recent study of popular images of children, describes how such images lead to an 'enforced irrationality' and suggests that children themselves make use of the imagery 'to define themselves and their experiences' (p. 174). It is hardly surprising, then, that in the course of my research it was adults, rather than children themselves, who used the concept of 'responsibility' in relation to children's work. (Of course, this is not to say that the children are not themselves proud of or pleased with being given responsibility, even if they do not use the term 'responsibility'. After all, these tasks, which seem to be specifically theirs, are significant enough for them to detail.) For example, an employer I interviewed (the direct sales manager of a local newspaper employing about 100 school children) described newspaper delivery very much as a 'proper job' in itself. From his point of view, it clearly is employment in the formal sense of the word, and he described how the children involved are made aware that they have a responsibility to their customers and to the newspaper. Two different headteachers of schools in inner-city Birmingham commented on the 'responsibilities' that many of their pupils had in taking their younger siblings to school. Interestingly, this was perceived negatively by one of the headteachers, who commented that such responsibilities interfered with attendance and punctuality requirements, while the other headteacher saw these as positive responsibilities that should be included on the children's 'records of achievement'. Indeed, the most usual cases where 'responsibility' was likely to be a prime concern for adults were of children looking after other younger children, whether for their own families or for other people's families. This leads me on to discuss children's work caring for their younger siblings/relatives, and baby-sitting outside the family.

Sibling Caretaking

Evidence from oral history and childhood autobiography shows that in the past, children, especially girls, helped at home by looking after younger siblings to a significant extent, particularly in working-class families (Gamble, 1979; Jamieson, 1986; Jephcott, 1942; Parr, 1980; Roberts, 1975 and 1976; Thompson, 1981). However, the recent literature on domestic labour rarely mentions children as sources of assistance in their homes, and children's contribution to domestic labour (whether in the form of routine housework or sibling caretaking) has not been the focus of attention for contemporary British research (Morris, 1988), except to a minimal extent in the literature on (girls') socialization where such work is seen entirely as role rehearsal for future adulthood and not intrinsically useful or valuable in any way (though see Solberg, 1990, for Norway). Yet many children in my study would appear to provide a good deal of help in the form of caretaking to relatives, and while women might be primarily responsible for arranging this, from the children's perspective, they were taking on responsibilities. Several mentioned that they babysat while their parents were at work, as in the following two examples:

During the holidays I look after my little brother on Mondays, Tuesdays and Wednesdays from 9 till 3.30 as my mum goes out to work. (12-year-old boy)

When we are on school holidays I babysit for my little sister in the mornings while my mum and dad are at work (9–12) . . . (13-year-old girl)

Other children described collecting their younger siblings from school, and others alluded to their parents' shift work, which meant they helped by looking after siblings at other times of the day. Children also described babysitting when relatives wanted to go out in the evening, providing a considerable amount of free time to adults. One 14-year-old girl described a good deal of childcare she undertook for relatives:

I get a video either Friday or Saturday evenings . . . because my mum and dad sometimes goes out for a drink so I get lumbered looking after my sister, and I find it a bit boring sometimes. . . . Mostly some Fridays my auntie comes round my house and picks me up from after school because I go round hers for the whole weekend to look after my baby cousin who is only two months old.

Some girls mentioned the childcare (and other tasks) they undertook in the context of their family's health problems, like this 15-year-old girl:

At home I help out to a degree; by running errands to family and friends . . . I also do some shopping depending on the times of school; (and) occasionally I do the week's grocery shopping for our family of seven. Other things which I do at home include babysitting the other five children, two of which are (adopted) babies and one of 16 who has a mental age of 7. I do this when my Mum goes out (my Dad died when I was 4). I also help with the cleaning and cooking as well as stimulating my two adopted baby brothers who are both Downs. When my Mum is ill I take care of the whole family until she has recovered.

More exceptionally, perhaps, several children mentioned responsibilities they had towards their grandparents. For example, a 12-year-old girl wrote 'My nan isn't well so I have to help look after her and keep check on her in case anything happens'. One girl I talked to in Birmingham said 'I started doing baby-sitting but I don't do any more work like that now because I look after my nan' (14-year-old). Two girls in the sample explicitly mentioned that they 'looked after' a parent (see also Aldridge and Becker, 1993).

Looking After Other People's Children

Baby-sitting involves providing an informal irregular childcare service to parents who want to go out, usually in the evenings and usually for leisure purposes. Again, it is a system of childcare that has not been the focus of much sociological attention (though see Gullestad, 1988 for Norway). Baby-sitting was a common form of work for girls. For example, a 15-year-old girl described how:

> Most of my nights from 8.00 till 12.00 I babysit for different families. I have six baby-sitting jobs, I enjoy doing it as I love to be with them the youngest is six weeks which I've looked after since it was born and the oldest is 12. So I get quite a lot of money but I don't do it because of that. I get on well with the children and I can communicate with them. There are fifteen children in all I look after . . .

Another 15-year-old girl wrote:

> Saturday evenings usually once a month I babysit for a regular couple. I take on the responsibility of looking after a 4-year-old girl and an 8-month old baby. I enjoy this and take care to make sure they are happy . . .

Childminding, on the other hand, is more formal, regular caring for children while the mother (typically) is out at work. At a common sense level, it is a form of caretaking, often of quite small babies and young children, and as such involves a good deal of responsibility. One 15-year-old girl described how:

> In the summer holidays I babysit for two boys aged 8 and 12. I do this from 8.30 am until around 6.30 pm I have to make them lunch and . . . tea and take them out to places such as the cinema, bowling etc . . .

It seems plausible to suggest that older children who babysit or undertake childminding are, in fact, taking over the role of 'parent' for a period of time though they are not technically 'in loco parentis' in the eyes of the law. The Royal Society for the Prevention of Accidents have issued a four page charter for babysitters and parents which assumes not only that baby-sitters are over 16 but also that they are 'responsible' people:

> For the baby-sitter: Are you aged 16 years and over and able to accept the responsibilities of looking after a child? Remember that parents are seeking good childcare in their absence. Can you offer such a service? (ROSPA, 1991)

In a recent discussion of job content and skill, it has been suggested that accepting responsibility 'for property, output, standards and people' is one of many attributes required of jobs holders at varying degrees of intensity: '. . . the burden of responsibility has an important bearing on the value of a job, a fact which is fully recognized in job evaluation' (Burchell *et al.*, 1990, p. 10). To a large extent, however, this seems only to apply to mainstream jobs done by men. In these examples, children are temporarily 'responsible' for 'people' (in this case, younger children) but this is not recognized (not surprisingly, given that childcare workers, whether child or adult, are notoriously badly paid), and it appears that the valuation of responsibility varies according to gender.

It also seems likely that the skills involved in childcare are relevant in the valuation of the work. Feminist writers have pointed out that skill is often 'an ideological category imposed on certain types of work by virtue of the sex and power of the workers who perform it' (Phillips and Taylor, 1986). Children are generally seen as irresponsible but perhaps girls are seen as more responsible than boys because they are likely to be 'naturally' more skilled at childcare, and this of course relates to social constructions of femininity and masculinity. Adult women are not generally seen as 'more responsible' than adult men, but childcare is the specific nature of the 'work' at issue here and it is seen as an exclusively feminine role. Furthermore, it is likely that fewer boys babysit than girls because there is some idea that boys cannot be trusted. A recent report in *The Guardian* about young abusers cited the case of a 14-year-old boy who set up a baby-sitting service in his neighbourhood and was sexually abusing young girls in his care (*Guardian*, 16 August 1991). Of course, there is a danger of circularity here, whereby the argument becomes a self-fulfilling prophecy. Boys are not given responsibility because they are boys and cannot be trusted because of stereotypes of masculinity. Hence, boys never learn to be caring individuals.

Taking on responsibility might be a positive thing for many children, an 'adult' attribute bestowed early on. As Barbara Hudson (1984) has suggested,

> the problem of adolescence for teenagers is that they must demonstrate maturity and responsibility if they are to move out of this stigmatised status, and yet because adolescence is conceived as a time of irresponsibility and lack of maturity they are given few opportunities to demonstrate these qualities which are essential for their admission as adults. (p. 36)

It is interesting that supposedly 'incompetent' children are given responsibility for looking after younger children and babies. Thus, the social construction of childhood and the reality of children's activities do not correspond, with the result that children who do assume responsibility are hidden from view, and occupy an ambiguous, and unacknowledged, place between adulthood and childhood.

Rethinking Childhood

These examples of children helping their families, and children taking on responsibilities outside their families, have implications for the way in which childhood is conceptualized within sociology and link with the argument that children can be seen as social actors in their own right. As discussed earlier, sociology broadly assumes that children are dependent beings. It is a truism to say that dependency in childhood is physically determined by the biological state of immaturity but children tend to be regarded, in sociological terms, as an undifferentiated category of 'all those under 16 or 18 years old'. The assumption is that children are 'dependent' whatever their age. However, a child's physical dependency diminishes as he/she grows older, and this dependency is gradually displaced by a dependency that is socially determined. This means that children are effectively prevented from attaining independence until they reach the appropriate chronological age. As Qvortrup (1990) suggests, children's status as dependents 'is so naturally ingrained in adult belief systems as not to be questioned at all' (p. 84). Dependency in late childhood is a reflection of the pressures of economic, social and psychological structures rather than a biological fact (cf. Walker, 1982, on old age), although it is frequently overlooked that the age at which one is considered to be a 'child' (at least in terms of social and economic dependency) has gradually increased during this century as a result of a range of social policies. In some cases, older children provide help and services to their families, both in the form of domestic labour and in family businesses, but because we classify the relationship between children and parents as one in which the former are dependent on the latter, we ignore what may well be elements of exchange.

The social construction of childhood dependency, based as it is on conceptions of children as 'developing', and therefore as incompetent and irresponsible, precludes us from acknowledging the extent to which children are capable, competent and have agency and responsibility in their own lives. Children's involvement in work is not mere role rehearsal in preparation for adulthood, though of course it may have an important socialization effect. It seems likely that there is a kind of continuum, from children who appear to make virtually no contribution to the domestic economy, to children whose contribution is total and on whom the functioning of the household depends, with the majority of children making contributions that fall somewhere in between the two extremes (cf. Shamgar Handelman, 1986). Some children also appear to be part of the labour market, albeit in a marginal way, and again there is probably a continuum of childhood experiences, from children who never have any involvement in paid work (whether formal or informal) to children whose activities out of school are structured around their roles in paid employment. I am questioning the norm that makes us see children as dependent, and I suggest that this socially constructed 'dependence' has prevented us from detecting what may well be, at the very least, reciprocal relations between family members, and the extent to which children are indeed part of the labour market (cf. Jones, 1992).

Why Do Children Work? The Children's Point of View

Why do children choose to take on the responsibility of paid employment, whether in formal wage labour or earning money informally by baby-sitting? The assumption is often made that children take on paid work out of necessity because of the inadequacy of the family income to meet the whole family's needs. Working-class children were indeed important contributors to the family income until the Second World War (Morrow, 1992a). However, it is problematic to argue that this is still the case for *all* children who work today and the contemporary relationship between children's employment and family income is by no means straightforward. Children may indeed be contributing to family incomes indirectly by purchasing consumer items with their earnings which parents would otherwise have to pay for directly or through the allocation of pocket money. However, the idea that poverty 'forces' children to find paid work is one that recurs in the press and political rhetoric. For example, the Labour Party's Spokesperson on Children, Joan Lestor, often claims that 'the reason why so many children have entered the workforce prematurely is, of course, family poverty. And this Government has been directly responsible for impoverishing families during more than a decade of mismanagement' (quoted in *The Guardian*, 8 March 1991). *The Observer* carried a report in December 1990 which claimed that 'more children are working because declining family incomes force them into jobs to supplement what their parents can provide'. Paradoxically, the same article gave details of a prosecution case in Bristol, where 'intriguingly . . . the ten children working (in a supermarket, illegal hours) were not from a poor, largely immigrant community, but from prosperous middle-class Portishead, a West Country town, popular with commuters to nearby Bristol . . .' (*Observer*, 16 December 1990).

It would be satisfying to point to a simple, direct link between poverty and children's employment. However, the fact that there are multiple wage earners in a household does not necessarily mean that the wage of the 'main' wage earner, the breadwinner, is inadequate (Siltanen, 1986). Children may be contributing their labour for very low pay or free to family businesses which cannot afford to pay for 'outside' labour. Some children may well be working out of necessity. However, in most cases, the link appears to be more complex. In my sample, the children least likely to be working were in the poorest areas (Birmingham inner city, 25 per cent) whilst a higher percentage of children (48 per cent) were working in a relatively affluent part of Britain. These data are reinforced by findings from elsewhere. Hutson, for example, in her study of sixth formers' Saturday jobs in Swansea, found that considerable numbers were 'educational achievers from affluent homes' (Hutson, 1990, p. 18).

There may be a number of reasons for the differences between rates of employment among children in the inner-city of Birmingham and Cambridgeshire. First, of course, the labour market for children is likely to be highly localized and employment opportunities will differ widely between vicinities. There may be more jobs available for children in affluent areas, and people may be able to afford to have their newspapers delivered, hire baby-sitters, pay for their cars to be washed and lawns mowed. Shops may be busier on Saturdays in a prosperous district, and there may be a higher demand for traditional services which demand cheap, unskilled workers. Greenberger and Steinberg (1986) make a similar point when they suggest that 'teenage work' in the USA is essentially a suburban rather than urban or rural phenomenon. They also suggest that job opportunities for young people in retailing and services have expanded over the past two decades, and the same may well be true in the UK. There may be correspondingly fewer such jobs available in deprived inner-city areas, or the jobs that are available may be filled by other members of the labour market, women or young people, for example, who have no alternative but to accept low pay and poor working conditions.

Secondly, children are a relatively immobile labour force. Children in inner-city areas may not have access to private transport or, indeed, the available income to pay for public transport to, say, the city centre where jobs are available. One girl in my sample who had a very busy schedule at weekends and worked on Sundays in a riding stables described her mother as 'a taxi-driver' for herself and her sister. Affluent children may also be more 'attractive' employees, or may have better connections and networks which they may use to find their jobs, and the labour market for children may mirror the adult labour market in terms of divisions according to class, ethnicity and gender.

Thirdly, norms and values in respect to children's work may differ between cultural and social groups. Asian girls, for example, may not be allowed out to deliver newspapers in the streets and may not want to anyway. The 'ethic' of children's employment may also differ according to the relative prosperity of an area, and there may be a different social class perception of the 'value' of children, and what they are expected to do. Expenditure on one's children is very important, and spending money on children's consumer items may be one way in which the 'poor pay more'. Children are an important expression of hope in the future for many people, almost status markers in their own right. There may be some ignominy attached to one's children working, a notion that 'they shouldn't need to', and conversely a certain amount of prestige to be gained by *not* having one's children working in the family shop, for example. Affluent families can afford to buy their children almost anything, but the point is that they may choose not to, and instead encourage (or allow) the child to have a job as an educational experience to 'learn' the value of hard work and money. These 'enterprising' children contradict the stereotypical view of children who work as 'exploited victims' and 'child slaves', and they may be advantaged over their less well-off peers, not only by their relative affluence, but also by their informal experience at work, when it comes to competing for jobs later on.

Finally, one of the main reasons that children seek paid employment is that 'consumerism and the advent of teenage markets created a need for money amongst this age group' (Greenberger and Steinberg, 1986, p. 76). Currently children's total spending power in the UK must be considerable, though figures are not available. MacLennan (1982) and MacLennan *et al.*, (1985) found that children spent their earnings on toys, sweets, fashions and other children's products. Hutson (1990) found that sixth-formers tended to work in order to pay for luxuries, while their parents paid for necessities. Many children in my sample did not say what they spent their money on, and it was not the intention of the research to elicit this information. Some children did, however, mention why they wanted to earn. Whilst some children spent their money, others described saving their earnings, often for quite specific purposes, for example, 'my holidays', 'a colour TV', 'my fishes and my car'. The 15-year-old factory worker quoted above described how 'This summer holiday I earnt £700+ and I saved £600 of that, as I am saving for a VW Polo Coupé hatchback sport for about £1500 as I'm nearly half way, and I have a year and a half until I can drive'.

Several children mentioned other benefits from working, for example, that it gave them confidence and independence, or it was useful experience for the future, and a source of references for future job applications. Many wrote that they enjoyed their work. Several children described working for charities, and one girl in the interview sample was using part of her income to sponsor a child in Ruanda. Others mentioned that they wanted to find jobs but realized that working might interfere with their social life, or their school work and homework. However, the main reason for working appeared to be, not surprisingly, generating pocket money to spend on consumer items.

In a critique of teenage consumerism in Sweden, Henriksson (1983) has argued that the only meaningful economic role children have left is as consumers, pointing out that children's situation and needs are well recognized by the market: 'It gives children a role and a function, and it creates an artificial participation, in exchange for the participation denied to children in the rest of everyday life. The role of consumer is at least a role' (pp. 62–3). To an extent, this is undoubtedly the case, but there is a danger in going too far, and arguing that children should be protected from themselves and their frivolous spending habits. Henriksson is right to point out that society denies (or ignores) children's active participation in many spheres of everyday life, but this underestimates the extent to which children are social agents. I have attempted to show that they are, in many ways, more than mere consumers. The problem with Henriksson's argument is that it denies young people any autonomy, and they appear to be materialistic yet manipulated objects in a process beyond their control. It also assumes that children cannot be altruistic;

but some examples contradict this view. Children are social actors in a much broader sense than in Henriksson's 'artificial participation' as 'child consumers'. Whilst social institutions construct an (artificial) function for children as 'adults-in-preparation', some children appear to choose not to accept this role and actively take steps to participate in adult society by earning as well as consuming. It also seems likely that children do not work merely in order to consume, but in order to give themselves a feeling of being responsible and more 'grown-up' generally, which accords with other aspirations they may have towards greater emotional/sexual maturity, besides 'material' maturity. However, the structural constraints on children are considerable, and these constraints define where children may work if they want to.

Conclusion

In conclusion, I have argued that the social construction of childhood as a period marked by dependency and an absence of 'responsibility' prevents us from 'knowing' about those cases of children working and taking responsibility. An analysis of children's everyday lives outside school reveals that children have continued to work, but their labour has been made 'invisible' behind a conception of 'the child' as dependent, non-productive, and maintained within the family unit. The responsibilities of 'productive work', whether formal paid labour, working for family firms, or domestic labour within the home, have become something to be undertaken in adulthood, not childhood. That a substantial proportion of secondary school age children have paid jobs, demonstrates the ways in which children's work roles articulate with those of adults as well as mirror adults' 'work'. However, much of children's paid employment has the characteristics of a segregated and specialized labour market where their roles are acted out in 'unsocial' hours in home and neighbourhood, and are structured by gender, age and ethnicity. Some children are also involved in carrying out domestic chores to a considerable degree, again articulating with and mirroring adults' roles. This contradicts the notion that children and adults occupy 'separate' worlds. Society (and indeed sociology) at best ignores and at worst denies children's active participation in many spheres of everyday life.

This suggests that we should move away from the sociological view of children as burdens who, as social actors, do little more than consume goods and services, whether within their families or in the education system. Throughout this century, there has been an interplay between where children should be (at school), and where they have actually been located in response to various familial, national and personal needs. Firstly, they worked out of necessity for their families, as contributors to the family income, as was the case in the early part of this century. Secondly, they worked for the needs of the economy as a whole (for example, working in agricultural production during the Second World War). Thirdly, they work nowadays in response to

The most teasing and tantalizing of these characteristics, that most of us would like to see in children, is that of resourcefulness in making use of their environment, simply because it involves those other attributes of responsibility and reciprocity. Every city was once rich in both incidental and intentional resources for children (Ward, 1978). Our problem is that some children exploit them, and others do not. Forty years ago, a geographer, James Wreford Watson, plotted on a map of a Canadian city, the facilities and cultural organizations available to citizens, and compared them with a map registering the concentration of case loads of the Department of Relief, the Unemployment Bureau and the Juvenile Court, and confirmed that a 'social Himalaya' prevented the city's poor inhabitants from making use of the facilities taken for granted by middle-class residents next door (Watson, 1951). Twenty years ago, Ashley Bramall, leader of the then Inner London Education Authority. confided to me, that whatever new facility was provided for children, he and his committee knew in advance which children would utilize it.

A researcher into leisure made the same point in a different way:

> In my leisure research, more of the children who took part in sports, than non-sporty children, said they lived near open country, to parks and to swimming-pools. But what their answers meant was, not that the nearer you get to facilities the more you like sport, but that the two groups perceived the world differently and those who used facilities knew where those facilities were: the facilities were part of their universe. (Emmett, 1975)

Those children whose universe does contain an understanding of the topography of the local environment, the manipulation of the facilities it offers, and the social assurance to use them, need increasingly as the century ends, the money to pay for them. Sporting facilities which were once available free, or at a nominal entrance charge as part of the community services provided by local authorities or voluntary bodies, are increasingly becoming more elaborate, more centralized and more expensive. For example, there was an assumption in the 1930s and 1940s, that councils should provide cheap and simple 'lidos', or open-air swimming pools, and that it was society's duty to ensure that every child should have a chance to learn to swim. By the 1990s, they have mostly been closed and replaced by high-quality 'leisure centres', incorporating pools of a far better standard of comfort and luxury, but further from home and at a price for admission that the children who most need them cannot readily pay.

It is not surprising that the division between users and non-users has become more obvious, nor that some feel automatically excluded, while others, in both acceptable and unacceptable ways, seek the purchasing power to utilize the goods and services that every urban centre provides, at a price.

The child as customer has a regard from the adult world quite different from that given to the child as beneficiary or supplicant, and this lesson is not lost on children. It is part of everyone's experience, that those most gratifying occasions in childhood were those when we were not treated as children, but met the adult world on equal terms. Some activity, in say, sport or music, was recognized as worthy of uncondescending respect without regard to age, and the children's self-esteem blossomed. In everyday life, this accolade is most often given to the child with a job, as important for the feeling of responsibility involved, as for the independent earnings that ensue.

This is a topic that is hard to discuss, since our predecessors had to campaign against the exploitation of children, since trade unionists have had to claim that child labour is used as a cheap substitute for that of adults, and since teachers are accustomed to complain that the reason why some child falls asleep in class is not through watching night-time television, but through the early morning paper round or cleaning job. Children themselves tell a different story, which is one of pride in the responsibilities accorded to them, and their feelings of satisfaction in a task accomplished and their right to the income it brings. The issue has, of course, to be seen in a world context. Peter Lee-Wright conducted a television examination of the way in which the rich world's consumers are dependent on the labour of sixty million child workers. He later wrote a book with detailed accounts of his interviews, in several continents. One interview encapsulates both the admiration we feel for the resourcefulness of child workers, and our fears for their safety. This was at the Ataturk Sanayi Siksi workshop in Istanbul, where:

> Ahmet, 13, and Emit, 14, are normally working late, cutting and arc-welding fuel tanks from quarter-inch steel plate. These small boys handle the heavy metal and the lethal power of the welding torch with insouciant ease. The earthing wire is casually dropped on to the base plate as the intense blue flame fuses the panels together. Just weeks before, their boss had kicked the wire away and was still in hospital with the burns received from the resulting near-fatal shock. The boys did not anticipate making the same mistake, and professed to be happy with their work, despite a 55-hour week, for which they made 20,000 Turkish lira (£6.50) each. Certainly in their case, the pride of a craft well done and a considerable amount of self-determination made them appear fulfilled in their work. Both expressed the wish to own a workshop of their own in due course, and Emit surprised us by saying how sorry he felt for African children who starved 'and were not lucky enough to work like us'. Not so many children have such realistic ambitions or such global awareness. But if they were unlucky enough to have the same accident befall them as their boss, they would not be entitled to treatment, since they cannot be legally registered. (Lee-Wright, 1990)

The story, and the manner of its telling, illustrate our mixed feelings about the economic lives of children. We are likely to conclude that our ethical objection to their undertaking both the kind of work and the hours of labour described, is that those boys had been 'deprived of their childhood'. By this we mean, not only that play as an end in itself is the proper business of children, but that between the ages of 5 and 16 the child should be occupied in institutionalized education between prescribed hours. We feel that these are years properly devoted to exploring our own potentialities, our relationships with others in the great art of living together, our physical environment and above all, our own enlarging autonomy and independence.

These various definitions of the criteria we use to shape our attitude to child labour apply with equal force to another measure of the extent to which children are 'deprived of their childhood'. This concerns the age at which children are granted freedom of movement to travel and use public facilities unaccompanied by adults. Somehow this topic arouses less adult emotion than the idea of children being gainfully employed. A recent study unearthed the history of a forgotten group of children from the nineteenth century: Italian street musicians in Paris, London and New York. They came from poverty-stricken mountain villages, specializing in the manufacture of hurdy-gurdies, barrel organs, fiddles and harps, whose children were sent off to the world's cities, walking, except for sea crossings, often taking monkeys and white mice with them, and sending back the postal orders that kept the family alive back home. Moral crusades were mounted in the host cities and this trade in children was brought to an end, although 'opponents showed no concern for Italian child glass workers and sulphur miners subject to far worse conditions' (Zucchi, 1992). The modern reader, with contemporary perceptions of the capacities of children, finds it hard to imagine how these children survived at all, even though we read, every day, reports of campaigns in Latin American cities, to murder street children because their presence is an embarrassment to trade and to the tourist industry.

But children in families with a secure income once had the freedom of the street in ways we find inconceivable today. I found in several countries, while addressing teachers and students on the urban environment as a learning experience, that they would dig into their bags and briefcases and produce a reprint on translation of an article by Albert Parr about 'The happy habitat'. Dr. Parr was the former director of the American Museum of Natural History, who in his retirement became a campaigner for a more diversified and interesting street scene than the one we know, which is a commercial townscape redeveloped for the benefit of the out-of-town, male, middle-aged and middle-class motorist. He died in his nineties in 1991. The passage that we all remembered was his account of the environmental diversity of a small Norwegian port, Stavanger, in his childhood:

Not as a chore, but as an eagerly desired pleasure, I was often entrusted with the task of buying fish and bringing it home alone. This involved the following: walking to the station in five to ten minutes; buying a ticket; watching train with coal-burning steam locomotive

pull in; boarding train; riding across long bridge over shallows separating small-boat harbour (on the right) from ship's harbour (on the
left), including small naval base with torpedo boats; continuing through
a tunnel; leaving train at terminal, sometimes dawdling to look at
railroad equipment; walking by and sometimes entering fisheries
museum; passing central town park where military band played during mid-day break; strolling by central shopping and business district,
or, alternatively passing fire station with horses at ease under suspended harnesses, ready to go, and continuing past centuries-old town
hall and other ancient buildings; exploration of fish market and fishing
fleet; selection of fish; haggling about price; purchase and return home.
(Parr, 1972)

The important thing about his story is that Parr was 4 years old at the
time. We all seized upon this tale as anecdotal evidence of the fact that the
deformation of cities and towns to meet the demands of the motorist has
stolen childhood experience from every subsequent generation of children.
The most recent reproduction I have seen of Parr's recollection was in a
journal that reprinted it without comment juxtaposed with a quotation from
a book of rhyming survival tips for the nineties child: 'Never play with foot-
balls in the middle of the street/Don't take anything from strangers — money,
games or sweets' (Simeon and Stewart, 1992). The item was headed 'Progress
of enclosure', linking the historic private sequestration of common ground
with the situation of the contemporary child with considerably less unaccompanied access to public space in today's environment than was taken for
granted by earlier generations.

This deferment of independent access to anywhere outside the home can
be verified in conversation with different generations of any family. Ask a
grandparent, a parent or a child, the age at which they were first allowed to
play in the street, to go on an errand, or to the local park, or ride their
bicycles unaccompanied, and the age of independence gets higher in every
generation. An attempt was made to evaluate this in 1971, with a comparison
in 1990 in five areas of England, replicated by a study in West German
schools. The researcher, Mayer Hillman, explained the work in terms of the
idea that 'universal' car ownership was a guarantee of personal mobility:

In a statement about the role of the car in today's society, travel
was described by Paul Channon, a former Transport Secretary, as 'a
barometer of personal independence'. Measured by this barometer,
there has been a marked improvement in personal independence
over the last two decades for those adults who have acquired cars.
What happens if *children's* personal independence is measured on
this barometer? The study . . . approached this issue through the
medium of perceptions of safety as reflected in parental regulation of
their children's freedom to get around on their own, and the resulting

effect both on children's and parent's patterns of activity. The research was given a temporal dimension by focussing on changes during the two decades in the six 'licences' given to children by their parents — to cross roads, use buses, go to school and other places on their own, to cycle on the public highway, and to go out after dark. (Hillman, 1993)

The conclusions that these surveys reported were that 9½-year olds in 1990 had typically the same freedom of movement that 7-year-olds did in 1971. And the authors of the survey report noted that this change had happened 'largely ... unremarked and unresisted' and that 'children have lost out ... without society apparently noticing' (Hillman, Adams and Whitelegg, 1991). Their findings are that:

Whereas nearly three-quarters of the children in 1971 were allowed to cross roads on their own, by 1990 the proportion had fallen to a half. There was an even more marked decline in the proportion allowed to use buses on their own: half were allowed to do so in 1971 in contrast to only one in seven in 1990. In comparing the proportion of children allowed to cycle on the roads, it should be noted that, whereas two-thirds owned a bicycle in 1971, ownership had increased to nine in ten by 1990. However, two-thirds of the cycle owners in 1971 said that they were allowed to use them on the roads: by 1990, this proportion had fallen to only a quarter. Perhaps, most disturbingly, very few children are allowed out after dark by their parents — effectively a curfew for them. Younger children are most affected, with the difference, as would be expected, declining with age: few 11 or 12-year-olds now or indeed then would accept such restrictions on their independence. Although more journeys are made for social and recreational purpose than for school, only about half of the 7 to 10-year-olds who were allowed to go to these places on their own in 1971 were allowed to do so in 1990. And no parents of the 7-year-olds allow their children to go out alone after dark, a restriction that is removed only for 6 per cent of the 11-year-olds. (Hillman, 1993)

It was found that the comparable German children had much greater freedom and that the gender distinctions that in England allowed far more independence to boys than to girls, were far less evident in Germany, apart from that of being allowed out after dark. Parents in England tended to give the unreliability of their children or the fear of their being assaulted or molested by an adult as the reason for restriction of their independent mobility, but traffic dangers were more frequently cited by the German parents. Some kind of balance has to be struck. But does it lie in yet more restriction of children's freedom of movement or in 'taming' traffic? Mayer Hillman tentatively asks a key question, which is whether 'the damaging outcomes of the growing parental restrictions on children revealed in our surveys may be associated with some of the anti-social behaviour observed among the current generation of teenagers?'

Earlier investigators of the experience of childhood, John and Elizabeth Newson, found that they got an instant response to the very simple question, 'Would you call him/her an indoor or an outdoor child?' Mothers responded with answers that revealed both class and sex differences in their 7-year-olds (Newson and Newson, 1978). Today it is almost taken for granted that to have an outdoor child means endless worry and trouble. The outdoor child is up to no good. The indoor child takes advantage of the same home-centred lifestyle enjoyed by adults: central heating, television with an infinite choice of channels or videos, computers and computer games. Our assumption of course is that the child has access to all these alternatives to traditional experiences in a wider environment, or will find them in the homes of more affluent friends.

But if we are attempting to evaluate the opportunities for childhoods in late twentieth-century Britain we are bound to conclude that something precious has been lost in the range of environmental experiences open to children. The press reported in 1993 on the case of a 14-year-old with thirty-eight convictions for burglary who had absconded for the thirty-sixth time from a children's home. He was nicknamed Rat Boy, because he had developed the habit, like an urban jungle child, of making a lair for himself in the heating ducts of high buildings. Somehow adult choices have created a world in which we only trust the indoor child, safely at home with all that consumer software. The outdoor child is automatically suspect, often for very good reason. Is that the children's fault or ours?

10 Childhood as a Mode of Production

David Oldman

Introduction

A recent cartoon in *The Guardian* consisted of three separate sketches arranged along a diagonal ladder. The topmost sketch showed a man, the *pater familias*, fleeing from the home, heading for his workplace with his briefcase and papers in his hand. He is looking over his shoulder and down at the second sketch — identical except that it is the wife and mother who is similarly dashing out of the door. She, in her turn, looks back and down at the third sketch, composed of two tearful children. She is waving her handkerchief, to show her more direct involvement with the deprived children. The cartoon (Krauze, 1993) was drawn to accompany an article giving publicity to the recent study by Patricia Hewitt and Penelope Leach (1993), which argues that social justice for children begins in the home, but is impossible without a national policy of support for parenting. Such a policy must recognize the reality of modern labour markets, and the real costs of bringing up children.

The cartoon encapsulates beautifully the interplay of three systems of differential power and corresponding inequality — employers and employees, husbands and wives (or, more generally, gender within the domestic economy), and adults and children. Notice that I have called the third system 'adults and children' rather than 'parents and children'. If the cartoon has a limitation, it is one which it shares with the article that it illustrates and that is its particular emphasis on the family home. They locate the key site for the interplay of the three stratification systems in the relationships between parents and their own children. Important though this site is, it is not the only one. Relationships within the school would be another obvious example. In what follows, I shall concentrate on an analysis of this 'third stratification system', which for the moment I shall simply label as 'adults and children'. In its interplay with the other two stratification systems of employment and gender, it will, as one of its manifestations, produce a system of social relationships that we might recognize as modern parenting, but it will help to shape other systems of relationships as well. Correspondingly, analyses of parenting and current family and household forms must involve a closer look at how adults and children form a stratification system, if indeed they can be considered so to do. But an undue concentration on *parents* and children runs the risk of becoming enmeshed in a family ideology which sees the child as having no other economic role than that of dependent, and no other social role than that of an object of care and concern (or their opposites, abuse and neglect). Many observers have complained about this 'invisibility' of the child within the family. The recent project Childhood as a Social Phenomenon, based at the European Centre, in Vienna, has attempted to combat this 'invisibility'. Participants from sixteen countries produced a series of national reports and a collection of theoretical papers (Qvortrup *et al.*, 1994). As one of the participants and as a contributor to the final volume, I made a start on this problem of how children fit into a multi-dimensional stratification system (Oldman, 1994). This chapter reworks the material of the earlier one, in the light of more recent, and British, developments, and in the light of criticisms received (Furstenberg, 1993; Dumon, 1993; Wintersberger, 1992).

My claim is that children constitute rather more than a minority group defined by an absence of rights (Sgritta and Saporiti, 1989), although minority group status is certainly an emergent feature of childhood. I suggest that we might consider adults and children as constituting *classes*, in the sense of being social categories which exist principally by their *economic* opposition to each other, and in the ability of the dominant class (adults) to exploit economically the activities of the subordinate class (children). Obviously, this will require some justification, which I hope it will receive in the sections that follow. For the time being, I want merely to point to the fact that I shall be exploring childhood through the value that children's activity can have for adults. Thus, to recapitulate, childhood is to be defined by its opposition to adulthood, and the family is but one site amongst others in which this opposition finds expression. It may not even be the most important one. This perspective is an attempt to tackle the question formulated by Jens Qvortrup, as follows:

> The question that should be raised is therefore whether there are any objective socio-economic grounds for the general attitude of adult society towards children. (Qvortrup, 1987)

Childwork

Dumon (1993) has detected a conceptual weakness in the Childhood as a Social Phenomenon project in that the attempt to rescue the 'child' from its definition within a kinship system has left the social location of this category 'child' fatally vague. Opposing the category 'child' to that of 'adult' seems to presume a set of relationships defined by age, and yet, as we know, age-related rights for children and the age-related behaviour of children varies enormously within and between societies, albeit always the subject of vigorous debate and moral panic. Yet it is this diversity, and the active concern of adults to monitor and control what children can do, and what they actually do, which form the social relationships that define my 'third stratification system'. Age-related rights and obligations imply some notion of immaturity operating below whatever age is in question, and a further notion that children must acquire the skills, knowledge, experience and character to justify their attainment of a degree of adulthood. Adults control the process of 'growing up', and herein lies its economic significance.

Children create *childwork*, that is, work done by adults on the organization and control of child activities. I want to make clear that childwork is adult work, not work done by children ('children's work'). I want to use the term 'childwork' because of its theoretical closeness to 'housework', and even 'shitwork', the evocative term used by some feminist writers to describe the low-status labour involved in the care and maintenance of others. In childwork, the child is the object of others' labour, whether paid or unpaid. At the same time, however, the child is an active subject. More precisely, it is the child's activity, the child's own labour, which becomes the object of adult labour. Childwork provides the means of subsistence for a significant proportion of the adult population.

A feature of childwork is the reduction of the child to a psychological or pedagogical 'object', and one that is in the process of 'becoming' not 'being'. This emphasis on development is itself a sociological phenomenon of interest and is part of the 'normalization' of childhood by which the cultural rules for the perception and definition of children are given social legitimation and their manifest sense of 'obviousness' (Sgritta, 1987). The reduction of the child to a self-evident developing personality, or to a half-empty container for knowledge, could be seen to be the ideological representation of an underlying state of affairs in which the class that is childhood is characterized by an essential and inevitable 100 per cent individual upward social mobility (children grow up!). Children's activities are thus categorized and then organized with this feature in mind. One can say that child activity is integral to the reproduction of adult society, but to say this is to say far more than that today's children form the next generation of workers. What is being claimed here, is that their 'growing up' is constituted as a pattern of activities that define, and are defined by, many of the private profit-making service industries, provide many jobs in the public sector, and which also form part of adults' leisure and consumer choices. This activity, 'growing up', creates value both for children, in that it provides them with the human capital they will require for investing in their own adult labour, but also for adults, in that it provides the rationale for the wages and salaries of childwork. If we can show that the value to adults grows at the expense of the value to children, then it becomes possible to talk of exploitative relationships between adults and children. These would be the hallmark of what we might call a 'generational' mode of production. What is being 'produced' is human capital through the activity of children, but much of its value is expropriated by adults.

The rules that constitute 'normalization' are also the rules around which childwork is both instituted and professionalized. The exploitability of children, as a class, will depend upon the maintenance of complex, and perhaps increasingly complex, theories of individual development and the bodies of skill and expertise that are associated with them. To give a crude example, a child psychiatrist earns more than a care-assistant in a children's home, yet both may be working with the same raw material of a particular child's behaviour. The professionalization of psychiatry allows a greater exploitation of that same behaviour than is available to the relatively 'unskilled' worker. What I am arguing here, then, is that the techniques of normalization are the achievements of class fractions of adults, whose power to exploit the activities of children is greater than that of other fractions. Professionalization is a good example of this process at work. It is difficult to find a convincing explanation of the pressure for increased professionalization in terms of any objective demonstration of increasing danger to children. The increased sensitivity to children's needs, and the successive discoveries of high prevalence of non-accidental injury and sexual abuse of children seem to be almost entirely an organizational product. If this is indeed so, the growth of child protection work must be explained by changes in the adult labour market and in the credentials offered to that labour market, not in any recent change in the conditions of childhood itself (Parton, 1985). As Heyns (1991) points out, there is almost no rational connection between the growth (or cut-back) in service provision to children and any calculation of their needs.

The invisibility of the child within the family, and within family-oriented statistics (Saporiti, 1994), is paralleled by a generally increasing visibility of the child outside the family, through the proliferation of forms of childwork. The correlates of this proliferation, in Western countries, are the well documented decline in family size, the decline in the proportion of children in the population, the rise of service industries relative to manufacturing industries, and the increasing proportion of women in the labour market. In Britain, particularly, women's jobs tend to be part-time and so exacerbate the double burden that women face — of being committed to both paid employment and unpaid domestic labour. During 1994, the number of women in the British labour market will come to exceed that of men. The question becomes whether this increases the significance of childwork, or merely shows it to be representing itself in new forms. Another form of this question is whether family life is becoming generally less significant for children, or whether the family relationships in which children are involved are becoming more dominated by an economic calculus. Furstenberg (1993) has queried the thesis of the declining role of parents, pointing out that there is very little hard evidence for it. I certainly agree that there is a clear need for more research into the nature and amount of paid childwork outside the family setting, but I think that there is little doubt that not only do children spend less time in the company of one or other parent than, say, a generation ago, but that there has also been a qualitative shift in the kinds of control exercised by parents over children. Whilst moral panics are poor indicators of the reality of the changes they lament, they usually indicate that some change is in the offing. The current obsession with the violence of uncontrolled and uncontrollable children seems to show that people are having to face up to some mismatch between ideology and reality.

This section has suggested that adult control over children's activity has become more self-evidently about the creation of paid employment for adults, and that this allows us to highlight what might be considered as an underlying situation of class conflict and exploitative relations between adults and children. Before proceeding any further, it is important to discuss how far I am arguing for a more comprehensive theory of stratification, or whether I am merely flagging certain relatively ignored issues of childhood for discussion by the use of a metaphor of class drawn from a quite separate area of social analysis.

The Limits of Class Analysis

A theory of class, in the Marxist sense, is also a theory of social change applicable to the level of the total society. Class conflict provides the motor of social change. Moreover, a class analysis proper is the analysis of a particular mode of production, or combination of modes of production, each with their distinctive modes of exploitation of the economic value of the labour of subordinate classes by dominant classes. If adults and children are to be conceptualized as classes, it has to be decided whether we are claiming that they are classes in a separate mode of production, such as might be claimed for husbands and housewives in a domestic mode of production (Walby, 1986; Delphy and Leonard, 1986). If they do constitute a separate 'generational' mode of production, then what is being produced is the human capital that children acquire through their activities in school, home or street. If we can talk of such a mode of production then we must examine how it articulates with the capitalist and domestic modes already well documented and analyzed.

Some criticism of the possibility of incorporating both gender and age into a theory of stratification can, perhaps be forestalled. Critics of the view that patriarchy is a crucial component of stratification (Goldthorpe, 1983; Lockwood, 1986) argue that women, and presumably by extension, children, appear to have made no difference to the overall shape of economic classes or to how that shape has changed since the emergence of fully-fledged capitalist societies from the seventeenth century onwards. But it depends on one's initial question. Delphy and Leonard (1986) argue that the critics' point is only valid if it is economic classes in a narrow sense that are the focus of analysis. Since economic classes, as hitherto defined, are oppositions between groups of working men, it is hardly surprising that women and children seem irrelevant. In the history of the continuing oppression of women, and by analogy the history of childhood, it is men's classes that are irrelevant. I accept the general point, if not the specifics of women's argument. The initial question is crucial, but should centre around whether we are interested in the fact of stability of strata, or their instability. It could be argued against Goldthorpe and Lockwood that the contribution of women and children has been to slow down the pace of change, and thereby they are just as crucial to a theory of stratification as if they had been powerful agents for change in history. What is crucial for an overall theory of stratification is the identification of the different kinds of economic production in a given society, the social relations characteristic of each kind of production, the categories of actor as defined by those relations of production, and the interrelationships between the separate modes of production.

An alternative approach would be a more traditional one, and would claim that the social relations of the family, the school, and the child agencies are the relations of *reproduction* of the capitalist mode of production. But let me say at once that I think this perspective is unduly limiting. To begin with, whatever is 'reproduced' by children growing up is the full complexity of adult society and not merely its economy. Put crudely, children grow up to become parents and home makers, as well as players in a labour market. Second, it will often prove quite hard to argue that a particular form of organization and control, or lack of control, over children's activity has some direct and obvious *reproductive* function for the social relations of capitalism, whereas it may well have some direct and obvious input into the well-being of some fraction of the present generation of adults. Childminding would be a fairly good example of this. On the one hand it flourishes because it makes large numbers of mothers available for low paid work — thus enhancing the exploitative possibilities of modern capitalism — yet, at the same time, it is a service industry of small-scale entrepreneurship which provides a certain level of income, however small, for women through the medium of the active nature of children. I have chosen this example precisely because it is going to be very hard to see childminding as *exploitative* of children in the sense that the minders gain at the children's expense. It can, and has been, criticized for providing a level of care for children that we feel is often less than ideal, or even less than adequate, but this is not the same thing as claiming it to be exploitative in a class sense. What I shall try to argue in a later section is that childminding is enmeshed in an exploitative class-like system in that when, with the best of motives, we try to improve the level of care in the interests of the children's development, we find it hard to prove that increased resources actually benefit the children more than the adults. In other institutions, such as child protection, it is actually claimed that increased resources have disadvantaged children (King and Trowell, 1992).

A third possible way of seeing adult-child relations as class relations is to deny any attempt to integrate them into a theory of stratification, and simply use the metaphorical strength of the concepts of class to highlight certain features of childhood which might otherwise have been ignored. A recent feature article in *The Guardian* newspaper shows that the metaphorical use of class has a polemical force that is well understood. In a critique of the recent emphasis on children's rights, the author equates a concern for rights with a confrontational view of the relations between children and adults (Bennett, 1994). One of her anxieties about such a view of childhood is that it encourages children to be oppositional, and she quotes concerned policemen and teachers who have become aware of a new militancy in children — a militancy which trades on the language of exploitation and deprivation in which the claim for rights is expressed. But this analysis reduces class to confrontational attitudes, and ignores the possibility that children might indeed suffer from material exploitation in the interests of adults. For the time being, therefore, I will remain with the theoretical status of adults and children as classes, and will explore further the explanatory value of a theory of class as applied to the relations between the generations.

Modern class analysis has abandoned the unidirectional view of social change through the increasing polarization of class conflict, in favour of an attempt to understand an increasingly diverse set of 'contradictory class locations' in capitalist society. The work of Wright and Roemer has restored the notion of exploitation to the centre of class analysis, but has given it a multi-dimensional character (Roemer, 1982; Wright, 1985). Exploitation has acquired a game-theoretic character, and is defined as a state of affairs whereby the 'exploited' would be better off, and the 'exploiters' worse off, if the former were to withdraw their productive assets (whatever they may be) from the relation of productions in which they are involved. Assets, under capitalism, are the ownership of the means of production, productive skills, and organizational control. It is the last of these, the control of organizational assets, which will prove most useful in understanding the exploitative character of adults' relations with children.

Exploitation Under a Generational Mode of Production — The Case of Schooling

To illustrate the nature of exploitation via the control of 'organizational assets', let us look at the example of teachers and children. Where, it seems to me, that children's labour can be said to be exploited through the agency of teachers in a compulsory school setting is through the maintenance of an essentially undemocratic organization of classroom activity. Children are deliberately limited in the range of self-capitalization that they can undertake, and there is no way that each individual child could be said to have an optimal learning environment. First and foremost, this is because the bulk of resources put into the organization of schooling goes in the direction of teachers' salaries, rather than as direct service provision to children. As a consequence, the high pupil-teacher ratios and the shortage of educational materials mean that teachers are forced to implement forms of classroom organisation that prevent each child from maximizing his/her educational opportunity. It can be quite hard to take this point seriously, although it was often argued by the radical critics of schooling of the 1960s.

What I want to make absolutely clear at this point is that I am *not* arguing that teachers should be paid less or that, as an occupational group, they work to exploit the children in their care. Teachers have enough problems at present dealing with a hostile government to have to defend themselves against charges of exploiting children in their own interests. What I would argue is that teachers are caught up in a system of essentially exploitative relationships that are a product of the interaction of the three types of stratification I mentioned in the introduction — employment, gender and generation. The result is that, *de facto*, their working conditions and remuneration can only be salvaged to anything like a tolerable level through having to accept less than optimal conditions for the self-capitalization of children. The fact of over-large classes is perhaps the most obvious example. And one never quite loses the feeling that the alienation in most children's experience of school (characterized by the subjective feelings of boredom and irrelevance, and by occasional attempts at subversion) is generated by those organizational features of schooling that the staff are compelled to use in order to rationalize and justify the salaries they take from the system (compulsory and regular attendance, timetables, examinations, syllabuses, maintained equipment, and so-on). These are the features that create manageable working conditions for teachers, and legitimacy in public opinion, and are not necessarily the optimal conditions for the self-capitalization of each child.

My argument is that much of the value of children's scholastic labour is realized, in the present, by the childwork it represents — work by teachers, ancillary staff in schools, educational administrators, and so on — and in most educational systems this value is realized merely through the presence of a disciplined child in the classroom, and is relatively independent of the degree of success of the self-capitalization of the child through his/her school work. It is not surprising that there is only the most tenuous connection between educational expenditure (expressed mostly as salaries) and educational output (expressed as the achievements of children). Hence the bitter struggle in Britain at present between the Government, who are trying to reduce public expenditure (and the value of childwork) and simultaneously raise the amount of self-capitalization by children by imposing more structured teaching and assessment, and the teaching profession who are trying to maintain the value of their childwork and, at the same time, preserve their professional autonomy. That this battle can take place at all is due to the absence of any rigorous relationship between the value extracted from children's work in the short-term, and the long-term value of the human capital acquired by the children through their own efforts. The present Government also believes that it can restore reality to what is, at heart, an ideological argument, by reversing the usual assumption that there ought to be some causal connection between expenditure on education and the human capital created. It believes that the publication of the scholastic achievements of pupils will attract parental productive assets to those schools that show the highest achievements, thus trading on the obvious fact that middle-class parents will invest more in middle-class schools. We are effectively returning to a system of 'payment by results', and the nature of the exploitation of children's scholastic labour might change. Just as in late nineteenth century elementary education, the value extracted by childworkers will depend on the skills of the most successful children — instead of merely the compliance of all children — and we can predict that, just as in the 1880s, the total amount of human capital created, as measured by statistics of educational achievement, will fall.

If we then ask who are the immediate losers, the answer must be the children. The long-term value of their human capital, when realized in an increasingly international labour market, will be less — both directly, in terms of their ability to trade credentials for wages, and indirectly, in that the overall success of the national economy is inherently at risk through 'under-capitalization' in the human sense. At the same time, the present generation of childworkers are forced to try to increase both status and income by direct and targeted attraction of parental assets.

The particular form of exploitation, under this scenario, becomes the maintenance of a low average level of achievement for children, and the use of the achievements of a selected few as indicative for claims for enhanced resourcing of childwork. The 'few' concerned tend to be precisely those children who bring to the school system significant amounts of cultural and economic capital generated within their families of origin.

Exploitation in a Generational Mode of Production — The Case of Childcare

The next area of childwork to be examined is the supervision of children outside school. Childcare is a major issue in all Western countries. It is nearly always the case that provision is less than that required, under-invested through the public purse, and seen ultimately as a parental responsibility. The extent of these features, of course, varies from country to country, but there is more or less general agreement that childcare increasingly takes place outside the nuclear family, and that this is largely due to the still-increasing incorporation of mothers into the labour force. One also notes that childcare by siblings and grandparents is increasingly problematic because of smaller family sizes and the particularly high rates of economic activity of middle-aged women. What seems to be missing from most of these analyses is any recognition that a fair proportion of the paid work that mothers do is childwork, and that, of course, includes childcare — either as nursery teachers, crèche attendants, registered and unregistered childminders, and so on. A reasonable conclusion, then, is that as children are increasingly cared for by non-family members who draw some direct economic advantage from doing it, so the nature and meaning of that care will be increasingly dominated by the need to maximize the earning power of the carer.

In Britain, if nowhere else, childcare and child health services, far from being, as the Government claims, targeted at those most in need, tend to be increasingly privatized and marketed towards just those children whose need is actually least, or whose 'need' demonstrates the value of high status professional knowledge and advanced technology (as in children's hospitals). Thus the self-disciplined child, and the dramatically ill child (rather than the chronically impaired or deprived child), provide the most value to childwork, whilst those children who have potentially most to gain from childwork are progressively ignored. This skewing of resources away from the most needy children, both in schooling and in childcare, is a very distinctive form of exploitation within the generational mode of production.

Within this framework of exploitation, come all the arguments as to what is the best kind of care for children. It has become almost impossible to extract the pros and cons of this debate from their ideological context. The immediate post-war history of the debate is well documented in Riley (1983). In this period, the ideological battle centred on the woman's right to work, but in its most recent versions, as in the work of Hewitt and Leach (1993), the battleground has shifted slightly so as to include the rights of children to the best possible conditions for their development. Thus, what might have been seen as once largely a form of class-conflict within a domestic mode of production, now includes a new form of class-conflict within a generational mode of production. The two forms interpenetrate in varied and complex ways, but the overall effect is to ensure that women and children cannot easily improve their lot together.

When I argue that the commercialization of childcare is essentially exploitative of children, I do, of course, recognize that those women who get paid for looking after children are themselves excessively exploited. But their exploitation comes from the interplay of capitalism and patriarchy. The force of the cartoon I described in the introduction comes from its suggestion that children are triply exploited — by capitalism, patriarchy and generation. This is actually too simplistic. Mothers, whether childworkers or not, can and do often act in the interests of children, in the sense that they try very hard to optimize the conditions under which children grow up. That is, in the terms of this chapter, they act as *class agents* on behalf of children. However, they can do so only by ceasing to be effective agents on behalf of their own class position within either the capitalist or domestic mode of production. Something of this dilemma can be seen in yet another article from *The Guardian* (Langdon, 1993). Here, the author, who works as a journalist, is describing the problems she had when she hired a nanny for her children. The young woman she employed not only seemed inadequate as a nanny, but also stole from her employer, and was portrayed as being in the grip of massive social and psychological pathology. The author claims her experience as an employer is not untypical. The tension between the two is graphically depicted in the sub-title, 'Jayne had the self-belief of the successful confidence trick-ster. She was mad, bad and dangerous to know — and the children called her nanny'. Readers' letters to the paper in response to the article showed little sympathy for the author; she had clearly challenged the conventional way in which mothers struggle to serve both their gender and their children. That is, she chose to promote the two sets of interests in a quite distinctive way. First, she maintained her right as an employer to extract value from the labour of her employee, ignoring what they might share as women employees. Thus, she acted on behalf of her children by reacting strongly to the admittedly unconventional and illegal attempts by the childworker to exploit the childwork situation. By taking this position, she challenged the 'impossible' burden of simultaneously trying to improve the lot of both children and childworker. Notice, though, that she did not try to challenge the position of her own employer, or the position of the father of the children. What this example shows is how difficult concerted or collective action is for women who are trapped in contradictory locations in this three-dimensional stratification system.

The Generational Mode of Production Elaborated

I think there is a case for saying that adult-child relations are relations of production in which the labour of one class (children) is exploited by another (adults). It is a big claim to make, but it amounts to saying that the quality of life enjoyed by adults is enhanced by their control over the process of growing up that constitutes the activities of childhood, and that the quality of life for children as they grow up is thereby reduced. That is the nature of the exploitation of one class by the other.

The claim for a generational mode of production of human capital answers a criticism, already levelled at an earlier draft of this chapter, to the effect that children are no different from the elderly, or any ethnic minority group, in their tendency to generate high status service work for others. The essential difference between children and the elderly or the ethnic minorities is that children and their childworkers are engaged in a distinctive type of production, that of making or preserving human capital in the minds and bodies of the children themselves. Thus, 'childworkers' and 'child workers' are constituted, as categories, by the relations of production, and this is not true of the 'elderly' or the 'black'. Of course, adults capitalize themselves as well as do children, just as both managers and workers under capitalism are wage-earners, but this does not affect the distinctiveness of the relations between managers and workers, on the one hand, nor between children and adults, on the other. A further criticism which might be levelled at my ap-proach, and also at the notion of a domestic mode of production, is that just as not all women are housewives, nor all domestic labourers women, so only few adults do childwork, and children do many other things than self-capitalize themselves. But this is equivalent to arguing for the inappropriateness of conventional class analysis on the grounds that some workers own capital, some workers are unemployed, and some capitalists may labour. It is important to remember that the relations of production exist independently of the particular actors involved, and any one person may occupy more than one site in more than one mode of production. It should be clear from my analysis so far that I regard the concept of class as an analytic and relational concept: it does not define empirical aggregates of people.

Child labour is exploited through the superiority of childworkers' organizational assets, in Wright's (1985) terms. The proof of exploitation should ideally lie in the demonstration that if children's schooling and the care of children were to be organized in a truly democratic fashion, then children would acquire a greater amount (value) of human capital, and adults would get less income or status out of childwork. This was, of course, a central tenet of 1960s educational radicalism, but since this was essentially a political stance, rather than an economic analysis, it failed to provide itself with a demonstrable material base. Perhaps this demonstration is inherently impossible. One would somehow have to conduct a mental experiment that would compare the loss in wages and salaries earned by adults through abandoning their control over their childwork with the human capital gained by children once they shared control with childworkers and were simply able to use their superior expertise. Even if such a calculation was possible, the result might well show that children were not, in fact, exploited. However, I want to draw attention to the point I made in the previous paragraph about the built-in alienated quality of much of children's experience. One suspects that most children, at most times, would rather be doing something other than what we, as adults, are making them do. Of course, we have to argue that what we make them do is in their own best interests but, interestingly, the quantitative proof of this argument is just as hard and just as immeasurable as the proof of exploitation. Both rely on mental experiments about states of affairs that are not going to materialize, because we as adults are not going to allow them to happen.

Perhaps the best argument for exploitation in the essential relationship between adult and child is the knowledge that the form of that relationship is more easily demonstrated to be some feature of the adult labour market that is concerned with the preservation or enhancement of jobs in childwork, than it is to be some provable consequence from some theory of child development or education. It is worth considering the proposition that nothing 'normal' that children do is not in the short-term economic interest of the adults that supervise it. My claim to the essentially exploitative relationship between childwork and children's activity is, first, the relatively weak one that any gain in the value of childwork (or political pressure to achieve such gain) is not accompanied by any measurable gain or loss in the value of the human capital attained by children. Thus, children are, per se, the objects of childwork, and the activities of children are often largely irrelevant. But I do have, in addition, a claim to a stronger version of exploitation. Childworkers in education bid for higher income and status through the production of highly *selective* results. Teaching status has always depended to a large extent on the demonstration of achievement by a minority of children, and precisely those children for whom childwork is less necessary. For 'clever' children or 'motivated' children, self-capitalization, whether cultural or economic, is largely assured by their class position within capitalism (Bourdieu and Passeron, 1977). Similarly, the childcare that gives high income and status is limited to the few children whose parents can pay, or who are 'rewarding' because they allow the exercise of professional knowledge and skills.

Finally, I want to make a few remarks about the relations between modes of production. We are talking of the possibility of articulation among three quite separate modes of production: a capitalist mode in which owners, managers and administrators exploit the labour of workers in the production of goods for the market: a patriarchal mode in which husbands exploit the labour of wives in the domestic production of goods and services within the family: finally, a generational mode in which adults exploit the labour of children in the production of the human capital that constitutes the process of growing up. The essential feature of the articulation of these three modes is that each can be considered as contributing to the reproduction of the others.

Much has been written on the way in which patriarchy serves capitalism, usually through the argument that domestic labour reproduces industrial labour at a cheaper rate than could be achieved by industry itself. In the same way, the self-capitalizing labour of children is structured so as to assist the reproduction of both industrial labour power (through differentiated schooling) and female domestic labour power (through the culture of femininity engendered in girls both formally, informally and even counter-culturally). But the relations of capitalist production themselves have reproductive functions for the other modes. It is the middle-class's own attempts to reproduce its advantages for itself through the generations that produces much of the childwork that allows the exploitation of children's self-capitalization. Childwork is predominantly middle-class work and, at the same time, its benefits are expropriated disproportionately by middle-class families. Last but not least, childwork is mostly done by women, yet managed by men. It is the power of men in families which structures much childwork as part-time work that is relatively low-paid, and taken by women who are not allowed to relinquish the demands for their domestic labour. It is reasonable to argue that this creates extremely inflexible conditions for most childwork, which correspondingly alienates further the child activity it exploits.

I am aware that this analysis must seem highly conservative in that it offers very little in the way of a theory of social change, or of any explanation of current social trends, nor provides any guidelines for policy or political action. But I think it provides an extra clue as to why the various forms of inequality prove so resistant to change. The generational mode of production, through its articulation with the other modes, stifles the development of effective class-based action. First, it has the potential to put every exploited adult, whether exploited as an employee or as a housewife, into a further contradictory class location through the possibility of becoming an exploiter of childwork. Second, children do not, of course, have the capacity to do much to further their own class interests and initiate major structural change. They cannot democratize the conditions of their self-capitalization: they cannot organize their own growing-up. They have to rely on adults as class agents, and we are not terribly reliable. To work for the interests of children is, so often, to do childwork and, as I have pointed out, this is first and foremost dominated by the interests of adults.

Notes on Contributors

Priscilla Alderson is a Senior Research Officer at the Social Science Research Unit, Institute of Education, University of London. Her PhD investigated parents' consent to children's heart surgery in two London hospitals. This was followed by a study of 120 children having orthopaedic surgery in London and Liverpool and their experiences of consent to surgery. She has also researched consent to breast cancer treatment and research, and information and decisions about childhood immunization.

Lise Bird is a Senior Lecturer in Education at Victoria University of Wellington in Aotearoa/New Zealand. She is currently writing a critique of issues in educational psychology from post-structural feminist viewpoints.

David Buckingham teaches in the Department of English, Media and Drama at the Institute of Education, University of London. He is currently conducting further research into children's use and understanding of television, and into classroom practice in media education. His publications include: *Public Secrets: 'EastEnders' and its Audience* (British Film Institute, 1987); *Watching Media Learning: Making Sense of Media Education* (Falmer Press, 1990); *Children Talking Television* (Falmer Press, 1993); and *Reading Audiences: Young People and the Media* (Manchester University Press, 1993).

Gunilla Halldén is Associate Professor at the Department of Education, University of Stockholm and at the Department of Child Studies, University of Linköping. She has carried out research on parental ideas and common sense psychology. Her work deals with the construction of childhood and of the 'good parent'. She is now studying concepts of parenthood and childhood from child and youth perspectives.

Gerison Lansdown is Director of the Children's Rights Development Unit. She was a social worker in the early seventies in Kirklees and in Liverpool and then worked at One Parent Families as a social worker/social policy officer. She taught social work for a couple of years and then moved to the National Association for CABs where she initially worked on the information system held by all bureaux and subsequently in the social policy unit and as their Parliamentary Liaison Officer. Her last post was with the London

Borough of Barnet producing their Community Care Plan. She was Chair of the Management Committee of Family Rights Group for several years, has also been on the Management Committees of One Parent Families, Maternity Alliance and Day Care Trust and has recently been elected onto the Executive Committee of Child Poverty Action Group.

Berry Mayall is Assistant Director of the Social Science Research Unit, Institute of Education, University of London. Her work has been concerned with divisions of labour between parents and others for the care and education of pre-school children, and more recently with children's participation in constructing and negotiating their daily lives.

Virginia Morrow is a Research Associate in the Centre for Family Research at the University of Cambridge, currently working on a literature review for a research project on transitions to adulthood. She completed her PhD in the Faculty of Social and Political Sciences, Cambridge in 1992 and is currently publishing a number of articles arising from her doctoral work. Her main areas of research interest are the sociology and anthropology of childhood and youth/adolescence. She is Director of Studies in Social and Political Sciences at Wolfson College, Cambridge, and teaches on the social and historical construction of childhood.

Ann Oakley is Director of the Social Science Research Unit, and Professor of Sociology and Social Policy at the University of London, Institute of Education. She has been researching in the fields of gender, the family and health for many years. Her books include: *The Sociology of Housework* (1974), *Becoming a Mother* (1979), *Subject Women* (1981), *The Captured Womb* (1984) and *Social Support and Motherhood*, (1992).

David Oldman is a psychotherapist in private practice in London and a part-time Senior Lecturer in Sociology in the Department of Sociology, University of Aberdeen.

Colin Ward is a writer with a background of architecture and further education. In the 1960s he edited the magazine *Anarchy* and in the 1970s he directed the Schools Council Project 'Art and the Built Environment'. His many books explore the relationship between people and their surroundings and include *The Child in the City* and *The Child in the Country*.

References

ADAMS, R. (1991) *Protests by Pupils*, Lewes, Falmer Press.

ALANEN, L. (1993) 'Standpoint in the sociological study of childhood', paper presented at the 17th Nordic Congress of Sociology, 13–15 August, Sweden, Gävle.

ALANEN, L. (1994) 'Gender and generation: Feminism and the "child question"', in QVORTRUP, J. *et al.* (Eds) *Childhood Matters: Social Theory, Practice and Politics*, Aldershot, Avebury Press.

ALANEN, L. and BARDY, M. (1991) *Childhood as a Social Phenomenon: National Report for Finland*, Eurosocial Report, 367, Vienna, European Centre.

ALDERSON, P. (1990) *Choosing for Children*, Oxford, Oxford University Press.

ALDERSON, P. (1992) 'Rights of children and young people', in COOTE, A. (Ed) *The Welfare of Citizens — Developing New Social Rights*, London, Institute for Public Policy Research/Rivers Oram Press.

ALDERSON, P. (1993) *Children's Consent to Surgery*, Buckingham/Philadelphia, Open University Press.

ALDRIDGE, J. and BECKER, S. (1993) *Children Who Care: Inside the World of Young Carers*, Loughborough, Loughborough University, Department of Social Sciences.

ANDERSON, J.A. (1981) 'Research on children and television: A critique', *Journal of Broadcasting*, 25, pp. 395–400.

APTER, T. (1990) *Altered Loves: Mothers and Daughters During Adolescence*, Hemel Hempstead, Harvester Wheatsheaf.

ARIES, P. (1979) *Centuries of Childhood*, Harmondsworth, Penguin.

BARKER, M. (1984a) *A Haunt of Fears*, London, Pluto.

BARKER, M. (1984b) (Ed) *The Video Nasties*, London, Pluto.

BARKER, M. (1989) *Comics: Ideology, Power and the Critics*, Manchester, Manchester University Press.

BARRETT, M. (1980) *Women's Oppression Today*, London, Verso.

BAUMEISTER, R.F. (1986) *Identity: Cultural Change and the Struggle for Self*, Oxford, Oxford University Press.

BEAUCHAMP, T. and CHILDRESS, J. (1983) *Principles of Biomedical Ethics*, New York, Oxford University Press.

BELENKY, M.B., CLINCHY, B.M., GOLDBERGER, N.R. and TARULE, J.M. (1986) *Women's Ways of Knowing*, New York, Basic Books.

BELOTTI, E.G. (1975) *Little Girls*, London, Writers and Readers Publishing Co-operative.

BENHABIB, S. (1987) 'The generalized and concrete other', in CORNELL, D. and BENHABIB, S. (Eds) *Feminism as Critique*, Oxford, Polity Press.

BENNETT, C. (1994) 'Underclass of 94', *The Guardian*, 16 March.

BETTELHEIM, B. (1971) *The Children of the Dream*, London, Paladin.

BIRD, L. (1992) 'Girls taking positions of authority at primary school', in MIDDLETON, S. and JONES, A. (Eds) *Women and Education in Aotearoa*, Vol 2. Wellington, Bridget Williams Books.

BIRKE, L. (1986) *Women, Feminism and Biology*, Brighton, Wheatsheaf Books.

BODEN, M. (1979) *Piaget*, London, Fontana Books.

References

BOULTON, M.G. (1983) *On Being a Mother*, London, Tavistock.

BOURDIEU, P. and PASSERON, J. (1977) *Reproduction in Education*, Society and Culture, London, Sage.

BOWLBY, J. (1964) *Childcare and the Growth of Love*, Harmondsworth, Penguin.

BRADLEY, B. (1989) *Visions of Infancy: A Critical Introduction to Child Psychology*, Cambridge, Polity Press.

BRANNEN, J. and WILSON, G. (1987) (Eds) *Give and Take in Families: Studies in Resource Distribution*, London, Allen and Unwin.

BROVERMAN, I., BROVERMAN, D., CLARKSON, F., ROSENKRANTZ, K. and VOGEL, S. (1970) 'Sex role stereotypes and clinical judgements of mental health', *Journal of Consulting and Clinical Psychology*, 34, pp. 1–7.

BROWN, J. and WEINER, B. (1984) 'Affective consequences of ability versus effort ascriptions: Controversies, resolutions, and quandaries', *Journal of Educational Psychology*, 76, 1, pp. 146–58.

BROWN, L. and GILLIGAN, C. (1993) 'Meeting at the crossroads: Women's psychology and girls' development', *Feminism & Psychology*, 3, 1, pp. 11–33.

BROWN, R. (1976) (Ed) *Children and Television*, London, Collier MacMillan.

BRYANT, J. and ANDERSON, D.R. (1983) (Eds) *Children's Understanding of Television*, New York, Academic Press.

BUCHANAN, A. and BROCK, D. (1989) *Deciding for Others: The Ethics of Surrogate Decision Making*, New York, Cambridge University Press, p. 220, quoting Piagetian psychologists.

BUCKINGHAM, D. (1987) *Public Secrets: 'EastEnders' and its Audience*, London, British Film Institute.

BUCKINGHAM, D. (1993a) *Children Talking Television: The Making of Television Literacy*, London, Falmer Press.

BUCKINGHAM, D. (1993b) (Ed) *Reading Audiences: Young People and the Media*, Manchester, Manchester University Press.

BURCHELL, B., ELLIOTT, B.J., RUBERY, J. and WILKINSON, F. (1990) 'Job content and skill: managers' and employees' perspectives', unpublished paper to XXIIth International Working Party on Labour Market Segmentation, Trento.

BURGESS, R.G. (1984) (Ed) *The Research Process in Educational Settings: Ten Case Studies*, London, Falmer Press.

BURKITT, I. (1991) *Social Selves: Theories of the Social Formation of Personality*, London, Sage.

CARDOZO, JUDGE (1914) In *Schloendorff v. Society of New York Hospitals*, 211, NY 125.

CARLEN, P., GLEESON, D. and WARDAUGH, J. (1992) *Truancy: The Politics of Compulsory Schooling*, Buckingham, Open University Press.

CARPENTER, M. (1853) 'Juvenile Delinquents', quoted in PINCHBECK, I. and HEWITT, M. (1973) *Children in English Society*, London, Routledge and Kegan Paul.

CHILDREN'S RIGHTS DEVELOPMENT UNIT (1994) *UK Agenda for Children*, London, CRDU.

CHODOROW, N. (1978) *The Reproduction of Mothering: Psychoanalysis and the Sociology of Gender*, Berkeley, CA, University of California Press.

CHODOROW, N. (1989) *Feminism and Psychoanalytic Theory*, London, Yale University Press.

CRAIB, I. (1993) *Modern Social Theory: From Parsons to Habermas* (2nd edn), London, Harvester Wheatsheaf.

CULLINGFORD, C. (1984) *Children and Television*, Aldershot, Gower.

Davies, B. (1989) 'The discursive production of the male/female dualism in school settings', *Oxford Review of Education*, 15, 3, pp. 229–41.

DAVIS, A.G. and STRONG, P.M. (1976) 'Aren't children wonderful? A study of the allocation of identity in developmental assessment', in STACEY, M. (Ed) *The Sociology of the National Health Service*, Monograph 22, Keele; University of Keele.

DELPHY, C. and LEONARD, D. (1986) 'Class analysis, gender analysis and the family', in CROMPTON, R. and MANN, M. (Eds) *Gender and Stratification*, Cambridge, Polity Press.

DOBASH, R.P., DOBASH, R.E. and GUTTERIDGE, S. (1986) *The Imprisonment of Women*, Oxford, Basil Blackwell.

DONALDSON, M. (1978) *Children's Minds*, Edinburgh, Fontana.

DONZELOT, J. (1980) *The Policing of Families: Welfare Versus the State*, London, Heinemann.

DORR, A. (1986) *Television and Children: A Special Medium for a Special Audience*, Beverly Hills, CA, Sage.

DUMON, W. (1993) 'Childhood matters: A critique', in QVORTRUP, J. (Ed) *Childhood as a Social Phenomenon: Lessons from an International Project*, Vienna, European Centre.

DU BOIS-REYMOND M., BUCHNER P. and KRUGER H.-H. (1993) 'Modern family as everyday negotiation: Continuities and discontinuities in parent-child relationships', *Childhood*, 1, pp. 87–99.

DUNN, J. (1984) *Sisters and Brothers*, London, Fontana.

DUNN, J. and KENDRICK, C. (1982) *Siblings: Love, Envy and Understanding*, London, Grant McIntyre.

DURKIN, K. (1985) *Television, Sex Roles and Children*, Milton Keynes, Open University Press.

EDWARDS, D. and POTTER, J. (1992) *Discursive Psychology*, London, Sage.

ELLIS, R. and LEVENTHAL, B. (1993) 'Information needs and decision-making preferences of children with cancer', *Psycho-oncology*, 2, pp. 277–84.

EMMETT, I. (1975) 'Masses and masters: A brief comparison of approaches to the study of work and leisure', in HAWORTH, J. and SMITH, M.A. (Eds) *Work and Leisure*, London, Lepus Books.

ENGLEBERT, A. (1994) 'Worlds of childhood: Differentiated but different', in QVORTRUP, J. *et al.* (Eds) *Childhood Matters: Social Theory, Practice and Politics*, Aldershot, Avebury Press.

ENNEW, J. (1982) 'Young hustlers, work and childhood in Jamaica', unpublished report, London, Anti-Slavery Society.

ENNEW, J. (1985) 'Juvenile street workers in Lima, Peru', unpublished report, London, ODA.

ENNEW, J. (1994) 'Time for children or time for adults?', in QVORTRUP, J. *et al.* (Eds) *Childhood Matters: Social Theory, Practice and Politics*, Aldershot, Avebury Press.

ENNEW, J. and MORROW, V. (1994) 'Out of the mouths of babes', in VERHELLEN, E. and SPIESSCHAERT, F. (Eds) *Children's Rights: Monitoring Issues*, Gent, Belgium, Meys and Breesch.

ERIKSON, E. (1971) *Identity, Youth and Crisis*, London, Faber.

FADEN, R. and BEAUCHAMP, T. (1986) *A History and Theory of Informed Consent*, New York, Oxford University Press, p. 257.

FAIRCLOUGH, N. (1989) *Language and Power*, London, Longman.

FARQUHAR, C. (1989) *Exploring AIDS-related Knowledge Amongst Primary School Children*, London, Thomas Coram Research Unit.

FIRESTONE, S. (1972) *The Dialectics of Sex*, London, Paladin.

FLAVELL, J. (1977) *Cognitive Development*, Englewood Cliffs, NJ, Prentice-Hall.

FOUCAULT, M. (1977) *Discipline and Punish: The Birth of the Prison*, NY, Pantheon. (trans. Alan Sheridan).

FRANKENBURG, R. (1992) Contribution to Conference on the Consent of Disturbed and Disturbing Young People, London, Institute of Education, University of London.

FREUD, S. (1914) 'On narcissism: An introduction', in STRACHEY, J. (Ed) (1961) *Complete Psychological Works*, London, Hogarth Press.

References

FRØNES, I., JENSEN, A. and SOLBERG, A. (1990) 1990. Childhood as a Social Phenomenon: National Report for Norway, Eurosocial Report 36/1, Vienna, European Centre.

FURSTENBERG, F. JNR., (1993) 'Reflections on the sociology of childhood', in QVORTRUP, J. (Ed) *Childhood as a Social Phenomenon: Lessons from an International Project*, Vienna, European Centre.

GAMBLE, R. (1979) *Chelsea Childhood, An Autobiography*, London, BBC Ariel Books.

GIDDENS, A. (1972) (Ed) *Emile Durkheim: Selected Writings*, Cambridge, Cambridge University Press.

GIDDENS, A. (1979) *Central Problems in Social Theory: Action, Structure and Contradiction in Social Analysis*, London, Macmillan.

GILLIGAN, C. (1982) *In a Different Voice: Psychological Theory and Women's Development*, Cambridge, MA, Harvard University Press.

GILLIGAN, C. (1993) *In a Different Voice*, (new edn) Cambridge, MA and London, Harvard University Press.

GILLIGAN, C., LYONS, N. and HANMER, T. (1990) *Making Connections. The Relational Worlds of Adolescent Girls at Emma Willard School*, Cambridge, MA, Harvard University Press.

GOLDTHORPE, J. (1983) 'Women and class analysis: In defence of the conventional view', *Sociology*, 17, 4, pp. 465–88.

GOULD, S.J. (1977) *Ontogeny and Phylogeny*, Cambridge, MA, Belknap/Harvard University Press.

GRAY, A. (1992) *Video Playtime: The Gendering of a Lesiure Technology*, London, Routledge.

GREENBERGER, E. and STEINBERG, L.D. (1986) *When Teenagers Work. The Psychological and Social Costs of Adolescent Employment*, New York, Basic Books.

GREER, G. (1970) *The Female Eunuch*, London, MacGibbon and Kee.

GRIESHABER, S. (1989) 'A pilot study of parent and child conflict', paper presented at the *International Conference on Early Education and Development*, Hong Kong.

GRIMSHAW, J. (1986) *Feminist Philosophers*, Brighton, Harvester.

GULLESTAD, M. (1988) 'Agents of modernity: Children's care for children in urban Norway', *Social Analysis*, 23, pp. 38–52.

GUNTER, B. and MACALEER, J. (1990) *Children and Television: The One-Eyed Monster?* London, Routledge.

HACKER, H. (1969) 'Women as a minority group', in ROSZAK, B. and ROSZAK, T. (Eds) *Masculinity/Femininity: Readings in Sexual Mythology and the Liberation of Women*, New York, Harper and Row.

HALLDÉN, G. (1991) 'The child as project and the child as being: Parents' ideas as frames of reference', *Childhood and Society*, 5, 4, pp. 334–56.

HALLDÉN, G. (1993) 'Reproduction the essence of family life?', in MAYALL, B. (Ed) *Family Life and Social Control: Discourses on Normality*, Proceedings of a Conference held on 18 March at the Social Science Research Unit, Institute of Education, University of London.

HALLDÉN, G. (1994) 'Establishing order: Small girls write about family life', *Gender and Education*, 6, 1, pp. 3–17.

HAMMOND, J.L. and HAMMOND, B. (1923) *Lord Shaftesbury*, London, Penguin Books.

HARDYMENT, C. (1984) *Dream Babies: Child Care from Locke to Spock*, Oxford, Oxford University Press.

HARKNESS, S. and SUPER, C.M. (1983) 'The cultural construction of child development: A framework for the socialization of affect', *Ethos*, 11, 4, pp. 221–31.

HARTLEY, D. (1987) 'The time of their lives: Bureaucracy and the nursery school', in POLLARD, A. (Ed) *Children and Their Primary Schools*, London, Falmer Press.

HAUGLI, A. (1993) 'Muted actors — children in court', in MAYALL, B. (Ed) *Family Life and Social Control*, Proceedings of a Conference held on 18 March at the Social Science Research Unit, Institute of Education, University of London.

HEILIO, P.-L., LAURONEN, E. and BARDY, M. (Eds) (1993) *Politics of Childhood and Children at Risk*, International Expert Meeting, Kellokoski, Finland, 22–24 August 1992, Eurosocial Report 45, Vienna, European Centre.

HENDRICK, H. (1994) *Child Welfare: England 1872–1989*, London and New York, Routledge.

HENRIKSSON, B. (1983) *Not For Sale: Young People in Society*, Aberdeen, Aberdeen University Press.

HEWITT, P. and LEACH, P. (1993) *Social Justice, Children and Families*, London, Institute for Public Policy Research.

HEYNS, B. (1991) *Childhood as a Social Phenomenon*, National Report for USA, Vienna, European Centre.

HILLMAN, M. (Ed) (1993) *Children, Transport and the Quality of Life*, London, Policy Studies Institute.

HILLMAN, M., ADAMS, J. and WHITELEGG, J. (1991) *One False Move . . . A Study of Children's Independent Mobility*, London, Policy Studies Institute.

HODGE, B. and TRIPP, D. (1986) *Children and Television: A Semiotic Approach*, Cambridge, Polity Press.

HOIKKALA, T., RAHKONEN, O., TIGERSTEDT, C. and TUORMAA, J. (1987) 'Wait a minute, Mr. Postman! Some critical remarks on Neil Postman's childhood theory', *Acta Sociologica*, 30, 1, pp. 87–99.

HOLLAND, P. (1992) *What is a Child? Popular Images of Childhood*, London, Virago.

HOLT, J. (1969) *How Children Fail*, Harmondsworth, Pelican.

HUDSON, B. (1984) 'Femininity and adolescence', in MACROBBIE, A. and NAVA, M. (Eds) *Gender and Generation*, Basingstoke, Blackwell.

HUMPHRIES, S., MACK, J. and PERKS, R. (1988) *A Century of Childhood*, London, Sidgwick and Jackson.

HUTSON, S. (1990) 'Saturday jobs: Sixth formers earning and spending', paper to BSA annual conference, University of Surrey.

INGLEBY, D. (1986) 'Development in social context', in RICHARDS, M. and LIGHT, P. (Eds) *Children of Social Worlds*, Cambridge, Polity Press.

JAMES, A. (1993) *Childhood Identities: Social Relationships and the Self in Children's Experiences*, Edinburgh, Edinburgh University Press.

JAMES, A. and JENKS, C. (1994) 'Public perceptions of childhood criminality', paper presented at Childhood and Society Seminar, 15 April, University of Keele.

JAMES, A. and PROUT, A. (1990) (Eds) *Constructing and Reconstructing Childhood: Contemporary Issues in the Sociological Study of Childhood*, London, Falmer Press.

JAMIESON, L. (1986) 'Limited resources and limiting conventions: Working-class mothers and daughters in urban Scotland c. 1890–1925', in LEWIS, J. (Ed) *Labour and Love: Women's Experiences of Home and Family*, Oxford, Blackwell.

JENSEN, A.-M. and SAPORITI, A. (1992) *Do Children Count? Childhood as a Social Phenomenon: A Statistical Compendium*, Eurosocial Report 36/17, Vienna, European Centre.

JEPHCOTT, A.P. (1942) *Girls Growing Up*, London, Faber and Faber.

JONES, G. (1992) 'Short term reciprocity in parent-child economic exchanges', in MARSH, C. and ARBER, S. (Eds) *Families and Households: Division and Change*, Basingstoke, MacMillan.

KANT, I. (1948) *Groundwork of the Metaphysic of Morals*, London, Hutchinson.

KELLY-BYRNE, D. (1989) *A Child's Play Life: An Ethnographic Study*, New York, Teachers College Press.

KING, M. and PIPER, C. (1990) *How the Law thinks about Children*, Aldershot, Gower.

KING, M. and TROWELL, J. (1992) *Children's Welfare and the Law*, London, Sage.

References

KIRKWOOD, A. (1993) *The Leicestershire Inquiry 1992*, Leicester, Leicestershire County Council.
KITZINGER, J. (1990) 'Who are you kidding? Children, power and the struggle against sexual abuse', in JAMES, A. and PROUT, A. (Eds) *Constructing and Reconstructing Childhood: Contemporary Issues in the Sociological Study of Childhood*, London, Falmer Press.
KOHLBERG, L. (1981) *The Philosophy of Moral Development*, New York, Harper and Row.
KRAUZE, A. (1993) Cartoon in *The Guardian*, 13 December.
KUN, A. (1977) 'Development of the magnitude-covariation and compensation schemata in ability and effort attributions of performance', *Child Development*, 48, pp. 862–73.
LANGDON, J. (1993) 'The nanny from hell', *The Guardian*, 24 November.
LAVALETTE, M. *et al.* (1991) *The Forgotten Workforce: Scottish Children at Work*, Glasgow, Scottish Low Pay Unit.
LEE-WRIGHT, P. (1990) *Child Slaves*, London, Earthscan.
LEVY, A. and KAHAN, B. (1991) *Report of the Staffordshire Child Care Inquiry 1990*, Staffordshire County Council.
LEWIN, K. (1941) 'Self hatred among Jews', *Contemporary Jewish Record*, 4, pp. 219–32.
LEWIS, C.E., LEWIS, M.A. and IFEKWUNIGUE, M. (1978) 'Informed consent by children and participation in an influenza vaccine trial', *American Journal of Public Health*, 68, pp. 1079–82.
LEWONTIN, R.C., ROSE, S. and KAMIN, L.J. (1984) *Not in Our Genes: Biology, Ideology and Human Nature*, New York, Pantheon.
LIEDLOFF, J. (1986) *The Continuum Concept*, Harmondsworth, Penguin.
LIGHT, P. (1986) 'Context, conservation and conversation', in RICHARDS, M. and LIGHT, P. (Eds) *Children of Social Worlds*, Cambridge, Polity Press.
LOCKE, J. (1924) *Two Treatises of Civil Government*, London, Dent.
LOCKWOOD, D. (1986) 'Class, status and gender', in CROMPTON, R. and MANN, M. (Eds) *Gender and Stratification*, Cambridge, Polity Press.
LULL, J. (1982) 'The social uses of television', in WITHEY, C.D. *et al.* (Eds) *Mass Communication Review Yearbook*, Volume 3, Beverley Hills, CA, Sage.
LULL, J. (Ed) (1988) *World Families Watch Television*, Newbury Park, Sage.
LUSTED, D. (1985) 'A history of suspicion: Educational attitudes to television', in LUSTED, D. and DRUMMOND, P. (Eds) *TV and Schooling*, London, British Film Institute.
LUTTRELL, W. (1993) '"The teachers, they all had their pets": Concepts of gender, knowledge and power', *Signs: Journal of Women in Culture and Society*, 18, 3, pp. 505–46.
MACINTYRE, A. (1981) *After Virtue*, London, Duckworth.
MACLENNAN, E. (1980) *Working Children*, London, Low Pay Unit.
MACLENNAN, E. (1982) *Child Labour in London*, London, Low Pay Unit.
MACLENNAN, E., FITZ, J. and SULLIVAN, J. (1985) *Working Children*, London, Low Pay Unit.
MCLEOD, J. and BROWN, J.D. (1976) 'The family environment and adolescent television use', in BROWN, R. (Ed) *Children and Television*, London, Collier MacMillan.
MAY, D. and STRONG, P. (1980) 'Childhood as an estate', in MITCHELL, R.G. (Ed) *Child Health in the Community*, (2nd edn) Edinburgh, Churchill Livingstone.
MAYALL, B. (1990) 'Childcare and childhood', *Children and Society*, 4, 4, pp. 374–86.
MAYALL, B. (1993) 'Keeping healthy at home and school: It's my body so it's my job', *Sociology of Health and Illness*, 15, 4, pp. 464–87.
MAYALL, B. (1994) *Negotiating Health: Children at Home and Primary School*, London, Cassell.

MAYALL, B. and FOSTER, M.-C. (1989) *Child Health Care: Living with Children*, Working for Children, Oxford, Heinemann.

MEDVED, M. (1993) *Hollywood vs. America: Popular Culture and the War on Traditional Values*, New York, Harper Collins.

MELZAK, S. (1992) 'Secrecy, privacy, survival, repressive regimes, and growing up', *Bulletin of the Anna Freud Centre*, 15, pp. 205–24.

MERCHANT, C. (1982) *The Death of Nature*, London, Wildwood House.

MIDGLEY, M. (1981) *Heart and Mind: The Varieties of Moral Experience*, Brighton, Harvester.

MIDGLEY, M. (1989) *Wisdom, Information and Wonder: What is Knowledge For?* London, Routledge.

MILLER, J.B. (1976) *Toward a New Psychology of Women*, Boston, MA, Beacon Press.

MITCHELL, J. (1971) *Woman's Estate*, Harmondsworth, Penguin Books.

MOORE, R.C. (1986) *Childhood's Domain: Play and Place in Child Development*, London, Croom Helm.

MOOREHEAD, C. (1987) *School Age Workers in Britain Today*, London, Anti Slavery Society.

MORLEY, D. (1986) *Family Television: Cultural Power and Domestic Leisure*, London, Comedia.

MORLEY, D. and SILVERSTONE, R. (1990) 'Domestic communication: Technologies and meanings', *Media, Culture and Society*, 13, 1, pp. 31–55.

MORRIS, L. (1988) 'Employment, the household and social networks', in GALLIE, D. (Ed) *Employment in Britain*, Oxford, Blackwell.

MORROW, V. (1992a) 'A sociological study of the economic roles of children, with particular reference to Birmingham and Cambridgeshire', Ph.D. dissertation, University of Cambridge.

MORROW, V. (1992b) Family values: Accounting for Children's Contribution to the Domestic Economy, Sociological Research Group Working Paper No 10, Social & Political Sciences Faculty, University of Cambridge.

MORROW, V. (in preparation) 'Invisible children: Towards a reconceptualisation of childhood dependency and responsibility', in AMBERT, A.-M. (Ed) *Sociological Studies of Childhood*.

MORSS, J. (1990) *The Biologising of Childhood*, Hillsdale, NJ, Lawrence Erlbaum.

NEWELL, P. (1989) *Children Are People Too: The Case Against Physical Punishment*, London, Bedford Square Press.

NEWSON, J. and NEWSON, E. (1978) *Seven Years Old in the Home Environment*, Harmondsworth, Penguin.

NICHOLLS, J.G. (1989) *The Competitive Ethos and Democratic Education*, Cambridge, MA, Harvard University Press.

NICHOLLS, J.G., PATASHNICK, M. and METTETAL, G. (1986) 'Conceptions of ability and intelligence', *Child Development*, 57, pp. 636–45.

NICHOLSON, R. (Ed) (1986) *Medical Research with Children: Ethics, Law and Practice*, Oxford, Oxford University Press.

NOBLE, G. (1975) *Children in Front of the Small Screen*, London, Constable.

O'NEILL, W.L. (Ed) (1969) *The Woman Movement: Feminism in the United States and England*, London, Allen and Unwin.

OAKLEY, A. (1974) *Housewife*, London, Allen Lane.

OAKLEY, A. (1979) *Becoming a Mother*, Oxford, Martin Robertson.

OAKLEY, A. (1982) 'Conventional families', in RAPOPORT, R.N., FOGART, M.P. and RAPOPORT, R. (Eds) *Families in Britain*, London, Routledge and Kegan Paul.

OAKLEY, A. (1986) 'Feminism and motherhood', in RICHARDS, M. and LIGHT, P. (Eds) *of Social Worlds*, Cambridge, Polity Press.

OAKLEY, A. (1991) 'Women's studies in British sociology: To end at our beginning?', *British Journal of Sociology*, 40, 3, pp. 442–70.

References

OAKLEY, A. (1992) *Social Support and Motherhood: The Natural History of a Research Project*, Oxford, Basil Blackwell.

OAKLEY, A. and OAKLEY, R. (1979) 'Sexism in official statistics', in IRVINE, J., MILES, I. and EVANS, J. (Eds) *Demystifying Social Statistics*, London, Pluto Press.

OLDMAN, D. (1991) Childhood as a Social Phenomenon, *National Report for Scotland*, Eurosocial Report 36/9, Vienna, European Centre.

OLDMAN, D. (1994) 'Adult-child relations as class relations', in QVORTRUP, J. *et al.* (Eds) *Childhood Matters: Social Theory, Practice and Politics*, Aldershot, Avebury Press.

PAHL, R.E. (1968) 'The rural-urban divide', in PAHL, R.E. (Ed) *Readings in Urban Sociology*, London, Weidenfeld and Nicholson.

PAHL, R. (1984) *Divisions of Labour*, Oxford, Basil Blackwell.

PARR, A.E. (1972) 'The happy habitat', *Journal of Aesthetic Education*, July, cited in WARD, C. (1978).

PARR, J. (1980) *Labouring Children. British Immigrant Apprentices to Canada, 1869–1924*, London, Croom Helm.

PARTON, N. (1985) *The Politics of Child Abuse*, London, MacMillan.

PFEFFER, N. and COOTE, A. (1991) *Is Quality Good for You?*, London, IPPR.

PHILLIPS, A. and TAYLOR, B. (1986) 'Sex and skill', in Feminist Review (Ed) *Waged Work: A Reader*, London, Virago.

PIAGET, J. (1924) *The Language and Thought of the Child*, London, Routledge.

PIAGET, J. (1932) *The Moral Judgement of the Child*, London, Routledge.

PICKERING, W.S.F. (Ed) (1979) *Durkheim: Essays on Morals and Education*, London, Routledge and Kegan Paul.

PLANT, R. (1992) 'Citizenship, rights and welfare', in COOTE, A. (Ed) *The Welfare of Citizens: Developing New Social Rights*, London, IPPR/Oram Press.

POND, C. and SEARLE, A. (1991) *The Hidden Army: Children at Work in the 1990s*, London, Low Pay Unit/Birmingham City Education Department.

POSTMAN, N. (1983) *The Disappearance of Childhood*, London, W.H. Allen.

POSTMAN, N. and WEINGARTNER, C. (1971) *Teaching as a Subversive Activity*, Harmondsworth, Penguin.

POTTER, J. and WETHERELL, M. (1987) *Discourse and Social Psychology*, London, Sage.

PROUT, A. (1987) ' "Wet children" and "little actresses": Going sick in primary school', *Sociology of Health and Illness*, 8, 2, pp. 111–36.

PROUT, A. (1992) 'Children and childhood in the sociology of medicine', in TRAKAS, D.J. and SANZ, E.J. (Eds) *Studying Childhood and Medicine Use*, Athens, ZHTA Medical Publications.

PROUT, A. and JAMES, A. (1990) 'A new paradigm for the sociology of childhood? Provenance, promise and problems', in JAMES, A. and PROUT, A. (Eds) *Constructing and Reconstructing Childhood: Contemporary Issues in the Sociological Study of Childhood*, London, Falmer Press.

QVORTRUP, J. (1985) 'Placing children in the division of labour' in CLOSE, P. and COLLINS, R. (Eds) *Family and Economy in Modern Society*, London, MacMillan.

QVORTRUP, J. (1987) 'Introduction: The sociology of childhood', *International Journal of Sociology*, 17, 3, pp. 3–37.

QVORTRUP, J. (1990) 'A voice for children in statistical and social accounting: A plea for children's right to be heard', in JAMES, A. and PROUT, A. (Eds) *Constructing and Reconstructing Childhood: Contemporary Issues in the Sociological Study of Childhood*, London, Falmer Press.

QVORTRUP, J. (1991) 'Childhood as a social phenomenon — An introduction to a series of national reports', *Eurosocial Report 36*, Vienna, European Centre.

QVORTRUP, J. (1993) 'Nine theses about "Childhood as a social phenomenon" ' in QVORTRUP, J. (Ed) *Childhood as a Social Phenomenon: Lessons from an*

International Project, Proceedings from a Conference held on 24–26 September 1992 at Billund, Denmark, *Eurosocial Report 47,* Vienna, European Centre.

QVORTRUP, J. (1993) *Childhood as a Social Phenomenon: Lessons from an International Project,* Eurosocial Report 47, Vienna, European Centre.

QVORTRUP, J., BARDY, M., SGRITTA, G. and WINTERSBERGER, H. (Eds) (1994) *Childhood Matters: Social Theory, Practice and Politics,* Aldershot, Avebury Press.

QVORTRUP, J. and CHRISTOFFERSEN, M.N. (1990) *Childhood as a Social Phenomenon, National Report for Denmark,* Eurosocial Report 36/3, Vienna, European Centre.

RILEY, D. (1983) *War in the Nursery: Theories of the Child and Mother,* London, Virago.

ROBERTS, E. (1975) 'Learning and living — Socialisation outside school', *Oral History,* 3, 2, pp. 14–28.

ROBERTS, E. (1976) *Working Class Barrow and Lancaster 1890–1930,* Centre for North-West Regional Studies, University of Lancaster, Occasional Paper No 2.

ROBERTS, H., SMITH, S. and LLOYD, M. (1992) 'Accident prevention in Corkerhill', in WILLIAMS, G. and SCOTT, S. (Eds) *Private Risks and Public Dangers,* Wiltshire, Avebury Press.

RODGERS, G. and STANDING, G. (1981) *Child Work, Poverty and Underdevelopment,* Geneva, ILO.

ROEMER, J. (1982) *A General Theory of Exploitation and Class,* Cambridge, MA, Harvard University Press.

ROSE, N. (1990) *Governing the Soul: The Shaping of the Private Self,* London, Routledge.

ROSENBAUM, M. and NEWELL, P. (1991) *Taking Children Seriously: A Proposal for a Children's Rights Commissioner,* London, Calouste Gulbenkian Foundation.

ROSENHOLTZ, S.J. and SIMPSON, C. (1984) 'The formation of ability conceptions: Developmental trend or social construction?', *Review of Educational Research,* 54, pp. 31–64.

ROSENKRANTZ, P., VOGEL, S., BEE, H., BROVERMAN, I. and BROVERMAN, D. (1968) 'Sex role stereotypes and self-concepts in college students', *Journal of Consulting and Clinical Psychology,* 32, pp. 287–95.

ROSPA (1991) *Guide to Good Practice in Babysitting,* Birmingham, RoSPA.

ROSSITER, J.R. and ROBERTSON, T.S. (1975) 'Children's television viewing: An examination of parent-child consensus', *Sociometry,* 38, 2, pp. 308–26.

ROTHMAN, B.K. (1989) *Recreating Motherhood: Ideology and Technology in a Patriarchal Society,* New York, W.W. Norton.

SANDELS, S. (1975) *Children in Traffic,* London, Elek.

SANDIN, B. (1990) 'The use and abuse of the historical perspective on the history of children', Proceedings of the Conference on Historical Perspectives in Childhood, Jeloya/Moss, Norway, 8–11 September 1988, Norwegian Centre for Childhood Research, University of Trondheim.

SAPORITI, A. (1994) 'A methodology for making children count', in QVORTRUP, J. *et al.* (Eds) *Childhood Matters: Social Theory, Practice and Politics,* Aldershot, Avebury Press.

SARUP, M. (1989) *An Introductory Guide to Post-Structuralism and Postmodernism,* Athens, GA, University of Georgia Press.

SCHACHTEL, E. (1947) 'On memory and childhood amnesia', *Psychiatry: The Journal of the Biology and Pathology of Interpersonal Relations,* 10.

SGRITTA, G. (1987) 'Childhood: Normalisation and project', *International Journal of Sociology,* 17, 3, pp. 38–57.

SGRITTA, G. and SAPORITI, A. (1989) 'Myth and reality in the discovery and representation of childhood' in CLOSE, P. (Ed) *Family Divisions and Inequalities in Modern Society,* London, Macmillan.

SHAMGAR HANDELMAN, L. (1986) 'The place of children in the household division of labour', *Israeli Social Science Research,* 4, 1, pp. 65–83.

References

SIEGAL, M. (1991) *Knowing Children: Experiments in Conversation and Cognition*, Hove, Lawrence Erlbaum Associates.

SILTANEN, J. (1986) 'Domestic responsibilities and the structuring of employment', in CROMPTON, R. and MANN, M. (Eds) *Gender and Stratification*, Cambridge, Polity Press.

SIMEON, L. and STEWART, S. (1992) *The Streetwise Kid: A Keeping Safe Rap*, London, Blackie.

SKOLNICK, A. (1975) 'The limits of childhood: Conceptions of child development and social context', *Law and Contemporary Problems*, 39, pp. 38–77.

SMITH, D.E. (1979) 'A sociology for women', in SHERMAN, J.A. and BECK, E.T. (Eds) *The Prism of Sex: Essays in the Sociology of Knowledge*, Madison, WI, University of Wisconsin Press.

SMITH, D.E. (1988) *The Everyday World as Problematic: A Feminist Sociology*, Milton Keynes, Open University Press.

SOLBERG, A. (1990) 'Negotiating childhood: Changing constructions of age for Norwegian children', in JAMES, A. and PROUT, A. (Eds) *Constructing and Reconstructing Childhood: Contemporary Issues in the Sociological Study of Childhood*, London, Falmer Press.

SOLBERG, A. (1992) 'The social construction of childhood: Children's contributions', paper given at a Childhood Study Group seminar, Social Science Research Unit, Institute of Education, University of London.

SONTAG, S. (1983) *Illness as Metaphor*, Harmondsworth, Penguin.

SPRADLEY, J. (1979) *The Ethnographic Interview*, New York, Holt, Rinehart and Winston.

STACEY, M. (1981) 'The division of labour revisited or overcoming the two Adams', in ABRAMS, P. *et al.* (Eds) *Practice and Progress: British Sociology 1950–1980*, London, Allen and Unwin.

STEEDMAN, C. (1982) *The Tidy House, Little Girls Writing*, London, Virago.

STEEDMAN, C., URWIN, C. and WALKERDINE, V. (Eds) (1985) *Language, Gender and Childhood*, London, Routledge and Kegan Paul.

THOMPSON, T. (1981) *Edwardian Childhoods*, London, RKP.

TIZARD, B. and HUGHES, M. (1984) *Young Children Learning*, London, Fontana.

UNICEF (1993) *Progress of Nations*, Geneva, UNICEF, London, UNICEF UK Committee.

URWIN, C. (1984) 'Power relations and the emergence of language', in HENRIQUES, J., HOLLOWAY, W., URWIN, C., VENN, C. and WALKERDINE, V. (Eds) *Changing the Subject*, London, Methuen.

URWIN, C. (1985) 'Constructing motherhood: The persuasion of normal development', in STEEDMAN, C., URWIN, C. and WALKERDINE, V. (Eds) *Language, Gender and Childhood*, London, Routledge and Kegan Paul.

VIOLENCE AGAINST CHILDREN STUDY GROUP (1990) *Taking Child Abuse Seriously*, London, Unwin Hyman.

WAKSLER, F.C. (1991) *Studying the Social Worlds of Children: Sociological Readings*, London, Falmer Press.

WALBY, S. (1986) 'Gender, class and stratification: Toward a new approach', in CROMPTON, R. and MANN, M. (Eds) *Gender and Stratification*, Cambridge, Polity Press.

WALBY, S. (1988) 'Gender politics and social theory', *Sociology*, 22, 2, pp. 215–32.

WALKER, A. (1982) 'Dependency and old age', *Social Policy and Administration*, 16, 2, pp. 115–35.

WALKERDINE, V. (1984) 'Developmental psychology and the child-centred pedagogy: The insertion of Piaget into early education' in HENRIQUES, J. *et al.* (Eds) *Changing the Subject*, London, Methuen and Co. Ltd.

WALKERDINE, V. (1988) *The Mastery of Reason: Cognitive Development and the Production of Rationality*, London, Routledge.

WALKERDINE, V. (1990) *Schoolgirl Fictions*, London, Verso.

WALKERDINE, V. and LUCEY, H. (1989) *Democracy in the Kitchen*, London, Virago.

WARD, C. (1973) 'The future of vandalism', in WARD, C. (Ed) *Vandalism*, London, Architectural Press.

WARD, C. (1978 and 1990) *The Child in the City*, London, Architectural Press, Penguin Books and Bedford Square Press.

WARD, C. (1988 and 1990) *The Child in the Country*, London, Robert Hale and Bedford Square Press.

WARD, C. and FYSON, A. (1973) *Streetwork: The Exploding School*, London, Routledge and Kegan Paul.

WARWICK, I. and AGGLETON, P. (1990) 'Adolescents, young people and AIDS research', in AGGLETON, P., DAVIES, P. and HART, G. (Eds) *AIDS: Individual, Cultural and Policy Dimensions*, London, Falmer Press.

WATSON, J.W. (1951) 'The sociological aspects of geography', in TAYLOR, G. (Ed) *Geography in the Twentieth Century*, London, Methuen.

WEBSTER, D. (1989) '"Who dunnit? America did": Rambo and post-Hungerford rhetoric', *Cultural Studies*, 3, 2, pp. 173–93.

WILLIS, D. and BIRD, L. (1993) Links between Learning, Motivation and Assessment in Fifth Form Modular Science, Interim Report to the Ministry of Education, Wellington, NZ, Victoria University Department of Education.

WINTERSBERGER, H. (1992) 'Children as a social group: Workshop report', in *Child, Family and Society*, Luxembourg, 27–29 May 1991, Report of the Conference, Brussels, Commission of the European Communities.

WRIGHT, E.O. (1985) *Classes*, London, Verso.

YOUNG, A. (1990) 'Moral conflicts in a psychiatric hospital', in WEISZ, G. (Ed) *Social Science Perspectives on Medical Ethics*, Dordrecht, Kluwer.

YOUNG, M. (1968) *The Rise of Meritocracy 1870–2033: An Essay on Education and Equality*, Harmondsworth, Penguin (first published 1958).

YULE, W. (1992) 'Post traumatic stress disorders in children', *Current Opinion in Paediatrics*, 4, 4.

ZUCCHI, J.E. (1992) *The Little Slaves of the Harp*, Montreal, McGill-Queen's University Press.

ZUCKERMAN, M. (1993) 'History and developmental psychology, a dangerous liaison: A historian's perspective' in ELDER, G.H., MODEL, J. and PARKE, R.D. (Eds) *Children in Time and Place: Developmental and Historical Insights*, Cambridge, Cambridge University Press.

Index